MARINE LIFE

OF THE
GALÁPAGOS

The Diver's Guide to
Fishes, Whales, Dolphins and
Marine Invertebrates

Pierre Constant studied at the University of Pierre and Marie Curie-Paris VI where he received his degree in Biology-Geology in 1975, followed by a Master's in Geology in 1979. In 1980, he went to Ecuador to work as a naturalist guide on cruise boats around the Galápagos Islands. After two years living on the islands, he returned to France and published his first book: *Archipel des Galápagos*, and became the recognized French expert on the archipelago. Constant took up submarine photography in 1984 and produced a guide to the fishes, whales, dolphins and marine invertebrates of the islands. His involvement with the ocean became professional when he obtained his diving instructor certification in 1997. He has been a regular visitor to the Galápagos for the past 25 years, leading trips to the islands annually. His comprehensive knowledge and expertise on the Galápagos Islands has been made use of in various travel and active sports television productions, including French television (TF1: *Ushuaia*) and the Discovery Channel (XL Productions, 1991). Constant has published over 100 articles worldwide in a range of travel, science and diving magazines. He has been a guest lecturer on many occasions including at the Royal Geographic Society in Hong Kong. Pierre is a permanent resident of the Galápagos.

MARINE LIFE
OF THE
GALÁPAGOS

The Diver's Guide to
Fishes, Whales, Dolphins and
Marine Invertebrates

Pierre Constant

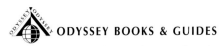
ODYSSEY BOOKS & GUIDES

Odyssey Books & Guides is a division of Airphoto International Ltd.
903 Seaview Commercial Building, 21–24 Connaught Road West, Sheung Wan, Hong Kong
Tel: (852) 2856 3896; Fax: (852) 2565 8004
E-mail: sales@odysseypublications.com; www.odysseypublications.com

Distributed in the USA by
W.W. Norton & Company, Inc.
500 Fifth Avenue, New York, NY 10110, USA
Tel: 800-233-4830; Fax: 800-458-6515
www.wwnorton.com

Distributed in the UK and Europe by
Cordee Books and Maps
3a De Montfort Street, Leicester LE1 7HD, UK
Tel: 0116-254-3579; Fax: 0116-247-1176
www.cordee.co.uk

Marine Life of the Galápagos, Second Edition
© Copyright Pierre Constant 2007, 2002
Library of Congress Catalog Card Number has been requested.
ISBN-13: 978-962-217-767-3
ISBN-10: 962-217-767-0

Readers who are planning to explore this destination are counseled to visit one of the following websites for safety information before travel:
US Department of State: www.travel.state.gov/travel_warnings.html
UK Foreign and Commonwealth Office: www.fco.gov.uk/travel
Canadian Department of Foreign Affairs & International Trade: www.voyage.gc.ca/dest/sos/warnings-en.asp
Australian Department of Foreign Affairs & Trade: www.dfat.gov.au/travel/

Persons interested in the matter of this book, sailing trips, diving cruises to the Galápagos Islands, or in the organization of any special trips, filming, television programs, may write to the author, who has regularly organized trips and expeditions to these islands since 1984.

Pierre Constant
Calao Life Experience, Le Trident, 74 rond point du Pont de Sevres, 92100 Boulogne, France
Tel: 331-4761-9329; Fax: 331-4621-7736
E-mail: calaolife@yahoo.com; www.calaolife.com; www.scubadragongalapagos.com

Color photographs and line drawings by Pierre Constant with exception of p.119 (photo 117), p.153 (photo 171), p.187 (photo 223) by Vivien Li.

Cover design: Au Yeung Chui Kwai
Editors: Kevin Bishop, Helen Northey
Production by Twin Age Limited, Hong Kong; E-mail: twinage@netvigator.com
Printed in China

Front cover photo: *Underwater scenery with black coral bush and seastars, Cousin's Roack, Galápagos Islands.*
Back cover photos—Top right: *Diver in 'black coral' bushes, observing a scorpionfish, Marchena Island.* Middle left: *"Galápagos Discodoris" nudibranch, Piedra Blanca, Santiago Island.*
Bottom right: *The crescent shaped tuff cone of Tortuga Island, dive site of southern Isabela.*

"In essence, it is harmony, sensitivity, a song of joy and a cosmic experience, it is the food of our cells, the depth of our subconscious, the primary need of our survival. Water is the source of life on earth."

CONTENTS

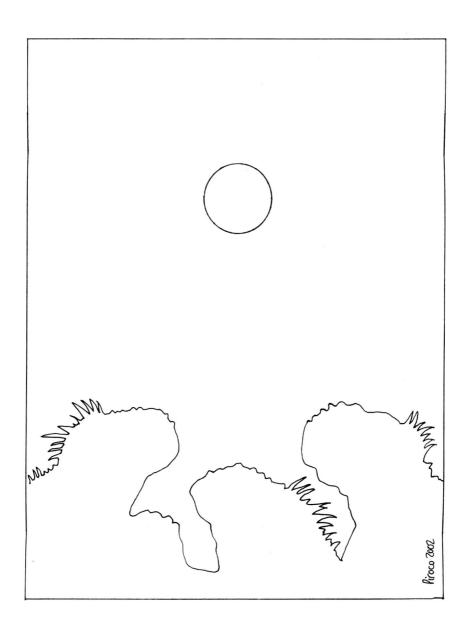

FOREWORD

My grandmother loved fish. She used to paint Chinese goldfish on lampshades and enjoyed doing tapestry. I was a secret admirer of her art and somehow it inspired me. At the age of 12, I was jumping from high boards at swimming pools and was involved in competition swimming. Later on, I did one and a half somersault dives and felt elated. I loved water and people jokingly compared me to a fish. I came to scuba diving in 1974, when I was a student in biology and geology at the University of Pierre & Marie Curie Paris VI. At that time, it took one year to become certified by the French Federation of Underwater Sports (FFESSM); training was then a very serious matter, suitable for 'commando types' and military frogmen. Nowadays it takes four days for a PADI Open Water diver to reach certification level. The earlier situation did not encourage me to take a chance nor did it inspire me to go diving in the sea.

Seven years passed. In 1981 my sister invited me to Corsica, where she was living with her boyfriend—a dive master. The next day, he took me out diving in 40 meters of water. I felt absolutely relaxed and safe. The visibility was great, but there was not much to see and I was a bit disappointed. I was still not hooked on diving.

In August 1980, I arrived in the Galápagos Islands to become a naturalist guide. However it took some time before I entered the water; in search of greater excitement, I first took up snorkeling and then skin diving. My initial encounter with a white tip shark in 1984, beneath the Pinnacle Rock of Bartolomé Island, filled me with awe and triggered my passion for underwater photography. Soon, I was diving to 15 meters to photograph hammerhead sharks at Gordon Rocks. But I could not dive on a single breath forever; a two-hour 'yoyo' experience skin diving at depth—waiting for a fish that hides in a hole—was a heart thumping exercise. By 1986 scuba diving was back on my agenda so, to regain confidence I completed an advanced diver course with the FFESSM.

As a logical progression, in 1984 I decided to write a book on the underwater world of the Galápagos. Secluded like a monk for three months, I wrote the manuscript and spent days at the Darwin Station. Simultaneously, I renewed my Galápagos Naturalist Guide's license. However, it took me a further six years to collect sufficient photographic material for a publication. In 1992, I self-published *Marine Life of the Galápagos*, the first book of this genre. Earlier, Godfrey Merlen had published a fish identification guide, using colored line drawings, but in my eyes his publication did not capture the glory of the Galápagos underwater world.

From 1984 onward, I led frequent trips to the Galápagos, on boats such as *Orca, Cachalote, Tigress* and finally *Sulidae*. I escorted the French television channel TF1 for underwater filming in 1990, for two productions of "Ushuaia" and took some French and Italian divers to Darwin and Wolf Islands in 1992. By this stage, it was clear to me that I had to turn professional. I became a PADI dive master in Borneo in 1994; a dive instructor in Tioman Island, Malaysia in 1997; and obtained cave diver certification from the CDAA, South Australia in April 2003.

Diving enterprises started in the Galápagos Islands in 1973 with the occasional dive cruises of Sea & Sea on *The Golden Cachalot*. David Day, an Englishman, was the pioneer dive guide. In 1974, Gerry Wellington and a group of scientists from the Peace Corps, with US photographer David Doubilet, led the first dive expedition on the CDRS boat *Beagle III* to Darwin and Wolf Islands to collect data. In 1978, Godfrey Merlen, a mechanic and autodidact, joined David Day as a dive guide. More boats became involved in dive cruises in the 1980s: *Cachalote, Symbol, Pirata*, and the company 'Quasar Nautica'. Ecuadorian dive guides soon showed up—Jimmy and Frederico Iglesias, Jenny Armas, and Macarena Ituralde, to name a few.

The first dive center opened in Puerto Ayora, Santa Cruz, in 1992, offering day trips and dive courses. It was followed by 'Scubaiguana' (Mathias Espinosa) in 1995 and 'Nautidiving' in 1998. The number of divers visiting the Galápagos slowly increased over the years from 5,000 (1991) to 8,000 (1993), 10,000 (1995), 15,000 (1996), 17,500 (1997), 20,000 (1998) and 22,000 (1999). In 2005 the number of visiting divers reached 25,000, which is one fourth of the annual total number of visitors to the Galápagos Islands. Without doubt, the dive business is booming.

The Galápagos became a Reserve of Marine Resources in 1986. The first Master Plan was issued in 1992, highlighting numerous conflicts of interest. Illegal fishing of shark fins and sea cucumbers was rampant. Declaration of the Biological Reserve in 1996 did not solve the problem; on the contrary it added fuel to the fire, so much so that UNESCO threatened to declare the Galápagos to be a World Heritage Site in danger of destruction. Seminars organized by the Galápagos National Park and the Darwin Station combined with the creation of the 'Grupo Nucleo' in 1997, brought local interests (fishermen, tourism, SPNG, CDRS, DIGMER) into the limelight. This Master Plan was revised in 1997–98, which lead to the promulgation of the 'Special Law for the Conservation and Sustainable Use of the Galápagos Province' in March 1998, and brought about the creation of the new Galápagos Marine Reserve, 140,000 square kilometers; an extension of the former limits from 15 miles to 40 miles off the extreme points of the islands.

The idea is that if the Galápagos ecosystem cannot survive without protection of the marine ecosystem, it is unrealistic to exclude artisanal fishermen whose survival depends on the sea and the local community that depends on tourism. Industrial fishing is excluded within the 40-mile boundary. In the long run, local participation in the management and conservation issues would protect the Marine Reserve against foreign interests in industrial fishing. Sadly, pirates are still at large in the Galápagos waters, and corruption is, as usual, part of the game. However, it was believed that the new strength of the Galápagos National Park, with the help of the Sea Shepherd Conservation Society and the patrol boat *Sirenian*, would balance the play and quell the insidious powers of destruction. Perhaps this is all but a dream?

Given the political involvement of the director of the Galápagos National Park, Dr. Fernando Espinosa, and subsequently, his sacking in November 2003, the situation in the islands is not improving. Conflicts of interest, a gradual degradation due to corruption and politics, two successive industrial strikes by the Galápagos fishermen and the takeover of the Galápagos National Park offices in 2004, have not helped allay concern about the future of the region. Fishermen, who suddenly claimed the exclusive right to run the recreational diving business, threatened dive operators in Puerto Ayora. From this event, it became obvious that the Lista 5 (the 'Democracia Popular' party of the fishermen) wanted to dictate its rule to the Galápagos National Park. The Autoridad Interinstitucional de Manejo de la Reserva Marina de Galápagos (AIM) decided in 2005–2006, that the sea cucumber population was under threat of extinction, and that only a harvest of 4 million pepinos per year (restricted to a two-month period) would be sustainable. The fishermen were unhappy with this edict and wanted a larger cut of the cake.

Although local residents well know that many of the fishermen waste their earnings in 'borracheras' (heavy drinking), fishermen still bemoan the fact that due to a "lack of business alternatives" as they call it, their industry is facing an economic and social crisis. Fishermen claim that they suffer unjustified discrimination from the government and from money-rich local and international conservation organizations; that 25 percent of the population—dependent directly on traditional fishing—cannot earn sufficient income or even feed their children. Their solution to the problem is to be allowed new fishing methods, such as 'el palangre corto' (a version of the long line with 80 hooks) to be able to catch tuna offshore. Everybody knows that industrial fishing, supported by the Asian market, uses these long lines for the prized capture of sharks, which curiously have been disappearing slowly from Galápagos Islands over the last 20 years.

The Fishing Sector in Galápagos considers that these NGOs are playing a dangerous game with local and national 'actors' alike; that—beyond the induced social crisis—NGO activities will trigger a negative outcome in terms of conservation; a somber warning indeed, that is manifest already, since illegal fishing is stronger than ever. A pirate-camp of fishermen holding 5934 pepinos was destroyed in Santa Cruz in June 2005 and the 'Cooperativa de Pesca Artesanal' (COPROPAG) has received reports that a small group of partners was involved in the illegal catch of sea cucumbers. Rumors continue to spread saying that the Government of Ecuador will allocate US$1.5 million for the creation of a fund to finance the 'occupational-change process' for the fishermen. Meanwhile, for the Galapagos Marine Reserve, the future looks grim.

In December 2005, to alleviate the pressure, a Galápagos National Park directive authorized the boat *Mi Esperanza* of the Copahisa (Cooperativa de Pesca Horizontes de Isabela) to undertake "Proyecto de Pesca de Altura", that is, the development of a Pilot Plan for high seas fishing in the RMG. Species targeted are big pelagics such as Scombridae (yellow fin tuna, bigeye tuna and wahoo) as well as larger species such as the swordfish, striped marlin and blue marlin.

We can only hope for peace in the Galápagos, a place that for many people has been a secret dream world since they were children, a believed paradise for which they are willing to cross the planet.

Let's keep this dream alive.

Pierre Constant, Paris, July 2006

Galápagos Islands

Pinta

Marchena

Genovesa

Roca Redonda

Isabela

Santiago

Cousin's rock

Bartolomé

Bainbridge

Sombrero Chino

Albany

Rabida

Pinzon

North Seymour

Baltra

Plazas

Giordan rocks

Santa Cruz

Santa Fe

4 Hermanos

Tortuga

Fernandina

Isabela

Devil's Crown

Champion

Caldwell

Gardner

Watson

Floreana

Leon Dormido

San Cristóbal

Gardner

Española

Darwin

Wolf

© Pikoso 2002

GENERAL SETTING

PART I: A VOLCANIC ARCHIPELAGO * OCEANIC CROSSROADS * ZOOGEOGRAPHIC AFFINITIES * BIODIVERSITY

A VOLCANIC ARCHIPELAGO

The Galápagos islands are a volcanic hotspot at the southwest end of the Carnegie Ridge, which heads towards Central America. Made of basaltic lava of the Hawaiian type, its earliest volcanoes emerged above the ocean floor roughly three to five millions years ago (Allan Cox 1983). These are known as 'shield volcanoes' that rise over 1,000 meters above the ocean surface. However the existence of sunken islands, discovered in 1992, to the south and east of the archipelago, bring the age of the islands much further back in time, to 90 million years ago.

Some of these islands have a flat top, locally known as *bajo*, which attract a good concentration of fish and marine life. These *bajos* are logically of high interest to fisheries, but also very valuable for the biodiversity of the Galápagos marine ecosystem.

The Galápagos islands lay exactly on the equator, in the South East Pacific, between the latitudes 1°40 North (Darwin Island) and 1°25 South (Española Island); and from east to west between longitudes 89°15 West (Punta Pitt, San Cristobal Island) and 91°40 West (Cape Douglas, Fernandina Island). Its geographical position from the mainland and other Pacific islands is 600 miles (966 kilometers) west of Ecuador, 1,000 miles (1,610 kilometers) south west of Panama, 2,100 miles (3,380 kilometers) south east from the tip of Baja California, 3,000 miles (4,830 kilometers) east of the Marquesas islands and 2,300 miles (3,700 kilometers) north east of Easter island. Hawaii, another famous hotspot, geologically related but much older than the Galápagos islands, lays 4,300 miles (6,920 kilometers) to the north west. (*see* maps, p.15).

The archipelago is an active group of islands located on the Nazca Plate, gradually moving eastward towards South America. The islands are built on a submarine platform, 1,300 meters deep, which is surrounded by greater depths of 2,000 to 4,000 meters. The western side of the islands, Isabela and Fernandina Islands, are an area of 'upwelling', where cold waters rise from the deep. The archipelago is composed of 14 main islands from 0.1 to 460 square kilometers on average and 107 islets (with a surface area of less than 0.1 square kilometers) most of them being rocks or remains of 'tuff' cones, a secondary volcanic activity in contact with salt water. Tuff cones, usually found offshore, have been shaped by erosion and wave action and offer very good dive sites for their richness in fish and marine life.

The littoral is not only made of basaltic lava. Beaches are found everywhere in the islands, made of black volcanic sand, red, brown or orange tuff material or even white sand of coral and organic origin. The coast is shaped with points, bays, coves, submarine caves, rock walls, channels, offering a great variety of underwater landscapes, depths and marine ecosystems.

OCEANIC CROSSROADS

The Galápagos have a very interesting geographical position in the Southeast Pacific, being the meeting point of at least three major currents:

- The cold Peru Oceanic current from the Southeast Pacific, which, in conjunction with the Peru coastal current, has often been called the Humboldt current.
- The warm Panama current, from the northeast.
- The equatorial undercurrent, also known as the Cromwell current, a bottom flowing cold water current from the central Pacific, upwelling on the west side of the Galápagos archipelago (Fernandina and Isabela islands).

Both the Peru Oceanic and the Panama current join on the equator and form the South Equatorial Current, flowing west across the islands.

These are the main avenues for immigration used by fish and larvae to reach the Galápagos. Flowing 5°North to 7°North of the equator, another current is significant in the transport of organisms which eventually make it to the Galápagos, providing conditions are favorable. This is the North Equatorial Countercurrent coming from the Central and Western Pacific (*see* maps opposite).

All these currents have a preponderant action at certain times of the year. With the help of the southeast and northeast trade winds, they have a definite influence on the air and water temperatures in the Galápagos and therefore induce two main seasons. The Peru oceanic and coastal currents, stronger from May to December (strongest in August–September), are responsible for the establishment of the cool season. The Panama current, strong from December to May, brings warm waters to the islands and gives rise to the hot season.

The eastward flowing North Equatorial Countercurrent shows a seasonal shift in size and intensity. From February to April (ie. the warm season in the Galápagos), the NECC is absent or nearly so. The rest of the year, it transports water from the Western and Central Pacific at a rate of two knots, or 55 miles per day (Abbott, 1966), with a peak from July to November. Reaching longitude 90° West, the NECC slackens. The residual flow goes northwest along the Mexican coast and towards the Gulf of California. At the apex of the season, this flow towards Central America ends and from Costa Rica heads south towards the Cocos Island. Eventually, its waters mix with the South Equatorial Current in the region northeast of the Galápagos.

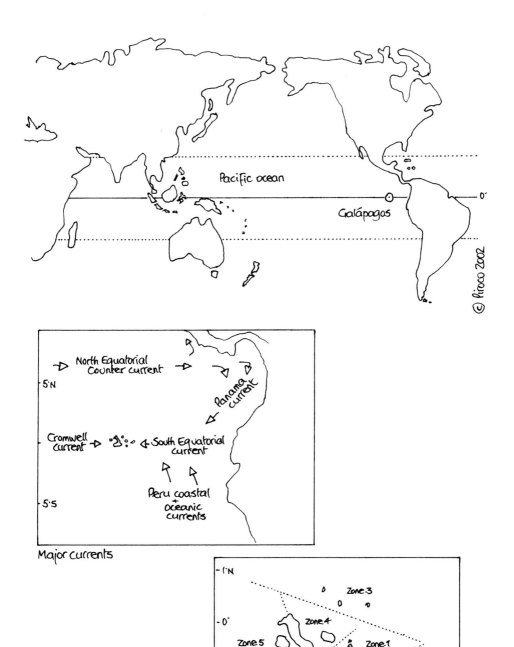

Pacific ocean

Galápagos

0°

© hiroco 2002

North Equatorial Counter current

5°N

Panama current

Cromwell current

South Equatorial current

Peru coastal + oceanic currents

5°S

Major currents

- 1°N

Zone 3

- 0°

Zone 4

Zone 5

Zone 1

- 1°S

Zone 2

Sea surface temperature zones [Harris, 1969]

ZOOGEOGRAPHIC AFFINITIES

These major currents obviously play a major role in the zoogeographic affinities of the Galápagos shore fish, and explain their origin, be it in the Pacific Ocean or in the Caribbean.

A record of origins and affinities of the Galápagos fish was made by Boyd W. Walker in 1966, and three main provinces came up. The Peru-Chilean, the Indo-west Pacific and the Panamic provinces, which appeared to be the main sources of the fish of the Galápagos. The Panamic province was related to the mainland Eastern Pacific area, and fish would come through chance from Panama, Colombia and Ecuador. Walker (1966) numbered 289 species, from 88 families, of which 77 percent were shore or shallow water forms. Twenty-three percent of the fish have been found then to be endemic to the Galápagos Islands.

Nevertheless, after Walker, a few studies and collections were made (Wellington, 1975) and the record was increased by McCosker, Taylor and Warner (1978), to a number of 306 species of fishes in the Galápagos, of which:

- 17 percent were endemic (51 species).
- Two percent insular endemic (seven species), only found in Galápagos and East Pacific offshore islands such as Cocos, Malpelo, Clipperton, Revillagigedos.
- 58 percent were Panamic (177 species).
- Seven percent were Temperate (21 species) or from the Peru-Chilean province.
- 14 percent from the western Pacific province (43 species).
- One percent from the Atlantic (four species).

McCosker called the Galápagos: a "biological bouillabaisse" (1978) in consideration of the striking difference of zoogeographic origins (*see* map p.18).

Research made by Jack Grove and R.J.Lavenberg of the Los Angeles County Museum, published in a huge volume, *The Fishes of the Galápagos Islands* (1997) brought the number of fishes up to 460 species, divided into 112 families, 304 genera and 51 endemic species. That means 9.2 percent of endemism in group and 11 percent endemism in species.

The degree of endemism varies with families. The highest degree of endemism is found in the snake eels, the grunts, the croakers, the gobies and eleotrids, the sand stargazers, the labrisomids and the tube blennies. Few endemic species are found in the morays, groupers, jacks, wrasses and the true blennies.

If the means of transport of the fishes from the Peru-Chilean province or from the Panamic province is obvious, things are rather different for the Western Pacific province.

It is very unlikely that any fish or larvae form have come via the cold Equatorial undercurrent or Cromwell current, which flows much too deep under the surface of the ocean. Its temperature is only 15°C. Any shore form would be dead long before arriving in the Galápagos.

Nevertheless, the fact that the Clipperton and Cocos Islands, far to the north, have a lot of Indo-West Pacific forms, indicate that the Galápagos may have been stocked the same way, ie. via the east flowing North Equatorial Countercurrent (NECC). This has been recently been given credence by the event of the last Niño (1982–83) which brought new Indo-West Pacific forms to the Galápagos, and a recurrence of the species *Zanclus cornutus*, the Moorish Idol.

As a matter of fact, whatever the zoogeographic province, the fishes have a tendency to look for the water temperature that suits them best in the Galápagos Islands. This is the case with the 21 species of the southeastern mainland of South America (Peru-Chile). These tend to be confined to the cooler waters of the islands (Fernandina, West Isabela).

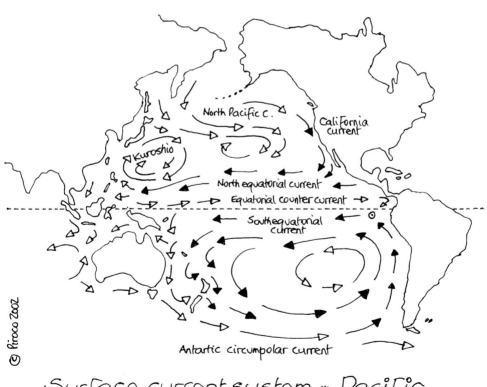

Surface current system * Pacific

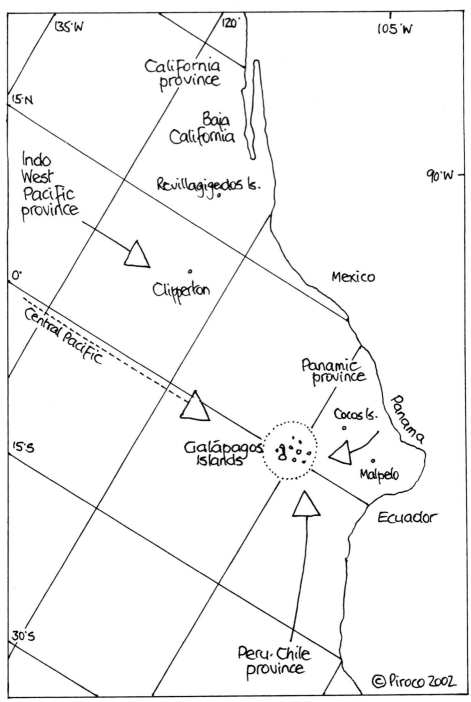

135°W

120°

105°W

California province

15°N

Baja California

90°W

Indo West Pacific province

Revillagigedos Is.

0°

Clipperton

Mexico

Central Pacific

Panamic province

Cocos Is.

Panama

15°S

Galápagos Islands

Malpelo

Peru·Chile province

Ecuador

© Piroco 2002

Zoogeographic affinities

For the marine biota as a whole, the greatest affinities of the Galápagos Islands appear to be with the American Pacific coast, from the lower reaches of Baja California to the region of the boundary between Ecuador and Peru. This fauna, in turn, shows a marked similarity to that of the Caribbean and West-Indies region (Abbott, 1966).

BIODIVERSITY

The major affinities of the Galápagos marine fauna are related to the tropical and subtropical regions of the American continent in the Pacific. The information prior to the 1982–83 Niño showed that the Panamic province provided 54 percent of the ichthyfauna, the Indo-Pacific 12 percent, the Peru-Chile province eight percent, the Atlantic two percent, and according to the actual knowledge 23 percent of the marine fauna is endemic to the Galápagos islands.

The primary productivity in general is high. Nutrients are available in the photic zone and produced by upwellings already well known. High concentrations of chlorophyllia are found in the west of Isabela as well as the benthic production of macrophytic algae. Within the archipelago productivity is also triggered by local upwellings.

The characteristics of the Galápagos marine environment are: the geographical isolation, a unique location with a southern ocean influence, specific climatic and oceanographic conditions with seasonal variations, a geographic position where horizontal currents are highly dynamic, a radical change of the environmental factors every three to seven years during Niño years.

The marine ecosystem is therefore gifted with a high degree of diversity, a high degree of endemism, a great number of species, mixed biogeographic affinities, species that are unique in the world and an abundance of marine invertebrates in shallow waters.

The Galápagos islands are consequently considered as one of the most complex oceanic archipelagos in the world. Already a Biosphere Reserve since 1995, the Galápagos Marine Reserve became a World Heritage Site in December 2001, following approval by UNESCO. This will not be treated as a separate entity from the Galápagos National Park, as it is intimately interrelated. The high degree of biological diversity and endemism has led to the discovery of 2,900 marine organisms so far, of which 18 percent are endemic. The endemism per biotic group is above 25 percent on average (see table of Marine Biodiversity on p.20).

MARINE BIODIVERSITY IN THE GALÁPAGOS ISLANDS

Groups	total no. of species	no. of endemic species	% endemism	richness in species.
Mammals	24	2	8.3	high
Algae	333	130	39.0	high
Seabirds	19	5	26.3	high
Fish	460	51	11.0	high
Polychaetes	192	50	26.0	medium
Brachiures	120	23	19.2	medium
Porcelanidae	12	1	8.3	low
Cirripeds	18	4	22.2	low
Mollusks	800	141	17.6	low
Opistobranchs	49	18	36.7	low
Echinoderms	200	34	17.0	high
Briozoans	184	34	18.5	high
Gorgonians	12	8	66.7	low
Corals	44	20	45.5	low

(after Plan de Manejo de la Reserva Marina de Galápagos, Galápagos National Park & CDRS 1998).

The biodiversity studies realized by the marine laboratory of the Charles Darwin Research Station have brought to evidence the fact that the majority of fish and invertebrates found in the islands show a distribution pattern that is related to the zonification proposed by Harris (1969) and the sea surface temperatures within different sectors of the archipelago. The biotic separation is clearly marked and is directly influenced by the action of the ocean currents that affect the Galápagos.

Specific ecosystems are recognized in the Galápagos. In the area of the Bolivar channel and Fernandina Island (west of the archipelago), known for the upwelling of the Cromwell current, lives 50 percent of the population of fur sea lions, endemic to the Galápagos. It is also the feeding ground of three cetaceans: Bryde's whale, Pilot whale and Bottlenose dolphin. For this reason, the islands have been declared a Whale Sanctuary.

To the south of Isabela is the biggest nesting site of marine turtles and a place of numerous lagoons. Cartago Bay, to the east of Isabela, is the biggest mangrove area of the Galápagos.

In the northern islands, Darwin and Wolf have the greatest coral reefs of the archipelago with eight species of hermatypic corals and the greatest diversity of tropical fish. In the islands of Marchena, Floreana and Española, coral reefs go in hand with colonies of seabirds. These make use of the numerous *bajos* known to exist near these islands— important feeding zones for seabirds.

The *bajos* are mostly found at the borders of the Galápagos submarine platform, in the south, southeast and east. These are sunken islands or old volcanoes at a depth of 100 meters below the surface of the ocean. These submarine mountains are surrounded by waters 2,000 to 4,000 meters deep. They generate local upwellings which attract land species such as sea lions, seabirds and turtles, but also marine species such as marlins, sharks and tunas. These are the main criteria which have led to the protection and conservation of the *bajos* in the extension of the marine reserve to a 40-mile limit around the archipelago within the 1998 Master Plan. The *bajos* are located between 20 to 40 miles from the islands.

PART II: OCEANOGRAPHY * EL NIÑO-LA NIÑA PHENOMENON

SEA TEMPERATURES

Harris (1969) identified five sea surface temperatures (SST) in the Galápagos:

Zone 1: Around Santa Cruz.
Zone 2: Northern islands (warmer).
Zone 3: Southern islands (cooler).
Zone 4: Similar to zone 3 in warm season; slightly cooler than zone 1 in cool season.
Zone 5: Western sector, coolest area in Galápagos.
(ref. map 2: SST zones, after Harris 1969).

In zone 1, the average temperature varies from 21°C to 26°C, between the cold and the warm season.

In zone 2, the temperatures show a mean of 23°C to 25.71°C in the warm season, a mean of 19°C to 21°C in the cold season. The warmest temperatures, over 26°C are recorded in Wolf , Darwin and in the northern islands (Marchena, Pinta and Tower).

In zone 3 and 4, the mean temperature varies from 23.2°C to 27.2°C during the warm season (Jan. 1975).

In zone 5, Caleta Iguana (West Isabela), mean temperatures are from 20.7°C to 24.6°C in the warm season. These drop to an average 16°C in the cool season and as low as 13°C depending on the Niña years.

As a whole we may conclude that sea surface temperatures in the Galápagos are a typically cold for an equatorial region, and show a strong similarity to austral temperatures of the southern hemisphere, comparable to a latitude of 10–20° south. As a consequence, the marine climate of the Galápagos is considered as subtropical, although the northern islands would be more tropical and the southern islands more temperate.

SALINITY, OXYGEN, NUTRIENTS AND TIDES

Salinity is on average 35ppm, for cold waters related to 'upwellings', or deep waters coming up to the surface. This phenomenon in turn explains a subsaturation of the waters in dissolved oxygen. Nutrients are good in the west of the archipelago and poor in the east. Phytoplancton is abundant all over. The productivity of the marine ecosystem is considered high.

The movement of tides rarely exceeds two meters in amplitude, but help the flow of coastal waters. Interior currents, i.e. within the islands, flow in every possible direction, with a speed of 35 to 62 centimeters per second.

EL NIÑO EFFECT

"El Niño" is a variation of the warm Panama current, which occurs every three to seven years, as a warming event in the eastern tropical Pacific.

The 1982–1983 Niño, which lasted for nine months, has been labelled the strongest such event known this century (Halpern 1983, Kern 1983). The sea temperature rose from 27.2°C to 30.4°C between November 1982 and August 1983. In Tagus Cove (Nov. 82) the water temperature, normally 17–19°C due to the Cromwell current, was measured at a uniform 27°C at a depth of 33 meters (Gary Robinson, 1985). The reduced salinities and nutrient regimes, high light intensities penetrating to greater depths due to water clarity, apparently triggered the loss of coral symbionts, through emigration or expulsion from coral tissues. Consequently, corals grew little and many died (Robinson, 1985).

Different drastic effects were to be seen during the 1982–83 Niño year. First, a widespread bleaching and mortality of hermatypic corals, such as Pocillopora damicornis, Pavona clavus and Porites lobata. Gorgonians, black coral, barnacles and ahermatypic corals showed the same evidence of increased mortality.

Many endemic fishes declined in abundance, but on the other hand the 1982–83 Niño favored the transport and establishment of fishes from warmer tropical regions. A significant factor contributing to the great diversity of marine forms found in the islands. Several species known to occur in the Indo-Pacific and Panamic regions were seen in abundance, such as the Moorish idol, the Filefishes, some species of Labrids (Wrasses) and Scarids (Parrotfish).

Species which showed decline in abundance: the sharks, noticeably absent; the bottlenosed dolphins, rare in the center islands; the baleen whales, which essentially disappeared from the southwest and northwest of Isabela ; and lastly, the sea lion colonies were deserted.

Data collected in the Niño year 1982–83 revealed a decrease in the population size of 17 species, 50 percent of which are endemic (Jack Grove, 1985). None are from the western Pacific origin (see list of species in lesser frequencies during El Niño 1982–83). To balance the previous fact, 19 species increased in population size and expansion range, 42 percent having zoogeographic affinities with the Indo-West Pacific (see list of species in greater frequencies p.24).

The Moorish idol was recorded for the first time on the west coast of Isabela. The Sunset wrasse was now found to be common, but was only registered in the northern islands before 1982–83. Now it is a conspicuous element of the reef fish fauna in the central and the southern islands. Two rare species, the Acapulco damselfish and the Dragon wrasse, were reported new and are now abundant. The Dorado, *Coryphaena hippurus*, which hold a commercial value for local fishermen, increased in number with the rising sea surface temperature. It came with the warm waters from the north, as its migration is latitudinal.

Jack Grove mentions 14 new records of Galápagos fishes, which were collected in May 1984 during a joint expedition of Los Angeles County Museum of Natural History and the University of Costa Rica to the islands of Wolf and Darwin.

SPECIES IN LESSER PREQUENCIES DURING EL NIÑO 1982–83

English name	Species	Family
Black-striped salema	Xenocys jessiae	Haemulidae (E)
White salema	Xenichthys agassizi	Haemulidae (E)
Black spot chromis	Azurina eupalama	Pomacentridae (E)
White spot chromis	Chromis atrilobata	Pomacentridae (PAN)
Rusty damselfish	Nexilosus latifrons	Pomacentridae (PC)
Cheekspot labrisomid	Labrisomus dentriticus	Labrisomidae (E)
Jenkins labrisomid	Labrisomus jenkinsi	Labrisomidae (E)
Castro's blenny	Acanthemblemaria castroii	Chaenopsidae (E)
Dusky chub	Girella fremenvillei	Girellidae (E)
Camotillo	Paralabrax albomaculatus	Serranidae (E)
Bacalao, Yellow grouper	Mycteroperca olfax	Serranidae (E)
Galápagos sheephead	Semicossyphus darwinii	Labridae (PC)
Loosetooth parrotfish	Nicholsina denticulata	Scaridae (PAN)
Spotted eagle ray	Aetobatus narinari	Myliobatidae (CIR)
Round stingray	Urotrygon sp.	Dasyatidae (CIR)
Requiem sharks	Carcharhinus spp.	Carcharhinidae (CIR)
Scalloped hammerhead	Sphyrna lewini	Sphyrnidae (CIR)

Distribution:
(E) = Endemic, (PAN) = Panamic, (PC) = Peru-Chile, (CIR) = Circumtropical

(after Jack Grove, 1985) in Gary Robinson's El Niño in the Galápagos.

SPECIES IN GREATER FREQUENCIES DURING EL NIÑO 1982–83

English names	Species	Family
Wahoo	Acanthocybium solandri	Scombridae (WP)
Yellowfin surgeonfish	Acanthurus xanthopterus	Acanthuridae (WP)
White tail surgeonfish	Acanthurus glaucopareius	Acanthuridae (WP)
Stripe tail aholehole	Kuhlia mugil	Kuhlidae (WP)
Scrawled filefish	Aluterus scriptus	Balistidae (WP)
Moorish idol	Zanclus canescens	Zanclidae (WP)
Sunset wrasse	Thalassoma lutescens	Labridae (WP)
Dragon wrasse	Hemipterodontus taeniourus	Labridae (WP)
	Pseudojulis notospilus	Labridae (PAN)
Bicolor parrotfish	Scarus rubroviolaceus	Scaridae (PAN)
Reef cornetfish	Fistularia commersonii	Fistularidae (PAN)
Trumpetfish	Aulostomus chinensis	Aulostomidae (PAN)
Sierra mackerel	Scomberomus sierra	Scombridae (PAN)
Acapulco damselfish	Stegastes acapulcoensis	Pomacentridae (PAN)
Blue bronze chub	Kyphosus analogus	Kyphosidae (PAN)
Cortez sea chub	Kyphosus elegans	Kyphosidae (PAN)
Pike needlefish	Strongylura exilis	Belonidae (PAN)
Dolphinfish	Coryphaena hippurus	Coryphaenidae (CIR)
Jacks	Caranx spp.	Carangidae (CIR)

Distribution:
(WP) = West-Pacific, (PAN) = Panamic, (CIR) = Circumtropical
water depth < or = 50 meters.

(after Jack Grove, 1985) in: El Niño en Galápagos, The 1982–83 event

EL NIÑO—LA NIÑA PHENOMENON

Recent knowledge shows that El Niño lasts on average 12 to 18 months. For the last 5,000 years, the event has been recurrent every two to eight years and its frequency is increasing. The global warming of the planet is almost certainly having an influence on this.

El Niño is part of a remarkable cycle that has for consequence a prolonged dry period—a cold event known as La Niña. Since 1965, five Niño events have been recorded: 1975–76, 1982–83, 1986–87, 1993–94 and 1997–98. These Niños have always been followed by periods of drought, that last for two or three years.

The 1982–83 and the 1997–98 events were the strongest reported in that century with very heavy rains in the islands. For the last 34 years the El Niño—La Niña oscillations have repeated every seven years. Following the recent Niño that ended in May 1998, the dry period stretched over 1999 and 2000. Marine life that normally suffers during Niño years (death of marine iguanas and sea lions, disappearance of fish species) recuperates greatly in Niña years thanks to cold waters rich in plankton, nutrients and various organisms. The scientific observations made by the Darwin Station (1999) confirm that the Niña events last longer within the Galápagos archipelago than in the Central Pacific.

The Niño phenomenon was mentioned in old writings from Peru dating back to 1525. The Inca themselves knew of its existence and built villages on hilltops with food caches in the mountains. Geological evidence from 13,000 years ago has also been discovered. The 1997–98 Niño was predicted months in advance by the scientific community.

PART III: CORAL REEFS * CORAL BIOLOGY * CORAL IN THE GALÁPAGOS

Expecting to find corals in mostly exotic tropical places, few people would believe that there are indeed corals in the Galápagos, not to mention coral reefs.

Coral development does actually need a minimum temperature of 18°C to 20°C, clear and well oxygenated waters, and a lot of light. Therefore corals tend to prefer shallow tropical waters in order to fill all these requirements for their establishment.

The development of coral reef structures is generally restricted to the warm tropical seas of the world between latitudes 20°N and 20°S.

A study on the matter revealed the presence of significant structural reefs in the Galápagos at several widespread locations in the islands (Glynn, Wellington, Jan. 1975). Their development is of course related to the temperature of the water, and gives us indications of the fish fauna present in a particular area. Indo-West Pacific fishes will show a definite preference for the corals or coral reef biota.

CORAL BIOLOGY

Corals belong to the Phylum Cnidaria, class Anthozoa, order Scleractinia. Anatomically, they are similar to sea anemones with the only difference being that corals secrete a calcium carbonate exoskeleton.

Coral reefs, like tropical rain forests, rank among the Earth's most complex biological systems (Peter Glynn). Any given coral contains a multitude of plant and animal species, representing a wide range of life forms. The association and interaction of these species to obtain food, shelter and other requisites, comprise the total reef community.

Simply defined, coral reefs are rigid structures formed in shallow warm seas from the calcareous skeletal remains of corals, coralline algae and other organisms. The internal structure of reefs may consist of coral skeleton undisturbed since growth, but more commonly it is made up of dislocated skeletons, skeletal sand and debris, that have been compacted and cemented together (Glynn).

Even though some coral reefs grow rapidly, building vertically at the rate of 10–15 meters every 1,000 years, a more common rate for that span of time is one to five meters.

The significant corals for reef building are called 'scleractinian' or stony coral, because the outer tissue layer deposits a calcareous skeleton. Other coelenterates that form calcareous deposits are the hydrocorals and the soft and horny corals.

The polyp is the basic functional unit of stony corals. This little animal has a hollow cylindrical body and a ring of tentacles surrounding a mouth (ref. fig.1), that functions as the only major opening to a sac-like gut. Stony corals are armed with stinging cells or nematocysts that are used for the capture of food, as well as for defense.

Coral can reproduce both sexually and asexually. In sexual reproduction, egg and sperm unite to produce a free swimming larva that eventually settles and develops into a polyp. Asexual reproduction occurs through budding, the outgrowth of an extension of the adult body cavity. The daughter polyp remains attached to the original polyp, and by constant addition of new buds, colonies are formed. In some species they may reach several meters in diameter, and achieve an age of 1,000 years.

There are two kinds of stony corals: the hermatypic and the ahermatypic. The reef building or hermatypic coral (from the Greek *hermatos*: mound) contains within the inner tissue layer a symbiotic alga, known as zooxanthellae, that speeds the calcification process. The ahermatype, the non-reef building coral, lacks the symbiotic alga and calcifies slowly. These are not confined to warm or sun lit waters. They may form extensive banks in calm deep waters of the higher latitudes.

In the coral-algal partnership, which is known to be 200 million years old (since Triassic times), the symbiotic algae zooxanthellae depend on light for photosynthesis. For this reason, hermatypic corals flourish only in shallow waters, seldom deeper than 100 meters.

The beneficial effects arising from the coral and zooxanthellae partnership are numerous and include:
    — Accelerated skeletal formation.
    — Availability of algal photosynthetic products to the coral host.
    — Efficient recycling of nutrients between partners.

Since both symbiont and host benefit from this association, it is described as a mutual form of symbiosis.

The fastest rates of skeletal formation occur when conditions are favorable for photosynthesis: that is, during midday hours, under cloudless skies, in clear water, and when the sun's rays are almost vertical.

CORALS IN THE GALÁPAGOS

In comparison to the Western Pacific reefs, the hermatypic coral fauna in the Eastern Pacific is considered depauperate, or poorly represented. Wellington (1975) numbered six genera of hermatypic corals present in the Galápagos Islands: Agaricella, Pavona, Porites, Pocillopora, Cycloseris, Psammocora. The last three genera are reef building.

In a later study *Coral and Coral Reefs in the Galápagos* (1983), Peter Glynn and G. Wellington recorded about 20 species of hermatypes, of which six are considered to be found only in the Galápagos and extreme eastern Pacific. The remaining species have an Indo-West Pacific distribution.

Coral growth is limited to the subtidal zone. White sandy beaches (Tortuga Bay, in Santa Cruz; Gardner Bay, in Española) often signify the nearby presence of actively growing corals, for their location is not apparent in the islands. The majority of coral growth in the archipielago constitutes coral communities or scattered patches of coral heads of variable density, which do little to influence or alter the physical conditions of the surrounding environments.

Structural reefs are not common. When they occur, they form impressive structures. At Onslow Island (also known as Devil's Crown) near Floreana, and along the adjacent side of Punta Cormorant, the branching coral *Pocillopora*, forms a one- or two-meter thick veneer over the underlying lava substrate. In Devil's Crown (remains of a half submerged volcanic cone), the reef covers an area of one hectare and constitutes a solid mass of branching corals, growing all about the same level. At extreme low water, the reef comes one meter below the surface. Towards the outer edges of the *Pocillopora* community, in deeper waters (three to four meters), massive colonies of *Porites* and *Pavona* are evident. Outside the north-east corner, in 20 meters of water, we find an extensive colony of *Cycloseris mexicana*, mixed with individuals of *Cycloseris elegans*.

On the northeast of Punta Cormorant, *Pocillopora* forms a non-continuous fringing reef which extends laterally along the point, a distance of approximately 150 meters. Seaward extension of the fringing reef averages ten meters from the shore (Glynn and Wellington, 1983).

Presence of coral reef formation in Galápagos / Dominating species:
- Champion Island (west coast)   *Pavona* and *Porites*
- Wolf Island (East Bay)   *Pavona* and *Porites*
- Darwin Island (tongue extension east)   *Pocillopora*
- Bartolomé Island (south coast)   *Porites* and *Pavona*
- Onslow Island (center part)   *Pocillopora*

In situations where the subtidal vertical profile is steep, *Porites* and *Pavona* predominate as reef building corals.

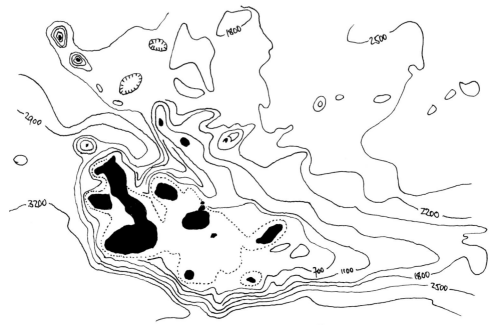

Bathymetry in the Galápagos

Cromwell current

Upwelling zones

© Piroco 2002

The *Pavona* coral is variable in form. Either large knobby or columnar colonies in massive groups or thin plate-like sheets often stacked like shingles. At Champion, near Floreana, the reef profile is seven meters thick.

The deepest record of reef building coral reported in the Eastern Pacific was made at Wolf Island, where *Pavona/Porites* corals extend from ten meters to 37.5 meters deep (Wellington, 1975). Both Wolf and Champion islands are characterized by clear water conditions with an average of 25 meters visibility.

At Champion Island, the vertical distribution of coral reef species down to 20 meters shows an interesting hierarchy scale: *Pavona, Porites, Pocillopora*. The slower growing corals, *Pavona* and *Porites* are dominant over the rapid accreting branching coral (Glynn, 1972):

- *Pocillopora* is found from 1.5 to three meters deep
- *Porites* from three to eight meters deep
- *Pavona clavus* from five to 15 meters deep
- *Pavona gigantea* from ten to 20 meters deep

The temperatures markedly affects coral growth and will determine its presence or absence in a given area (Glynn and Stewart, 1973).

The absence of a coral reef fauna along the west coast of Isabela and around Fernandina is related to the fact that average monthly temperatures from June to December (cool season) fall well below the minimum required to support coral growth. The usual temperature of 16–17°C is caused by the sporadic upwelling of the equatorial undercurrent (Cromwell current). At Punta Espinosa (north-east Fernandina), where the water temperature in a sheltered bay is around 20°C, the presence of *Pocillopora* branching coral has been made possible.

Due to the cool waters driven northward by the Peru current, for four to six months per year, the Galápagos is considered a marginal environment for reef development. From July to November, when the Peru current is flowing at its maximum, water temperatures in the central region vary from 19 to 23°C. It is only during the warm season, when the warm waters from the north raise the water temperature to 27–29°C, that the coral growth is accelerated.

If hermatypic coral growth does not occur in areas with an average temperature below 20°C the reef development is mostly restricted to areas with temperatures over 25°C (Stehli and Wells, 1971).

Applying Glynn's (1972) observation of one meter = 250 years, the age of the oldest reef known in Galápagos would be around 1,750 to 2,000 years. The greatest reef build up was found at Champion, Floreana, where the fathograms indicated a thickness of seven to eight meters. A small fragment of *Pocillopora* was also found near Villamil (Isabela) and estimated to be 5,000 to 6,000 years old.

As expected, there are quite a few coral predators in the islands, but the famous sea star, *Acanthaster planci*, responsible for heavy depredation in Australian waters and in the Western Pacific, is absent from the Galápagos islands. Instead, we find several actual and potential reef corallivores, among which:

• *Scarus ghobban* (Blue chin parrotfish) and *Scarus perrico* (Bumphead parrot-fish), both species from the Panamic province (family Scaridae) feed on *Pavona* and *Porites* corals.
• The Tiggerfish (*Sufflamen verres*), species from the Panamic province (family Balistidae), feeds on *Pocillopora* and *Porites*.

Other predators include pufferfishes, *Arothron hispidus*, the White spotted puffer and *Arothron meleagris*, the Guineafowl puffer; the hermit crabs, *Trizopagurus magnificus* and *Aniculus elegans*, both nocturnal species feeding on *Pocillopora*; and the Pencil sea urchin, *Eucidaris thouarsii*, as in Onslow Island, Floreana.

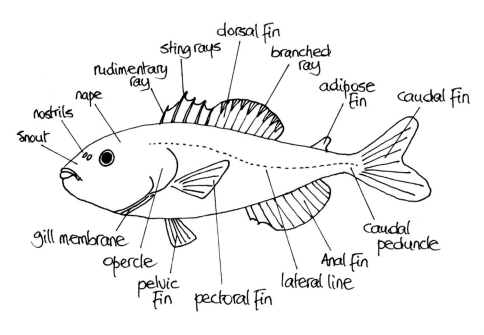

Parts of a fish

© Piraco 2002

FISHES

PART I: HISTORY * PACIFIC PROVINCES * ENDEMIC FISHES * INDEX OF FAMILIES * CLASSIFICATION BY SHAPES AND LOOKS

Aboard the *HMS Beagle*, bound for a five-year journey around the globe, was the famous english naturalist Charles Darwin, the first man ever to collect and record the fishes from the Galápagos Islands. At the time, in 1835, the 15 specimens he collected were all new to science. Later, in 1842, the Reverend Leonard Jenyns described and illustrated Darwin's collection, of which five species are today considered endemic to the Galápagos. He even gave Darwin's name to the Galápagos sheephead, *Semicossyphus darwini*, in honor of the collector.

Many expeditions followed Darwin's journey, among them the French expedition aboard the frigate *La Venus*, when 13 new species were described by Achille Valenciennes in 1855. Then we should mention Professor Louis Agassiz of Harvard, conducting the first American expedition in 1873, and the expeditions of the US Fisheries Service *Albatross* in 1888 and 1891. In 1898–99, two distinguished zoologists, Heller and Snodgrass, spent six months in the islands with the Hopkins Standford Galápagos Expedition and eventually published a record of 128 species (in 1905), of which 20 were new. Zoologist William Beebe, famous for his book *Galápagos World's End*, came to Galápagos in 1923 and 1925, and made a collection for the Harrison Williams Galápagos Expedition of the New York Zoological Society.

After the visits of Allan Hancock in 1928, and ichtyologists Seale and Myers during 1931–1935 on the *Veleros I–III*, and then Rosenblatt and Walker between 1961–1963 the total number of shore species recorded stood at 269 fishes. This was increased still further to 289 species by Boyd Walker in 1966.

For approximately the next 20 years the number remained the same (Wellington 1975). Peter Scott, aboard the *MS Lindblad Explorer* in 1976, made colorful drawings of 33 species of fishes. In 1984, Jack Grove, a Galápagos Naturalist guide, published with the Instituto Nacional de Pesca of Guayaquil, Ecuador, a very precise report including 105 black and white detailed drawings of fishes collected in the Galápagos. The same year, Mc Cosker and Rosenblatt reported a new list of 306 species from 91 families, following collections made in 1978. This number is very significant when compared to Easter Island (109 species), but less than the Hawaïan Islands where 471 inshore fishes have been recorded (Randall 1976, 1980).

The Galápagos definitely shows a high degree of affinity—almost 60 percent of the species (177)—to the eastern tropical mainland or Panamic province. A small number of eight percent is considered pantropical. An even smaller number is closely related to the Peru-Chile province, and only four species are common to the Atlantic (see List of the Peru-Chile province, p.33).

After the Panamic province, the second significant population of fishes comes from the western Pacific or Indo-West Pacific province with 14 percent (43 species) (see list of the Indo-West Pacific fishes, p.33).

In their publication *The Fishes of the Galápagos Islands* (1997), Jack Grove and R. Lavenberg brought the number of fish to 460 species. The endemism of the Galápagos shorefish fauna is very conspicuous: 51 species, representing 11 percent of the total number. Out of these 51 species, five are also found at Cocos Island and Malpelo (see List of endemic species, p.36).

The degree of endemism varies between families:
- Snake eels (Ophichtyidae)   3 endemic out of 9 species
- Grunts (Haemulidae)   4 endemic out of 9 species
- Croakers (Scianidae)   3 endemic out of 5 species
- Gobies (Gobiidae)   3 endemic out of 5 species
- Eleotrids (Eleotrididae)   3 endemic out of 5 species
- Sand stargazers (Dactyloscopidae)   3 endemic out of 4 species
- Labrisomid blennies (Labrisomidae)   4 endemic out of 7 species
- Viviparous brotulas (Bythitidae)   5 endemic out of 6 species
- Pike blennies (Chaenopsidae)   3 endemic out of 3 species
- Mullets (Mugilidae)   3 endemic out of 5 species

In these families we find a high degree of endemism.

The families showing none or few endemic species are:
- Morays (Muraenidae)   none of 16 species
- Groupers (Serranidae)   two of 23 species
- Jacks (Carangidae)   none of 23 species
- Wrasses (Labridae)   none of 12 species
- True blennies (Blenniidae)   none of 3 species

In 2004, the latest research of Dr. Philippe Bearez, of the French Museum d'Histoire Naturelle in Paris, revealed a total of 938 species of fish found in Ecuador, in which 448 species belong to the waters of the mainland only; 162 species belong to the Galápagos waters only and 288 belong to both Ecuador and Galápagos. This brought a total of 450 species of fish recorded in the Galápagos Islands, and 776 species of fish recorded for Ecuador (Jimenez-Prado P. & Bearez P. 2004, Peces marinos del Ecuador continental/Marine fish of continental Ecuador, SIMBIOE/NAZCA/IFEA, Quito, T.1 130 pages; T.2 401 pages).

In September 2005, 'fish base' indicated a total number of 465 species for Galápagos, including 86 endemic species. This means that now 17% of the fish are endemic to the Galápagos Islands (endemism is shared with Malpelo, Cocos and revillagigedos Islands for some species).

The vagility—or transport ability—of the larval and/or adult stages, and the duration of the larval stage are two important factors responsible for the arrival of an organism to an island. Jacks and tunas, for example, are strong pelagic swimmers and have no difficulty in crossing the 650-mile barrier separating the Galápagos from the mainland.

Larval stages well suited to pelagic life (serranids, blennies) and larval or adult stages that inhabit floating detritus (wrasses, blennies) find no difficulty covering a distance across water (Mc Cosker and Rosenblatt, 1984).

Short larval stages unsuitable to open water transport (croakers, grunts), but fortuitously arriving at an island, have an opportunity to differentiate (eg. Labrisomid blennies). The only labrisomid not endemic to the Galápagos, *Labrisomus multiporosus*, has an unusually long larval stage and is found largely distributed in the Pacific.

FISHES REPRESENTATIVE OF THE PERU-CHILE PROVINCE

English name	Family	Species
Galápagos hornshark	Heterodontidae	*Heterodontus quoyi*
Moray eel	Muraenidae	*Muraena panamensis*
White-spotted rock seabass	Serranidae	*Paralabrax albomaculatus*
Gray threadfin seabass	Serranidae	*Cratinus agassizii*
Pacific beakfish, tigris	Oplegnathidae	*Oplegnathus insigne*
Amberjack	Carangidae	*Seriola peruana*
Rusty damselfish	Pomacentridae	*Nexilosus latifrons*
Harlequin wrasse	Labridae	*Bodianus eclancheri*
Deep water wrasse	Labridae	*Pimelometopon darwinii*
Afuera goby	Labrisomiidae	*Malacoctenus afuerae*
Bonito	Scombridae	*Sarda chilensis*
Ocean whitefish	Branchiostegidae	*Caulolatilus princeps*

FISHES REPRESENTATIVE OF THE INDO-WEST PACIFIC PROVINCE

English name	Family	Species
Tiger shark	Carcharhinidae	*Galeocerdo cuvieri*
White tip reef shark	Carcharhinidae	*Triaenodon obesus*
Smooth hammerhead	Sphyrnidae	*Sphyrna zygaena*
Spotted eagle ray	Myliobatidae	*Aetobatus narinari*
Zebra moray	Muraenidae	*Gymnomuraena zebra*
Paint-spotted moray	Muraenidae	*Siderea picta*

continued overleaf

FISHES REPRESENTATIVE OF THE INDO-WEST PACIFIC PROVINCE (CONT'D)

English name	Family	Species
Black moray	Muraenidae	Gymnothorax buroensis
Green halfbeak	Hemirhamphidae	Euleptorhampus viridis
Reef cornet fish	Fistularidae	Fistularia petimba
Pipe fish	Sygnathidae	Doryrhampus melanopleura
Milkfish	Chanidae	Chanos chanos
Striped mullet	Mugilidae	Mugil cephalus
Stripetail aholehole	Kuhlidae	Kuhlia taenuria
Soldierfish	Holocentridae	Myripristis murdjan
Bigeye	Priacanthidae	Priacanthus cruentatus
Blue fin jack	Carangidae	Caranx melampygus
Bicolore parrotfish	Scaridae	Scarus rubroviolaceus
Blue parrotfish	Scaridae	Scarus ghobban
Halftoothed parrotfish	Scaridae	Calotomus spinidens
Green wrasse	Labridae	Thalassoma grammaticum
Dragon wrasse	Labridae	Novaculichthys taeniourus
Moorish idol	Zanclidae	Zanclus canescens
Convict tang	Acanthuridae	Acanthurus triostegus
Yellowfin surgeonfish	Acanthuridae	Acanthurus xanthopterus
Gold rim surgeonfish	Acanthuridae	Acanthurus glaucopareius
Speckled triggerfish	Balistidae	Canthidermis maculatus
Black triggerfish	Balistidae	Melichthys niger
Pinktail triggerfish	Balistidae	Melichthys vidua
Redtail trigerfish	Balistidae	Xantichthys mento
Blue striped triggerfish	Balistidae	Xantichthys caeruleolineatus
Scrawled filefish	Balistidae	Aluterus scriptus
Spotted sharpnose puffer	Tetraodontidae	Canthigaster punctatissima
Guineafowl puffer	Tetraodontidae	Arothron meleagris
White spotted puffer	Tetraodontidae	Arothron hispidus
Balloonfish	Diodontidae	Diodon holocanthus
Porcupinefish	Diodontidae	Diodon hystrix
Pacific burrfish	Diodontidae	Chilomycterus affinis
Pacific boxfish	Ostraciidae	Ostracion meleagris
Chaenopsid blenny	Chaenopsidae	Eklemblemaria
Sailfin leaffish	Scorpaenidae	Taenianotus triacanthus
Long nose hawfish	Cirrhitidae	Oxycirrhites typus
Coral hawkfish	Cirrhitidae	Cirrhitichthys oxycephalus

Endemic Fishes of the Galápagos

English name	Family	Species
Blacktip cardinalfish	Apogonidae	*Apogon atradorsatus*
Pink brotula	Bythitidae	*Ogilbia galápagosensis*
Orange brotula	Bythitidae	*Ogilbia deroyi*
new species	Bythitidae	*Ogilbia species*
Tailspot brotula	Bythitidae	*Calamopteryx jeb*
Castro's tube blenny	Chaenopsidae	*Acanthemblemaria castroii*
Galápagos pike blenny	Chaenopsidae	*Chaenopsis schmitti*
	Chaenopsidae	*Eklemblemaria species*
Bicollar false moray	Chlopsidae	*Chlopsis bicollaris*
Galápagos thread herring	Clupeidae	*Opisthonema berlangai*
Galápagos garden eel	Congridae	*Heteroconger klausewitzi*
Shortfin sand stargazer	Dactyloscopidae	*Platigillellus rubellulus*
Arrow sand stargazer	Dactyloscopidae	*Myxodagnus sagitta*
Milky sand stargazer	Dactyloscopidae	*Dactyloscopus lacteus*
Galápagos sleeper	Eleotrididae	*Eleotrica cableae*
Dusky chub	Girellidae	*Girella fremenvillei*
Red clingfish	Gobiesocidae	*Arcos poecilophtalmus*
Mystery goby	Gobiidae	*Chriolepis tagus*
Brokenband cleaner goby	Gobiidae	*Elecatinus nesiotes* (*)
Blue-banded goby	Gobiidae	*Lythrypnus gilberti*
Forbes grunt	Haemulidae	*Orthopristis forbesi*
Scalyfin grunt	Haemulidae	*Orthopristis lethopristis*
White salema	Haemulidae	*Xenichthys agassizi*
Black-striped salema	Haemulidae	*Xenichthys jessiae*
Galápagos razorfish	Labridae	*Xyrichtys victori*
Jenkins blenny	Labrisomidae	*Labrisommus jenkinsii*
Spotblenny goby	Labrisomidae	*Malacoctenus zonogaster*
Galápagos blenny	Labrisomidae	*Starksia galapagensis*
Four-eyed blenny	Labrisomidae	*Dialommus fuscus* (*)
Cheekspot labrisomid	Labrisomidae	*Labrisommus dentriticus* (*)
Yellowtail mullet, lisa	Mugilidae	*Mugil galapagensis*
Galápagos batfish	Ogcocephalidae	*Dibranchus species*
Galápagos snake eel	Ophichthyidae	*Callechelys galapagensis*
Pouch snake eel	Ophichthyidae	*Paraletharchus opercularis*
Thread snake eel	Ophichhytidae	*Apterichtus equatorialis*
Galápagos cusk eel	Ophidiidae	*Ophidion species*
Black spot chromis	Pomacentridae	*Azurina eupalama*
Yellowtail damselfish	Pomacentridae	*Stegastes arcifrons*
Galápagos croaker	Sciaenidae	*Umbrina galapagorum*

ENDEMIC FISHES OF THE GALÁPAGOS (CONT'D)

English name	Family	Species
Wide eye croaker	Sciaenidae	*Odontoscion eurymesops* (*)
Galápagos rock croaker	Sciaenidae	*Pareques perissa*
Stalkeye scorpionfish	Scorpaenidae	*Pontinus strigatus*
Bacalao, yellow grouper	Serranidae	*Mycteroperca olfax* (*)
White-spotted rock grouper	Serranidae	*Paralabrax albomaculatus*
Sideblotch bass	Serranidae	*Serranus stilbostigma*
Galápagos seabrim	Sparidae	*Archosargus pourtalesii*
Concave puffer	Tetraodontidae	*Sphoeroides angusticeps*
Galápagos cutlassfish	Trichiuridae	*Lepidopus manis*
Orange throat searobin	Triglidae	*Prionotus miles*
Finspot triplefin blenny	Tripterygiidae	*Lepidonectes corallicola*

50 species; (*) = Five species also found at Cocos Island and Malpelo Island.

FISHES FROM THE PANAMIC PROVINCE

8 species of sharks
4 species of rays
5 species of wrasse
5 species of parrotfish
3 species of blennies
3 species of clinid blennies
5 species of surgeonfishes
7 species of mackerels
2 species of gobies
2 species of scorpionfishes
1 species of sole
6 species of triggerfishes
3 species of puffers
2 species of porcupinefishes
2 species of frogfishes
1 species of boxfish
3 species of hawkfishes
6 species of damselfishes
3 species of butterflyfishes
3 species of pipefish
1 species of cornetfish
1 species of aholehole
5 species of grunt
1 species of porgy
1 species of goatfish
1 species of halfbeak

1 species of angelfish
11 species of jack
2 species of snapper
1 species of dolphin
4 species of mojarra
6 species of seabass
2 species of mullet
1 species of tilefish
1 species of bigeye
1 species of barracuda
1 species of bonefish
1 species of soapfish
2 species of cardinalfish
1 species of snook
3 species of needlefish
1 species of trumpetfish
4 species of snake eel
2 species of conger eel
14 species of moray
2 species of lizardfish
3 species of flying fish
1 species of silverside
3 species of herring
3 species of flounder
3 species of squirrelfish

INDEX OF FAMILIES OF FISHES

continued overleaf

INDEX OF FAMILIES OF FISHES (CONT'D)

CLASSIFICATION BY SHAPE AND LOOK

continued overleaf

CLASSIFICATION BY SHAPE AND LOOK (CONT'D)

PART II: Description of Families and Fishes

Cornetfishes, Trumpetfishes, Pipefishes

Cornetfishes (Fistularidae)

Long slender type of fish with depressed body. The mouth is at the end of a tubular snout. Dorsal and anal fins short-based, close together, posterior location. Caudal fin forked, giving way to a tail looking filament. No scales.

Occurs in tropical and subtropical coastal areas of the world.

REEF CORNETFISH *(Fistularia commersonii)*
Also known as Flutemouth. Apparently translucent, with pale whitish-greenish color and two thin blue stripes along the body. A rather shy species, solitary, found in coral reefs area (Devil's Crown, Floreana; Gardner Bay, Española). Shallow waters or near shore. Length around one meter.
Pacific range: Baja california to Ecuador, including Cocos and Galápagos islands (*see* photo 1, p.49).

Trumpetfishes (Aulostomidae)

Similar to previous family. Body elongated. Mouth at the end of a tubular snout. The only difference is a chin barbel, and isolated dorsal spines, looking like sails. Color variation brown or yellow. Tropical Pacific distribution.

TRUMPETFISH *(Aulostomus chinensis)*
Dorsally brown or gray; caudal fin yellow-pink with dark spots. Dorsal rays pink. Feed on shrimps and small fishes. Inhabits coral reef areas, and shallow water bays (Devil's Crown, Floreana; Punta Suarez, Española; Marchena Island). Length up to 75 centimeters (*see* photos 2, 3, p.49).
Pacific range: Panama, Costa Rica, Clipperton, Revillagigedos, Malpelo, Cocos, Easter Island and Galápagos.

Pipefish (Syngnathidae)

Small toothless mouth at the end of a tubular snout. Most species with pectoral and dorsal fins, pelvic fin is absent. Anal fin small, when present. Seahorses are included in this family of fishes, with small bodies encased in bony rings. A unique feature is the male's pouch in which the young are reared.

FANTAIL PIPEFISH *(Doryrhampus species)*
Color brown, dorsal fin yellowish. Uncommon species, timid. Shallow waters in coral and algae environment. Length five centimeters (Grove).
Pacific range: Indo-West Pacific, Eastern Pacific from Baja California to Ecuador, Clipperton, Cocos and Malpelo.

PACIFIC SEAHORSE *(Hippocampus ingens)*
Anal fin, small prehensile tail. Males have a brood pouch. Color may vary from red, black to light brown. Uncommon. Areas of coral development, marine algae, rocky substrates, rubble, volcanic sandy bottoms (Tagus Cove). Often found in the yellow branches of the Galápagos black coral (Cousin's Rock). Also seen at Punta Moreno, North Seymour *(see photos 4, 5, p.50).*
Pacific range: Baja California to Peru, including Galápagos.

Needlefishes, Halfbreaks, Flyingfishes
Needlefishes (Belonidae)

Elongate, cylindrical, compressed bodies. Jaws very long, beak-like, armed with sharp teeth. Pelvic fins abdominal. Dorsal and anal fins far back. Needlefishes are surface dwellers and skitter over the water. Feed on small fish.

PIKE NEEDLEFISH *(Strongylura exilis)*
Head and back green with black speckles. Ventrally silver-white. A dark stripe along side of body. Caudal fin black. Length up to 50 centimeters.
Pacific range: Indo-West Pacific, California to Peru, including Cocos and Galápagos islands. Found throughout the archipielago in bays and mangrove areas, at the surface. Common in the hot season, from January to March *(see photo 6, p.50).*

Halfbeaks (Hemirhampidae), Flyingfishes (Exocoetidae)

Halfbeaks are either belonging to the family Hemirhampidae (strict halfbeaks) or to the family Exocoetidae, which comprise of two groups: the Halfbeaks and the Flyingfishes. Cylindrical body, pectoral fins located high on the sides, abdominal pelvic fins, posterior dorsal and anal fins. Halfbeaks have long lower jaw.

HALFBEAK *(Hyporhampus unifasciatus)*
Elongate, slightly compressed. Greenish above, scales dark-edged, silvery below. Black lines on mid-dorsal area between head and dorsal fin. Tip of lower jaw bright orange red. Usually seen on surface near shore. Common in the warm season. Favorite bait for dolphins and sharks *(see photo 7, p.51).*
Pacific range: From California to Peru, including Galápagos. Indo-West Pacific.

FLYINGFISH *(Exocoetidae)*
Differs from the halfbeaks by having greatly enlarged pectoral fins and elongated pelvic fins. Flyingfish do not really fly but glide over the surface of the water on ther pectoral fins. Three species in the Galápagos Islands: *Cheilopogon dorsomaculata, Prognichthys seali, Exocoetus monocirrhus* (*see* photo 8, p.51).
Pacific range: Indo-West Pacific, and throughout the Pacific to the eastern border.

Parrotfishes, Wrasses

Probably the most common fish around the archipielago. All the scaridae are from the Panamic region (five parrotfish out of six), but two, *Scarus ghobban* and *Scarus rubroviolaceus*, also share the Indo-West Pacific province.

Out of eight labrids, five wrasses share the Panamic origin, two the Peru-Chilean: *Bodianus eclancheri* and the famous *Semicossyphus darwinii*, the Galápagos sheep-head. The *Novac0ulichthys taeniourus*, Dragon wrasse (McCosker, 1978) and *Thalassoma grammaticum*, the Green wrasse, originate from the Western Pacific. The latter became very common in the 1982–83 Niño year. Parrotfishes and wrasses are very colorful fishes, generally associated with coral development and coral reefs.

Parrotfishes (Scaridae)

Have the particularity of uncommon teeth that are fused to form beak-like plates in both jaws. They have a single uninterrupted dorsal skin, and large cycloid scales. Even though they are considered herbivores, they are potential, if not actual, reef corallivores.

BLUE CHIN PARROTFISH *(Scarus ghobban)*
Probably related to the Blue Parrotfish (*Scarus coerulus*) of the Caribbean, the Blue Chin Parrotfish is very common to the Indo-West Pacific and to the California shore fishes. Sexual dimorphism is conspicuous in this species, often found in schools. Females are bright orange with five irregular pale blue vertical stripes from head to tail. The male is more bluish-greenish all over the body, with tinges of orange and pink. Purple radiating lines behind the eyes. Known to be a predator on *Pavona* and *Porites* corals. Length up to 50 centimeters (*see* photos 9, 10, pp.51–2).
Pacific range: Indo-West Pacific, Gulf of California to Ecuador, including Galápagos.

BUMPHEAD PARROTFISH *(Scarus perrico)*
Unmistakably recognizable by its original bump on the head. Colors mix from green-blue to orange-yellow on the nose. Dorsal and caudal fins rather blue or dark green. Big jaws. Also a predator of the *Pavona* and *Porites* corals. Usually alone, sometimes in groups of three to four. Common in coral areas. Length up to 50 centimeters (*see* photo 11, p.52).
Pacific range: Gulf of California to Peru, including Cocos and Galápagos.

BICOLOR PARROTFISH *(Scarus rubroviolaceus)*
In both sexes, the body is clearly marked by two different colors. Males have dark green anterior and light red-green posterior. Females have brownish-red anterior and light brown posterior. Caudal fin square in male and female. Frequents coral reefs. Length about 40 centimeters (*see* photos 12, 13, pp.52–3).
Pacific range: Tropical Indo-Pacific, central Gulf of California to Panama, Galápagos.

AZURE PARROTFISH *(Scarus compressus)*
Males with bright green bodies, each scale outlined with orange. Green streaks radiate from eye ring. Juveniles are reddish-brown. Females light blue to blue-gray. Length about 50 centimeters (*see* photo 14, p.53). Pacific range: Gulf of California to Galápagos.

Wrasses (Labridae)

Another big family very present around coral development. Wrasses may change sex and their patterns. Males and females are usually shaded differently. Thick lips are very conspicuous, hiding strong canine teeth in the jaws. Single dorsal fin with weak spines. Lateral line following the dorsal contour, continuous or interrupted. Twelve species of labrids in Galápagos, one is endemic: *Xyrichtys victori*, the Galápagos razorfish.

MEXICAN HOGFISH *(Bodianus diplotaenia)*
Males have a slight bump on the head, a gray-green light brown body with a clear vertical yellow stripe behind the pectoral fin. Females have a more elongated body, with two horizontal black stripes, interrupted, rather reddish underparts, gray color, yellowish tail. Common around the islands over rocky substrates and coral reef areas. Length up to 40 centimeters (*see* photos 15, 16, 17, 18, pp.53–4).
Pacific range: Gulf of California to Central Chile, including Clipperton, Revillagigedos and Galápagos.

HARLEQUIN WRASSE *(Bodianus eclancheri)*
A large bright orange wrasse, with black markings in patches, usually found on the western side of the archipielago (Isabela, Fernandina) where waters are cooler. Locally known as Vieja, the species originates from the Peru-Chilean province. Color variations from orange to white and black, or mixture of a bit of everything. This harlequin coloration may be a distinct selective disadvantage (McCosker and Rosenblatt, 1984) in terms of survival/sexual signalling value. No apparent correlation of coloration with size or sex. Species of *Bodianus* are sequential protogynous hermaphrodites, whereby young fish are females which ultimately change sex to become males. In the genus *Bodianus*, species are sexually dimorphic and dichromatic, but in the species *Bodianus eclancheri*, this is not the case. Predators are the Galápagos sea lions and the Galápagos sharks. Can also be seen in the central islands at depth of 30 meters. Length up to 40 centimeters (*see* photos 19, 20, 21, p.55).
Pacific range: From Ecuador to mid-Chile, including Galápagos.

CORTEZ RAINBOW WRASSE *(Thalassoma lucasanum)*
Although of small size, this species is nevertheless highly colorful. Also known as the Yellow-belted wrasse (Peter Scott, 1976), because the male has a conspicuous yellow belt behind a blue purple head. The rest of the body is purple. Females are smaller, but high distinctive by their black-yellow-red horizontal coloration. Length up to 15 centimeters. Shallow waters near coral reefs (*see* photos 22, 23, p.56).
Pacific range: Gulf of California to Colombia, including Cocos, Malpelo and Galápagos.

GREEN WRASSE *(Thalassoma grammaticum)*
This species was in abundance in the Galápagos during the 1982–83 Niño year, when it was formerly known as the Sunset wrasse, *Thalassoma lutescens*. Salmon-red head with wavy conspicuous purple-blue lines radiating from the eye to the area of the pectoral fin. Green-blue body. Tail white, fringed with two pink-reddish lines. Common to coral areas. Length about 20 centimeters (see photos 24, p.56).
Pacific range: Eastern Pacific, Gulf of California to Panama, including Cocos, Revilla-gigedos and Galápagos.

CHAMELEON WRASSE *(Halichoeres dispilus)*
Males have a green head with wavy conspicuous blue lines radiating from the snout. Caudal fin blackish. Body striated with green and blue. Dark spot above center of pectoral fin. Females are light brown with a white stripe from head to tail. Dark spot on the caudal peduncle. Shallow reef areas. Length about 15 centimeters (*see* photo 25, p.57).
Pacific range: Gulf of California to Peru, Cocos and Galápagos.

SPINSTER WRASSE *(Halichoeres nicholsi)*
Also known as the Saddle wrasse (Peter Scott, 1976), for the female looks whitish with a black horizontal line, and a black vertical line extending to the dorsal area from the mid-point of the horizontal line. Males are darker, blue-gray with a golden spot on the posterior tip of the opercle and above pectoral fin. Juveniles with pale yellow bodies and dark blotches. Length up to 40 centimeters. Favors sandy bottoms (*see* photos 26, 27, p.57).
Pacific range: Gulf of California to Panama, Clipperton, Cocos and Galápagos.

DRAGON WRASSE *(Novaculichthys taeniourus)*
Formerly *Hemipteronotus taeniourus*. Color primarily brown to gray, with alternating pearly-white body scales. Dorsal and anal fins reticulated with white. Dark brown bars radiate from eyes. Breast rosy, ventral fin dark brown. Vertical white band at the base of the caudal fin. Juveniles greenish to brown, with irregular brown and white markings. Juvenile mimic floating filamentous algae, to which it is similar looking in shape and color. Adults more wary, keep distance. Feeds on tiny shrimps. Found on shallow sandy and rubble bottoms near reefs, this is a solitary fish that remains close to its shelter.

Frequent during Niño year 1982–83, when the islands where bathed in warm waters. Length 15 to 30 centimeters (*see* photo 28, p.58).
Pacific range: Indo-Pacific, Polynesia, Galápagos.

BANDED WRASSE *(Liopropoma fasciatum)*
Also known as the Rainbow basslet (Allen). Yellow, black and red bands horizontally on sides. A deep water wrasse, down to 54 meters. Hiding in cracks and holes in rocky areas. Length about 15 centimeters (*see* photo 29, p.58).
Pacific range: Baja California to Mexico, Galápagos.

GALÁPAGOS SHEEPHEAD *(Semicossyphus darwinii)*
Named in 1842 by Reverend Jenyns in honor of Darwin who first collected the fish in 1835. Of a fairly big size (45 centimeters), it is somewhat related to the Pacific red sheephead, but rather different in color. Basically gray with a yellow blotch above the pectoral fin. The Galápagos sheephead favours cool waters, and is therefore found on the western side of the archipielago (west Isabela and Fernandina), where one can see it in association with the Harlequin wrasse. In shallow waters less than 30 meters (*see* photo 30, 31, pp.58–9).
Pacific range: Ecuador to Central Chile, including Galápagos.

PEACOCK WRASSE *(Xyrichtys mento)*
Also known as razorfish. Hides on sandy bottoms where it disappears into the sediment.
Pacific range: Indo-Pacific, Gulf of California to Panama, Galápagos.

GALÁPAGOS RAZORFISH *(Xyrichtys victori)*
Males dark blue with iridescent blue-green hue and various black spots of variable size. Females red to pale orange, cheek dark red, some with yellow stripe across lateral line. Iris gold. Common on soft sand where garden eels occur, below ten meters (Marchena, Baltra). Protogynous hermaphrodite. Size below 14 centimeters. Found at depth between five and 12 meters.
Pacific range: Insular endemic, Cocos and Galápagos.

Oplegnathidae

PACIFIC BEAKFISH *(Oplegnathus insigne)*
Known locally as the Tigris. Body deep, head profile abrupt. Color black, speckled white. Monkey-like face is black. Ventrally white. Caudal fin like a fan. Dorsal and anal fins far to the back, above and under caudal peduncle. Often found in association with the Harlequin wrasse. Restricted to the western side of the archipielago, West Isabela and Fernandina, where the waters are cooler. Affinities to the Peru-Chile province. Common in shallow waters to depths of 30 meters. Length up to 45 centimeters (*see* photo 32, p.59).
Pacific range: From Peru to Chile, including Galápagos.

Surgeonfishes, Angelfishes, Damselfishes, Butterflyfishes

A very colorful family of fishes, usually the excitement of coral reefs, and by far the most pleasant for the snorkeller or skin diver to view. These families are common to warm tropical waters of the Caribbean, the Pacific and the Indo-West region. Surgeonfishes (Acanthuridae) number five species in the Galápagos, the Angelfishes (Pomacanthidae) only one species, the Damselfishes or demoiselles (Pomacentridae) about ten species, and the enchanting Butterflyfishes (Chaetodontidae) five species. The Galápagos Islands are obviously not the optimal place for coral reefs and genuine tropical fishes.

Surgeonfishes (Acanthuridae)

These fishes derive their name from scalpel like spines, located on each side of the caudal peduncle. They are also known as doctors or tang. Deep compressed body, uninterrupted dorsal fin with nine spines. Surgeonfishes may slash their scalpel spin out to other fish, either to warn or to injure. They are not harmful to divers, provided they are handled carefully.

YELLOW TAIL SURGEONFISH *(Prionurus laticlavius)*
Often found in shoals around the central islands. Gray body, yellow caudal fin, two black vertical bars on the head (one over the eye, the other between the eye and pectoral fin), three white spots in a horizontal line on the caudal peduncle. The latter tell you of the scalpel spines. A very common and curious species, usually found in shallow waters throughout the archipielago. Length about 35 centimeters (*see* photo 33, p.59).
Pacific range: Revillagigedos, Cocos and Galápagos.

WHITE TAIL SURGEONFISH *(Acanthurus glaucopareius)*
Also known as the Gold-rimmed surgeonfish for the yellow contours on the body along the base of the dorsal and anal fins. A beautiful dark blue fish with a distinctive horizontal white mark under the eyes. Tail is white, striped with a vertical yellow line. This surgeonfish was found in great numbers during the 1982–83 Niño year, and obviously originates from the western Pacific. Often seen in association with the Yellow tail surgeonfish, in shallow waters and coral reefs. Length about 20 centimeters (*see* photo 34, p.60).
Pacific range: Gulf of California, Revillagigedos, Cocos and Galápagos.

YELLOW FIN SURGEONFISH *(Acanthurus xanthopterus)*
An Indo-West Pacific species, very common during the 1982–83 Niño year. Turquoise, blue-green body. Tail blue, circled in white at the base. Thin light blue rim at the base of the dorsal and anal fins. A conspicuous yellow horizontal mark on the eyes, and yellow pectoral fins. Usually seen in small schools in the northern islands, where the waters are warmer. Length about 35 centimeters (*see* photo 35, see p.60).
Pacific range: Indo-west Pacific, Cocos, Galápagos.

Photo 1: Reef Cornetfish, Flutemouth, *Fistularia commersonii*

Photo 2: Trumpetfish, *Aulostomus chinensis*

Photo 3: Trumpetfish, *Aulostomus chinensis*

Photo 4: Pacific seahorse, *Hippocampus ingens*

Photo 5: Pacific seahorse, *Hippocampus ingens* (pregnant male)

Photo 6: Needlefish, *Strongylura exilis*

Photo 7: Halfbeaks, *Hyporhampus unifasciatus*

Photo 8: Flyingfish

Photo 9: Blue chin parrotfish, *Scarus ghobban* (male)

52

Photo 10: Blue chin parrotfish, *Scarus ghobban* (female)

Photo 11: Bumphead parrotfish, *Scarus perrico* (male)

Photo 12: Bicolor parrotfish, *Scarus rubroviolaceus* (male)

Photo 13: Bicolor parrotfish, *Scarus rubroviolaceus* (female)

Photo 14: Azure parrotfish, *Scarus compressus*

Photo 15: Mexican hogfish, *Bodianus diplotaenia* (male)

54

Photo 16: Mexican hogfish, *Bodianus diplotaenia* (female)

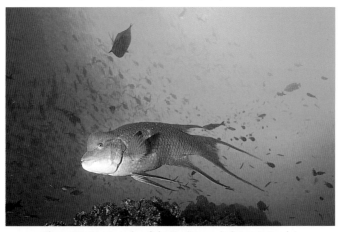

Photo 17: Mexican hogfish, *Bodianus diplotaenia* (male)

Photo 18: Mexican hogfish, *Bodianus diplotaenia* (male)

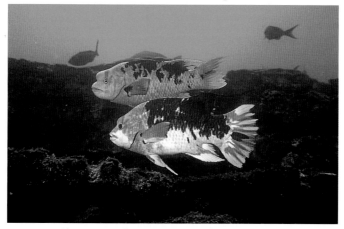

Photo 19: Harlequin wrasse, *Bodianus eclancheri*

Photo 20: Harlequin wrasse, *Bodianus eclancheri*

Photo 21: Harlequin wrasse, *Bodianus eclancheri* (juvenile)

56

Photo 22: Cortez rainbow wrasse, *Thalassoma lucasanum* (male)

Photo 23: Cortez rainbow wrasse, *Thalassoma lucasanum* (female)

Photo 24: Green wrasse, *Thalassoma lutescens*

Photo 25: Chameleon wrasse, *Halichoeres dispilus*

Photo 26: Spinster wrasse, *Halichoeres nicholsi* (male)

Photo 27: Spinster wrasse, *Halichoeres nicholsi* (female)

Photo 28: Dragon wrasse, *Novaculichthys taeniourus*

Photo 29: Banded wrasse, *Liopropoma fasciatum*

Photo 30: Galápagos sheephead, *Semicossyphus darwini* (male)

59

Photo 31: Galápagos sheephead, *Semicossyphus darwini* (female)

Photo 32: Tigris, Pacific beakfish, *Oplegnathus insigne*

Photo 33: Yellowtail surgeonfish, *Prionurus laticlavius*

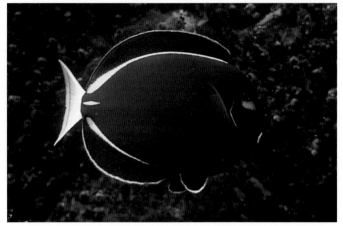

Photo 34: Gold-rimmed surgeonfish, *Acanthurus glaucopareius*

Photo 35: Yellowfin surgeonfish, *Acanthurus xanthopterus*

Photo 36: Convict tang, *Acanthurus triostegus*

Photo 37: Moorish idol, *Zanclus canescens*

Photo 38: King angelfish, *Holocanthus passer*

Photo 39: Barberfish, *Heniochus nigrirostris*

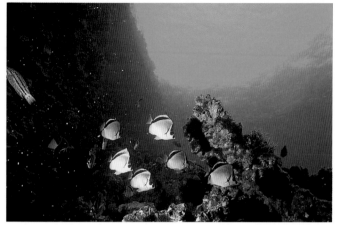

Photo 40: Barberfish school

Photo 41: Scythe butterflyfish, *Chaetodon falcifer*

Photo 42: Three-band butterflyfish, *Chaetodon humeralis*

Photo 43: Meyer's butterflyfish, *Chaetodon meyeri*

Photo 44: Panama sergeant major, *Abudefduf troschelli*

Photo 45: Dusky sergeant, *Abudefduf concolor*

Photo 46: Yellowtail damselfish, *Stegastes arcifrons*

Photo 47: Whitetail damselfish, *Stegastes leucorus beebei*

Photo 48: Acapulco damselfish, *Eupomacentrus acapulcoensis*

CONVICT TANG *(Acanthurus triostegus)*
Rarely seen. An Indo-Pacific species, more likely to be seen in the warm waters the northern islands. Body creamy in color with six vertical black stripes. Usually found in small numbers in shallow waters around coral reefs (Darwrin Bay, Genovesa). Length about 25 centimeters *(see photo 36, p.60)*.
Pacific range: Indo-West Pacific, Gulf of California to Panama, Revillagigedos, Galápagos.

MOORISH IDOL *(Zanclus canescens)*
For some specialists it is classified in the Acanthuridae family (Surgeonfishes), for others it is a distinct family known by the name of Zanclidae. Body color is basically black, white and yellow, in vertical stripes from the head to the tail, like it is dressed in striped pyjamas. A definite filament like dorsal fin, and a funny tube nose. An Indo-West Pacific species, numerous during the 1982–83 Niño year, where it was first seen in the cooler waters of western Isabela. Usually common to the warm waters of the northern islands. Found in pairs, or in small groups around coral reef formations. Length about 25 centimeters *(see photo 37, p.61)*.
Pacific range: Indo-West Pacific, Gulf of California to Panama, Revillagigedos, Cocos and Galápagos.

Angelfishes (Pomacanthidae)

Brightly colored fishes with deep compressed bodies. Closely related to the Butterflyfishes, but differ by their blunter snout and large spine on the angle of the preopercle. Rays of the dorsal and anal fins often filamentous. Diurnal activity around shallow reefs.

KING ANGELFISH *(Holocanthus passer)*
Dark blue, with white stripe behind pectoral fin, golden tail. Orange fringe above nape. Metallic blue pigmentation on the front. Females have yellow pelvic fins, males white. Common throughout the archipelago, often associated with the Yellow tail surgeonfish. Length about 30 centimeters *(see photo 38, p.61)*.
Pacific range: Gulf of California to Northern Peru, including Cocos and Galápagos.

Butterflyfishes (Chaetodontidae)

Rather small fishes, with disc-like shaped compressed bodies. Very colorful; adults and juveniles may have different patterns. Snout is pointed. Dorsal fin long and continuouous. Lateral line extends to caudal peduncle. Usually in shallow waters. Butterflyfishes are a reef dwelling family, well represented in the western Pacific.

BARBERFISH *(Heniochus nigrirostris)*
Black forehead and silvery-yellow body. Conspicuous black stripe coming down from base of dorsal fin to caudal fin. Eye circled in black. Shallow rocky areas and coral reefs to a depth of 12 meters. Length up to 20 centimeters *(see* photos 39, 40, pp.61–2). Pacific range: Gulf of California to Ecuador, Cocos, Malpelo and Galápagos.

SCYTHE BUTTERFLYFISH *(Chaetodon falcifer)*
A deep water butterfly, which seems to replace the shallow water Barberfish, from 11 to 75 meters. High spiny dorsal fin with conspicuous barbs. Silvery-yellow, with long snout, black nape and dorsal fin. Distinctive inversed V design, striping the sides from lower part of the opercle to dorsal barbs and down below the caudal peduncle. Length 15 centimeters *(see* photo 41, p.62). Pacific range: California to Galápagos.

THREE-BAND BUTTERFLYFISH *(Chaetodon humeralis)*
Conspicuous three black bars on a silvery body. Caudal fin striped, black and silver. Shallow waters, reef areas. Length 20 centimeters *(see* photo 42, p.62). Pacific range: Gulf of California to Peru, Cocos and Galápagos.

MEYER'S BUTTERFLYFISH *(Chaetodon meyeri)*
Bluish-white body fringed with yellow, with oblique black bands across the sides. Tail yellow with black vertical stripes. Face blue-gray with yellow and black rings. Found in coral reefs to a depth of 25 meters in the warm waters of the northern islands. Seen only on the east coast of Wolf Island. Length up to 18 centimeters. *(see* photo 43, p.63). Pacific range: Coral sea (Great Barrier reef), Indo-West Pacific, Galápagos.

Damselfishes (Pomacentridae)

Deep-bodied, compressed fish. Mouth small, protractile jaws. Single nostril on each side of snout a distinctive characteristic of the Pomacentridae family. Scales are ctenoïd (ie. with a spiny margin) and not smooth like in other bony fish (cycloid). The Demoiselles as they are also known, are well represented in the Galápagos archipelago.

PANAMA SERGEANT MAJOR *(Abudefduf troschelli)*
A very common fish in the islands, in association to the Yellow tail surgeonfish and the Parrotfishes. The scientific Latin name comes from the Arabic name for a Butterflyfish, named after Professor Troschel. Silvery underparts, yellowish uppersides and back. Five to six vertical black bars on the sides of the body. While guarding nest, adults turn blue. Small groups in shallow waters near coral reefs. Uncommon to the western part of the islands. Length up to 17 centimeters *(see* photo 44, p.63). Pacific range: Baja California to Peru, offshore islands, Galápagos.

DUSKY SERGEANT *(Abudefduf concolor)*
Light brown with six dark brown bars. Caudal fin forked. Agitated areas of the rocky shore along the lava coast. Length about 20 centimeters *(see photo 45, p.63)*.
Pacific range: Baja California to Peru, including Galápagos.

RUSTY DAMSELFISH *(Nexilosus latifrons)*
Dark brown dorsally, light brown on sides. Rusty-orange bar along body sides above anus. Rust color tint on head. Lava shore near the bottom. Restricted to west Isabela and Fernandina (Grove 1982). Dramatic reduction of population during Niño 1982–83. Length up to 16 centimeters.
Pacific range: Galápagos, Peru to Northern Chile.

YELLOW TAIL DAMSELFISH *(Stegastes arcifrons)*
Blackish fish with yellow tail and blue eyes. Conspicuous yellow lips. Common in rocky areas and coral reefs throughout the archipelago. Length up to 16 centimeters *(see photo 46, p.64)*.
Pacific range: Insular endemic, Cocos, Malpelos, Galápagos.

ACAPULCO DAMSELFISH *(Eupomacentrus acapulcoensis)*
Same shape and size as the Yellow tail damselfish, but quite distinct by its conspicuous two colors: pale to whitish anteriorly, dark to black posteriorly, including the dorsal, anal, pectoral and caudal fins. Conspicuous scales with dark margins. Eye is clear sky blue. On rocky substrates in shallow depths. Observed at Academy Bay (Nov. 1988). Rarely seen in Galápagos. Length up to 15 centimeters *(see photo 48, p.64)*.
Pacific range: Lower Gulf of California, to Peru.

GALÁPAGOS WHITE TAIL DAMSELFISH *(Stegastes leucorus beebei)*
Adults dark brown in color, orange-red-brown above eye. Caudal peduncle with white bar. Juveniles blue with bright chestnut upper head and back. Rocky areas and coral reefs around the archipelago. Length 15 centimeters *(see photo 47, p.64)*.
Pacific range: Panama, Malpelo, Cocos and Galápagos.

GIANT DAMSELFISH *(Microspathodon dorsalis)*
Adults gray-blue with long dorsal, anal, and caudal fin rays. Juveniles recognized by iridescent blue spots (three to five) on back and upper sides of the body. Throughout the islands. Length about 20 centimeters *(see photos 49, 50, p.81)*.
Pacific range: Baja California to Ecuador, Galápagos.

BUMPHEAD DAMSELFISH *(Microspathodon bairdi)*
Dark brown blackish body with a distinctive bump on the head, and blue eyes. Juveniles ressemble a young Beaubrummel, bright blue above and orange below. Around coral reefs. Length up to 30 centimeters *(see photo 51, p.81)*.
Pacific range: Gulf of California to Ecuador, Galápagos.

WHITE SPOT CHROMIS *(Chromis atrilobata)*
Also known as the Scissortail damselfish (Grove 1984). Usually found in shoals around coral areas. Dark gray with a conspicuous white spot at the base of the last dorsal ray. Deeply forked tail, black. Length 13 centimeters *(see* photo 52, p.82).
Pacific range: Baja California to Chile, Revillagigedos and Galápagos.

WHITE-STRIPED CHROMIS *(Chromis alta)*
Bluish-brown body with a white line at the base of the dorsal fin (looking like a crest of spines). Dorsal, caudal and anal fin black to brown. Eyes streaked above with bright blue lines. Found in rocky areas with Galápagos black coral (Tagus Cove, Punta Vicente Roca, on west Isabela), to depth of 35 meters. Length about five centimeters *(see* photo 53, p.82).

BLACK SPOT CHROMIS *(Azurina eupalama)*
Dusky gray dorsally with blue iridescence, sides of body gray, ventrally silver. Black blotch at the base of the pectoral fins (Grove 1984). Rocky shores, coral areas and drop-offs. Not common. Disappeared during El Niño 1982–83, replaced by the White-spot chromis. Length 16 centimeters.
Pacific range: Insular endemic to Galápagos, Cocos, Malpelo.

Puffers, Porcupinefishes, Boxfishes

Order Tetraodontiformes. Fishes showing a great diversity in form, size, color, scales and habitat. More than any order of fishes in the world.

Puffers (Tetraodontidae)

This family has the capacity to inflate the body with either air or water, rapidly, from which it derives the name 'puffer'. Head blunt and rounded, mouth terminal, with two teeth in each jaw. Tetraodontidae comes from the Greek, *tetra* (four) and *odontos* (tooth). Eyes are high up on the sides of the head. No pelvic fins, but very active ballet like pectoral fins, flapping and acting as stabilizers. Dorsal and anal fins close to caudal peduncle. Skin is unscaled, but spiny prickles may be present.

CONCENTRIC PUFFERFISH *(Spheroïdes annulatus)*
Probably the most common Puffer in the islands, also known as the Bullseye puffer in California. Often compared to the garbage fish for it is always around boats at anchor, especially around the kitchen area. Color light brown to gray with distinctive white rings on the back and over the sides. This concentric pattern is easy to recognize. Considered as highly toxic food, but the Japanese eat one of its relatives once the liver has been

removed. Usually found on shallow sandy bottoms, reefs and bays. Length 35 centimeters (*see* photo 54, p.82).
Pacific range: California to Peru, Galápagos.

GALÁPAGOS PUFFERFISH *(Spheroïdes angusticeps)*
Also known as Concave puffer. Dark green to brown-gray. Iris yellowish. A pair of black fleshy flaps on mid-back between pectoral fins. Base of dorsal and pectoral fins black. Dorsal, anal, pectoral fins dusky to transparent. Caudal fin pigmented. Deeply concave, uniform dark coloration. On rocky or sandy bottom where it burrows at night or during the day (Baltra, Gordon Rocks, Santa Cruz, Floreana, Isabela, Marchena. Length up to 25 centimeters (*see* photo 58, p.84).
Pacific range: Endemic to the Galápagos.

LOBESKIN PUFFER *(Spheroïdes lobatus)*
Gray or tan with 11 to 13 dark bars along sides. Olive on back and uppersides, brownish mottlings and numerous white spots. Small triangular flaps of skin scattered along sides. On sandy and weedy areas where it camouflages at depth of one to 20 meters. Forages on reef and sand (Baltra, Cartago Bay, Tagus, Marchena, Santa Cruz). Length up to 30 centimeters.
Pacific range: Eastern Pacific to Peru, including Galápagos.

GUINEAFOWL PUFFER *(Arothron meleagris)*
Globe-like body, like the former puffer, wholly black with white spots. Uncommon in the islands. Rocky shore and coral areas. The distinctive yellow phase of the juvenile may be mistaken for the Yellow Puffer (*Arothron nigropunctatus*), an Indo-Pacific species which is not present in the islands. Length about 30 centimeters (*see* photos 55, 56, p.83).
Pacific range: Tropical Pacific, Gulf of California to Ecuador, Revillagigedos, Galápagos.

WHITE-SPOTTED PUFFER *(Arothron hispidus)*
Another Indo-West Pacific species, also known as the Striped bellied puffer, Deadly death puffer or Miki maki (Halstead, 1970). Body color gray with white spots, black eye and black spot with thin white ring around base of pectoral fins. Longitudinal white bands on underparts. Considered toxic to eat, except by the Japanese, once the liver has been removed. Found on sandy bottoms and coral areas in shallow water. Length up to 40 centimeters (*see* photo 57, p.83).
Pacific range: Indo-West Pacific, California to Ecuador and Galápagos.

SPOTTED SHARP-NOSED PUFFER *(Canthigaster punctatissima)*
Large pointed snout. Reddish-brown body, with bluish-white spots. Solitary individual, in caves and under ledges in shallow waters. Length about ten centimeters (*see* photo 59, p.84).
Pacific range: Gulf of California to Panama, offshore islands, Galápagos.

Porcupinefishes (Diodontidae)

Small- to medium-sized puffers. A single tooth in each jaw. Name derived from Greek, *di* (two) and *odonta* (tooth). Pelvic fin absent. Dorsal and anal fins posteriorly placed. Spines like erectile quills (genus Diodon) or stout and fixed (genus Chilomycterus).

BALLOONFISH *(Diodon holocanthus)*
Longer spines on forehead. Elongate, robust, covered with long erectile spines. Light brown with scattered dark brown spots. Belly light yellow. Four dark bars on back. Snout blunt. Shallow sandy bottoms and around reefs. Length up to 50 centimeters (*see* photo 60, p.84).
Pacific range: Gulf of California to Peru, tropical seas, Galápagos.

PORCUPINEFISH *(Diodon hystrix)*
Quite similar to the previous species, except for the bars on the back. Pale olive color dorsally, white-brown underparts. The body is more spotted with dark brown or black points of same diameter as the spines. Single tooth in each jaw, fused at midline to form a parrot-like beak. Nocturnal habits, hides in caves and crevices during the day. Secretive, solitary fish, reef feeder. Length up to 90 centimeters.
Pacific range: Gulf of California to Chile, Galápagos.

GALÁPAGOS BLUE PORCUPINEFISH *(Chilomycterus affinis galapagoensis)*
Also known as the Pacific Burrfish. Similar to the porcupinefish, but with short spines, with three-part base (the genus Diodon is two-rooted base). Blue color dorsally, white ventrally. Body covered with small dark spots. Margin of eyes encircled with black. Uncommon in Galápagos. Length 50 centimeters. Rocky and coral areas (*see* photos 61, 62, p.85).
Pacific range: California to Ecuador, Galápagos.

Boxfishes (Ostraciidae)

The Ostraciidae family gets its name from the carapace formed of modified scales that totally encloses the fish, like a box. Openings for the mouth, eyes, gill slits and fins. Caudal peduncle unprotected. Small, slow swimming fish which depend on the shell to discourage eventual predators. Sometimes provided with horn-like spines on the forehead (cowfish). Lack pelvic fins. Frequent coral and rocky reefs.

PACIFIC BOXFISH *(Ostracion meleagris)*
Different colorations for the male and the female. Male is dark blue with golden spots on the sides, bluish on the back. Speckled golden lines from eyes to caudal fin. Female blackish, speckled white. Eyes circled with white dots. Two-thirds of the caudal fin is

speckled with white. Around shallow reefs, down to 15 meters. Length up to 20 centimeters. (*see* photos 63, 64, pp.85–6).
Pacific range: Tropical Indo-Pacific, Gulf of California to Panama, Galápagos.

Triggerfishes, Filefishes

The Leather jackets (family Balistidae) also belong to the order of the Tetraodontiformes which have a great diversity in size, body form, color, scalation and habitat. Some are scaleless, others are covered with spines. The pelvic fin is usually absent, as in the previously mentioned Puffers, Porcupinefishes and Boxfishes. The brightly colored Leather jackets are divided into two distinct groups: the Filefishes (one recorded species in Galápagos) and the Triggerfishes (seven recorded species in Galápagos). They both live around rocky and coral reefs and are considered pantropical fishes. The Galápagos species originate mainly from the Panamic province, even though a few are common to the Western Pacific. In all of them the pelvic fin is reduced to a spiny projection.

Filefishes (Balistidae)

Deep, highly compressed body. Velvety skin consisting of minute scales. Two dorsal spines, the first being larger. Six outer teeth in each jaw.

SCRAWLED FILEFISH (*Aluterus scriptus*)
Common in Galápagos during the Niño 1982–83. Indo-West Pacific species which eventually arrived with the North Equatorial Countercurrent. Light bluish-gray to olive color. Blue lines seem to originate from the pointed snout, past the pectoral fins, and scatter towards the caudal fin in broken light blue lines. Caudal peduncle with black spots. Caudal fin resembles a long comb-like tail. Around shallow reefs. Length 60 to 90 centimeters. Better seen in the northern islands (*see* photo 71, p.88).
Pacific range: Worldwide tropical seas, Gulf of California, Revillagigedos, Galápagos.

Triggerfishes (Balistidae)

Oval, compressed bodies. Large diamond-shaped scales. Three dorsal spines; the first can be locked into an upright position by the second. Eight strong outer teeth in each jaw. Some triggerfishes are good to eat; others are toxic.

YELLOW-BELLIED TRIGGERFISH (*Sufflamen verres*)
The most common Triggerfish in Galápagos. Easily recognized by its three-colored pattern. Back is blackish-gray, ventral part is yellow, becoming dark gray towards the front and snout. Solitary fish around sandy bottoms and coral areas. Shies away easily. Length about 35 centimeters (*see* photo 65, p.86).
Pacific range: Gulf of California to Ecuador, north Peru, Galápagos.

BLACK TRIGGERFISH *(Melichthys niger)*
Black body with bluish-white lines at the base of dorsal and anal fins. Solitary species over shallow reefs. Uncommon. An Indo-Pacific species. Easily seen at Mosquera and northern islands. Length about 30 centimeters (*see* photo 66, p.86).
Pacific range: Gulf of California, Revillagigedos, Cocos, Clipperton, Malpelos and Galápagos.

PINK TAIL TRIGGERFISH *(Melichthys vidua)*
Black colored triggerfish. Tail is white with a pink vertical margin. Dorsal and anal fins white with a black margin. A solitary fish seen in coral reefs, shy, hides in a hole at the first approach. Eat anything from coral, to algae, sponges, sea urchins, crustaceans (personal observation at Marchena Island, Punta Espejo, April 1990, February 1991). Length 17 to 30 centimeters. Very rare.
Pacific range: Indian and Pacific oceans, French Polynesia, Galápagos.

BLUNTHEAD TRIGGERFISH *(Pseudobalistes naufragium)*
Gray-brown or gray-blue body with distinctive dark bars on the sides. Prominent forehead. Around reefs and over sandy bottoms, down to 30 meters. Length up to 90 centimeters (*see* photo 67, p.87).
Pacific range: Gulf of California to Ecuador.

FINESCALE TRIGGERFISH *(Balistes polyepsis)*
Body deep, compressed. Dorsally dark brown, ventrally lighter. Drab coloration. Three dorsal spines in front of the dorsal fin, very conspicuous, giving the fish a dragon-like appearance. Reefs and sandy bottoms to a depth of 30 meters. Sleep on their side at night. Length up to 80 centimeters (*see* photo 68, p.87).
Pacific range: California to Chile, Galápagos.

RED TAIL TRIGGERFISH *(Xanthicthys mento)*
Body yellow-orange, with a dark head, blue lines on chin. Checkered pattern on sides with a black spot in each square. A black line with blue above, fringed with yellow at the base of dorsal and anal fins. Tail is red with a light blue fringe running vertically and along the profile. A solitary fish in rocky areas, to a depth of 30 meters. Length up to 25 centimeters. Personal observation at Wolf Island east coast (February 1991) (*see* photo 69, p.87).
Pacific range: Indo-Pacific, Japan, Hawaii, California, tropical east Pacific, Galápagos, Easter Island.

BLUE-STRIPED TRIGGERFISH *(Xanthichthys caeruleolineatus)*
Body gray and checkered with a white lateral line running from pectoral fin to upper caudal fin. Blue lines streak the chin. Tail white with upper and lower margins red. Solitary fish, on drop-offs, rocky areas, to depths of 25 meters. Length up to 30 centimeters. Personal observation at Wolf Island east coat (Feb. 1991). *(see* photo 70, p.88).
Pacific range: West Pacific, Galápagos.

Blennies, Labrisomid Blennies, Tube Blennies, Gobies

Blennidae (Combtooth blennies), Chaenopsidae (Tube blennies) Labrisomidae (Labrisomid blennies), Gobiidae (Gobies), are well represented in Galápagos. These families show a very high percentage of endemism, of at least 50 percent. In the Labrisomid, a family with a high number of species, 83 percent are endemic (five out of seven) (Grove and Lavenberg, 1997). All are small, bottom-dwelling fish.

True Blennies (Blennidae)

Blennies usually occur in shallow waters. Small, scaleless, blunt snout and steep head profile. Jaws have single row of incisor teeth. Dorsal fin long and continuous. Three species recorded in Galápagos, none is endemic.

LARGE BANDED BLENNY *(Ophioblennius steindachneri)*
Also known as the Pacific fanged blenny. Color brown, with several lighter yellowish bars on head and anterior part of body. Red circle around eye. Black spots posterior to eyes. On reefs in shallow waters down to 11 meters, also found on rocky shores. Length up to 20 centimeters *(see* photo 72, p.88).
Pacific range: Gulf of California to Peru, Cocos and Galápagos.

SABRETOOTH BLENNY *(Plagiotremus azaleus)*
Also know as the Parasitic blenny. Often attacks larger fish, taking bites out of fins or skin, pestering other fish like a horsefly on humans. Body elongate, yellow with two black stripes. Ventral area pale, just like the caudal and anal fins. Coral development area, tide pools around the central and southern islands. Length ten centimeters *(see* photo 73, p.89).
Pacific range: Gulf of California to Peru, Revillagigedos, Malpelo, Cocos and Galápagos.

Tube Blennies (Chaenopsidae)

Of the three species recorded, all are endemic: *Acanthemblemaria castroii, Chaenopsis schmitti, Eklemblemaria species.*

BARNACLE BLENNY *(Acanthemblemaria castroii)*
Also known as Castro's blenny. Body elongate, slightly compressed. No scales. Greenish-brown in color, with eight dark brown bars on sides. Yellow cirrus (finger-like protuberance) above snout. Dorsal fin longer than anal fin. Arrow-shaped tail. Around shallow waters in rocky areas. Length five centimeters (*see* photo 74, p.89).
Pacifc range: Endemic to Galápagos.

Labrisomid blennies (Labrisomidae)

Formerly known as Clinid blennies. Small elongate fishes. Long-based dorsal and anal fins. Head often has fleshy flaps on the nostrils above eyes. Pelvic fin reduced to inconspicuous spine with two to three rays. Body may be naked or with cycloid scales (i.e. with a smooth rounded margin). Bottom dwelling around rocky or coral reefs, in shallow waters. Seven species in Galápagos, four are endemic (*see* photos 75, 76, pp.89–90).

GALÁPAGOS FOUR-EYED BLENNY *(Dialommus fuscus)*
A famous fish in Galápagos. Small mottled fish crawling on shore or alighting upon volcanic rocks as waves recede. Amphibious capacity enables the Four-eyed blenny to search for small shore crabs and insects. May venture as far as 30 meters from shore. Adaptation to problems of vision, locomotion and respiration out of the water (aerial sojourn up to two hours). The corneas of the eyes are laterally flattened and meet a 100° angle along the vertical midline. The fish avoids myopia by equalling the refraction of light beams. Accomodation of the eye by the lens will result in a clearly focused image on the retina (Graham and Rosenblatt, 1970). Leaps on the ground by propelling itself forward with its tail curled towards head and then extended. Toughened skin pads along head and paired fins help locomotion on land. Length ten centimeters.
Pacific range: Endemic to Galápagos.

CHEEKSPOT LABRISOMID *(Labrisomus dentriticus)*
Also known as Bravo clinid. Dorsally gray, dark olive bars over head. Yellow blotches on cheeks and throat. Insular endemic found in quiet rocky areas. Length eight centimeters (*see* photos 75, 76, pp.89–90).
Pacific range: Insular endemic, Galápagos, Cocos and Malpelo.

Triplefin blennies (Tripterygiidae)

GALAPAGOS TRIPLEFIN BLENNY *(Lepidonectes corallicola)*
Characteristic three dorsal fins are distinctive. Color red to brown, with dusky longitudinal stripes and light spots. Breeding male has two yellow spots on the first black dorsal fin, otherwise normal adults have pale spots and females reddish marks. Pointed snout with bluish dots. Abundant, on rocky reefs, boulders, walls. Length up to ten centimeters (*see* photo 77, p.90).
Pacific range: Endemic to Galápagos.

Gobies (Gobiidae)

Unlike blennies, gobies differentiate themselves usually by a double dorsal fin. Small, robust, elongate fish. Variably colored and marked. Dorsal fin single or double. Scales usually present, but do not form a lateral line. Five species recorded in Galápagos, three are endemic.

GALÁPAGOS BLUE-BANDED GOBY *(Lythrypnus gilberti)*
Bright red with nine or ten blue bands on sides. Orange-red marking around eyes and on head. Common in Galápagos around rocky areas. Abundant in south James Bay (Santiago). Length up to five centimeters *(see* photo 78, p.90).
Pacific range: Endemic to Galápagos.

Bass-like fishes: **Groupers, Sea Basses, Grunts, Mojarras, Snappers, Sea Chubs, Soapfishes**

Sea Basses (Serranidae)

Includes the well known groupers. Perchlike fishes. Single slightly notched dorsal fin. Mouth large with exposed maxilla. Opercular spines. Many species change color pattern from juvenile to adult form. Twenty-three species of Serranidae have been recorded in Galápagos, of which only two are classified as endemic.

FLAG CABRILLA *(Epinephelus labriformis)*
Also known as the White-spotted grouper (Peter Scott, 1976). Basic color is gray-green with white spots all over the body. Tail and caudal peduncle of yellowish color. Shallow waters in rocky areas, down to 30 meters. Abundant in the western part of the archipelago. Length up to 30 centimeters *(see* photo 79, p.91).
Pacific range: Gulf of California to Peru, Galápagos.

SPOTTED CABRILLA GROUPER *(Epinephelus analogus)*
Color gray to reddish-brown with darker spots also reddish-brown. Ventrally milky-white. Seven dark bars on the sides of the body. Bottom living species on rocky shores, at depth greater than ten meters. Length about 20 centimeters.
Pacific range: Gulf of California to Peru, Galápagos.

PANAMA GRAYSBY *(Epinephelus panamensis)*
Crimson body with several bluish-white bars on the sides. Head blue with orange spots. Large darker blue spot behind eyes. Rocky reefs and crevices at great depth, up to 75 meters. Length about 30 centimeters *(see* photo 80, p.91).
Pacific range: Gulf of California to Colombia and Galápagos.

MUTTON HAMLET *(Epinephelus afer)*
Red-brown body with light spots and seven to eight transversal bars. Distinctive red eye. Solitary nocturnal species, around shallow reefs. Length 25 centimeters (*see* photo 81, p.91).
Pacific range: Gulf of California to Chile, Galápagos.

LEATHER BASS *(Epinephelus dermatolepis)*
Also known as the Flat grouper (Peter Scott, 1976). Grayish-brown with dark and light spots. Distinctive darker bars along the sides. Dorsal, anal and caudal fins fringed with conspicuous yellow. Species capable of changing color. Rocky coast and coral development. One or two individuals are often found in association with a school of Yellow tail surgeonfishes, hiding in the group. Length 25 centimeters (*see* photos 82, 83, 84, p.92).
Pacific range: Baja California to Ecuador, Galápagos, Revillagigedos.

BACALAO, YELLOW GROUPER *(Mycteroperca olfax)*
Well known by the local fishermen as one of the main fishery products. Dark gray fish to brown dorsally. Ventrally white with yellow-brown blotches. There is a brilliant yellow phase in the Bacalao. Open waters near the bottom. Abundant around Fernandina, Darwin and Wolf. First resource of the Galápagos fisheries, 50 percent of the fishing (Gunther Reck, 1986). Length about 35 centimeters (*see* photos 86, 87, p.93).
Pacifc range: Insular endemic, Cocos, Malpelo, Galápagos.

WHITE-SPOTTED ROCK SEABASS *(Paralabrax albomaculatus)*
Locally known as Camotillo. Gray-green dorsally, silver-gray ventrally. Horizontal alignment of white spots on the sides. Pectoral fins and opercle yellow. Dorsal fin dark. Abundant on the west of Isabela and Fernandina. Length about 25 centimeters (*see* photo 88, p.94).
Pacific range: Endemic to Galápagos.

BARRED SERRANO *(Serranus fasciatus)*
Six pairs of dark bars, condensed into a dark stripe above lateral line. Ventrally white. Dark yellow spots on caudal fin. Reefs, sandy bottoms to a depth of 60 meters. Length about 17 centimeters (*see* photo 89, p.94).
Pacific range: Gulf of California to Peru, Galápagos.

CREOLEFISH *(Paranthias colonus)*
Also known as the Five-spotted anthias (Peter Scott, 1976) for the conspicuous five white spots above the lateral line. Gray-green body, to red, according to depth. Tips of the forked caudal fin are red. Often found in large schools in deeper waters, around isolated rocks and drop-offs (e.g. Cousin's Rock, Gordon Rocks). Length up to 35 centimeters (*see* photos 90, 91, pp.94–5).
Pacific range: Gulf of California to Peru, Galápagos.

GRAY THREADFIN SEABASS *(Cratinus agassizi)*
Known locally as Plumero. Silver-gray dorsally. Dorsal, anal and pelvic spines with faint black markings. Pectoral fins light yellow (Grove 1984). Mangrove areas and shallow bays. Length about 25 centimeters (*see* photo 85, p.93).
Pacific range: Ecuador to Chile, Galápagos.

Soapfishes (Grammistidae)

Small bass-like fishes with few predators, due to an ability to secrete a toxin which hemolyzes red blood cells. Adopts a head-standing posture prior to feeding. A white line on back serves as a distraction to small fish. When approached, the soapfish darts forward and catches prey swiftly.

CORTEZ SOAPFISH *(Rypticus bicolor)*
Pale brown with lighter irregular mottling. Cream stripe on nape, from jaw to dorsal fin. Knife-shaped body with small rounded fins. Shy during the day when it hides in cracks and holes. Nocturnal feeder. Inshore, shallow waters (*see* photo 92, p.95).
Pacific range: Eastern Pacific, Gulf of California to Peru, Cocos, Galápagos.

Grunts (Haemulidae)

A family with a large degree of endemism in Galápagos (four species out of nine). Perch-like fishes with oblong bodies and large heads. Ctenoïd scales (i.e. with a spiny margin) all over the body, including opercle cheeks. Grunts inhabit shallow inshore waters. Habitat varies from coral reefs to sand bottoms. Their common name originates from the sound they make by rubbing the pharyngeal teeth together (like grunting). Grunts have teeth in the jaw and on pharyngeal bones. Four endemic species: the Forbes grunt, *Orthopristis forbesi* (rare, Fernandina, Santa Cruz), the Scalyfin grunt, *Orthopristis lethopristis*, the White salema, *Xenichthys agassizi*, the Black-striped salema, *Xenocys jessiae*.

FORBES GRUNT *(Orthopristis forbesi)*
Also known as Galápagos grunt. Back dark brown. Ventrally grayish with green-purple iridescence. Fins dark. Found in schools, sandy areas. Length 24 centimeters (*see* photo 95, p.96).
Pacific range: Endemic to Galápagos (Grove, 1997).

BRASSY GRUNT *(Orthopristis chalceus)*
Silver-gray with brass lines in waves on sides above lateral line. Iris yellow. Fins blue-black. Body deep, elevated back. Found over sand bottom and on rock walls (*see* photo 98, p.113).
Pacific range: Eastern Pacific to Peru, Galápagos.

GRAYBAR GRUNT *(Haemulon sexfasciatum)*
Silver-gray with six to eight irregular brown or yellow bands. Juveniles have three stripes and a tail spot. Vertical body bands separate Graybar grunt from all other grunts in the Eastern Pacific. Length up to 48 centimeters (*see* photos 96, 97, pp.96, 113).
Pacific range: Eastern Pacific, Gulf of California, Panama, Galápagos.

GRAY GRUNT *(Haemulon scudderi)*
Silver-gray to dark gray. Eye yellow. Two black stripes and a black spot on caudal peduncle in juveniles. Usually found in schools, sandy areas and coral reefs. Length about ten centimeters. (*see* photo 93, p.95).
Pacific range: Baja California to Peru, Galápagos.

YELLOWTAIL GRUNT *(Anisotremus interruptus)*
Also known as Burrito grunt. Color silvery-gray with yellow tail and fins. Head with sharp slanting profile. Fleshy lips. Large scales with dark spots on anterior margin. Around reefs and caves down to 23 meters. Usually seen in large groups, specially in the northern islands. Locally known as Zapatilla. Length up to 50 centimeters (*see* photo 94, p.96).
Pacific range: Gulf of California to Peru, Revillagigedos, Galápagos.

PERUVIAN GRUNT *(Anisotremus scapularus)*
Silver-gray, fins dusky. Dark blotch at angle of preopercular margin. Base of pectoral fin black. Snout blunt, mouth low. Common in small schools west of the archipelago (Isabela). Feed on bottom invertebrates and floating matter. Length up to 35 centimeters (*see* photo 99, p.113).
Pacific range: Eastern Pacific from Ecuador to Chile, Cocos, Galápagos

BLACK-STRIPED SALEMA *(Xenocys jessiae)*
A tropical grunt (Wellington, 1978), also known as Little snapper. Dark gray to blue dorsally. Ventrally silver-white. Seven conspicuous black horizontal stripes on the sides of the body extending to eyes. Often found in schools in shallow waters. Decreased in Niño of 1982–83. Used as main baitfish for local fisheries. Length 15 centimeters (see photo 100, p.114).
Pacific range: Endemic to Galápagos (Grove, 1984; Wellington, 1975)

WHITE SALEMA *(Xenichthys agassizi)*
Silver-gray dorsally. Ventrally silver-white. Schooling species in shallow waters. Population decreased during 1982–83 Niño year. Length 16 centimeters (see photo 101, p.114).
Pacific range: Endemic to Galápagos.

Mojarras (Gerreidae)

Small fishes with shiny silver scales. Deep compressed bodies with pointed snout, protractile jaws (projection of jaws forward). Ventral profile of head is concave. Shallow notch on dorsal fin. Caudal fin deeply forked. Mojarras are bottom dwelling fishes over sand or mud in shallow waters. Five species were recorded in Galápagos, all originate from the Panamic province.

PACIFIC FLAGFIN MOJARRA *(Eucinostomus californiensis)*
The Latin name means to 'move mouth well' and comes from the long snout and protusible mouth. Light brown body with dark vertical markings on sides. Dorsal fin with black and white rays. Shallow sandy bottoms in bays and mangrove areas. Length 15 centimeters.
Pacific range: Gulf of California to Peru, Galápagos.

SPOTFIN MOJARRA *(Eucinostomus argenteus)*
Also known as Silver mojarra (Grove, 1984). Silvery grayish-green. Dusky bars on sides of the body. Black spots on dorsal fin. Sandy shores to mangrove areas. Length 15 centimeters.
Pacific range: Baja California to Peru, Galápagos.

YELLOWFIN MOJARRA *(Gerres cinereus)*
Silvery blue. Seven dark bars on the sides. Pelvic fins are yellow. Beaches and sandy areas, including regions of coral development. Length ten centimeters.
Pacific range: Baja California to Peru, Galápagos.

Snappers (Lutjanidae)

Oblong compressed fishes. Large terminal mouth. Conical sharp teeth. Single continuous dorsal fin. Caudal fin deeply forked or truncate. Small ctenoïd scales cover the body, except between mouth and eyes. Carnivorous fishes living around coral reefs. Six species recorded in Galápagos.

BLUE AND GOLD SNAPPER *(Lutjanus viridis)*
Bright yellow with five horizontal turquoise-blue stripes fringed with black lines on the sides of the body. Caudal fin yellow. Found in schools around reefs. Large groups in the warm northern islands. Length 30 centimeters (*see* photo 102, p.114).
Pacific range: Indo-West Pacific, Baja California to Ecuador.

YELLOWTAIL SNAPPER *(Lutjanus argentiventris)*
Also known as Yellow snapper, Yellow tail snapper or Amarillo snapper. Body silvery. Dorsal, anal and caudal fins are bright yellow. Juvenile phase totally yellow with back eye circled in red. Found in small numbers. Habitat around reefs, inshore waters, sand bottoms, also in caves. Exploited in the Galápagos coastal fisheries. Length about 35 centimeters (*see* photo 103, p.115).
Pacific range: Gulf of California to Peru, Galápagos.

JORDAN SNAPPER *(Lutjanus jordani)*
Dark red to purple, with dark green back. Red iris. Deep bodied and elongated. Forehead sloping and rounded, tail truncate. A schooling species found in the northern islands (Wolf and Darwin). Length up to 55 centimeters.
Pacific range: Southern Mexico to north Peru, Cocos, Malpelo, Galápagos.

MULLET SNAPPER *(Lutjanus aratus)*
Large and elongated fish, color silvery-gray with conspicuous lines of apparent scales on sides. All fins are dark to black. Eleven spines on dorsal fin. Yellow eye ring, iris black. Usually in schools in open waters, over flat coral bottoms. Seen at Punta Espejo, Marchena, Gordon Rocks. Length up to 76 centimeters, to depths of 20 meters *(see photo 104, p.115)*.
Pacific range: Gulf of California to Ecuador, Galápagos.

PACIFIC DOG SNAPPER *(Lutjanus novemfasciatus)*
Silvery body, with nine dusky bars. Adults turn to reddish when out of the water. Large canine teeth visible, are an easy identification key. Hides in caves during the day (Los Tunneles, Isabela). Exploited as a resource of the Galápagos coastal fisheries. Night feeder around reefs to depth of 30 meters. Length up to 90 centimeters.
Pacific range: Gulf of California to Peru, Galápagos.

SPINDLE SNAPPER *(Lutjanus inermis)*
Fusiform in shape, color from rusty red to silver. A new record for the Galápagos first seen by the author at Gordon Rocks (Dec. 2000) and later at Darwin Arch (Dec. 2004). A rather continental species, endemic to the east Pacific, seen from Mexico to Ecuador, although very rare in the latter country. Clearly with tropical affinities, it should be found in warm water islands (Philippe Bearez, Museum of Natural History in Paris, personal communication). Length to 40 centimeters *(see photo 105, p.115)*.

Sea Chubs (Girellidae)

Formerly classified in the Kyphoslidae family (Wellington, 1975). Oval, compressed fish. Dorsal fin with spines and rays. Anal fin with three spines. Caudal fin almost truncate. Mouth is small: sea chubs mostly eat algae. Three species recorded in Galápagos, one endemic: *Girella fremenvillei*, the Dusky chub.

DUSKY CHUB *(Girella fremenvillei)*
Dark gray fish with two white spots on the nostrils in front of eyes—looks very serious minded. Thick lips and large head. Conspicuous black lines along the edge of the opercle, along the top of the dorsal fin. Usually found in shoals in shallow waters. Related to the Opaleye *(Girella nigricans)*, found in California and Baja California. Length about 40 centimeters *(see photo 106, p.116)*.
Pacific range: Endemic to Galápagos.

Photo 49: Giant damselfish, *Microspathodon dorsalis*

Photo 50: Giant damselfish, *Microspathodon dorsalis* (juvenile)

Photo 51: Bumphead damselfish, *Microspathodon bairdii*

Photo 52: White spot chromis, *Chromis atrilobata*

Photo 53: White-striped chromis, *Chromis alta*

Photo 54: Concentric pufferfish, *Spheroïdes annulatus*

Photo 55: Guineafowl puffer, *Arothron meleagris*

Photo 56: Guineafowl puffer, *Arothron meleagris* (yellow phase)

Photo 57: White-spotted puffer, *Arothron hispidus*

Photo 58: Galápagos pufferfish, *Spheroïdes angusticeps*

Photo 59: Spotted sharpnosed puffer, *Canthigaster punctatissima*

Photo 60: Balloonfish, *Diodon holocanthus*

Photo 61: Galápagos blue porcupinefish, *Chilomycterus affinis galapagoensis*

Photo 62: Galápagos blue porcupinefish, *Chilomycterus affinis galapagoensis*

Photo 63: Pacific boxfish, *Ostracion meleagris* (male)

Photo 64: Pacific boxfish, *Ostracion meleagris* (female)

Photo 65: Yellow-bellied triggerfish, *Sufflamen verres*

Photo 66: Black triggerfish, *Melichthys niger*

Photo 67: Blunthead triggerfish, *Pseudobalistes naufragium*

Photo 68: Finescale triggerfish, *Balistes polyepsis*

Photo 69: Red tail triggerfish, *Xanthichthys mento*

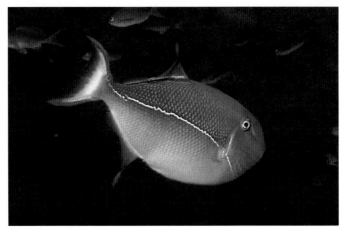

Photo 70: Blue-striped triggerfish, *Xanthichthys caeruleolineatus*

Photo 71: Scrawled filefish, *Aluterus scriptus*

Photo 72: Large banded blenny, *Ophioblennius steindachneri*

Photo 73: Sabretooth blenny, *Plagiotremus azaleus*

Photo 74: Barnacle blenny, *Acanthemblemaria castroii* (E)

Photo 75: Cheekspot labrisomid, *Labrisomus dentriticus* (female) (E)

Photo 76: Cheekspot labrisomid, *Labrisomus dentriticus* (male) (E)

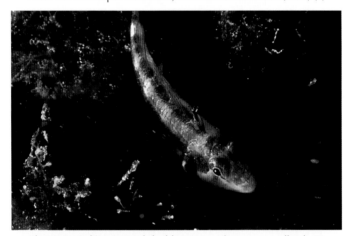

Photo 77: Galápagos triplefin blenny, *Lepidonectes corallicola* (E)

Photo 78: Galápagos blue-banded goby, *Lythrypnus gilberti* (E)

Photo 79: Flag cabrilla, *Epinephelus labriformis*

Photo 80: Panama graysby, *Epinephelus panamensis*

Photo 81: Mutton hamlet, *Epinephelus afer*

Photo 82: Leather bass, *Epinephelus dermatolepis*

Photo 83: Leather bass, *Epinephelus dermatolepis* (color variation)

Photo 84: Leather bass (juvenile) in diadema sea urchin

Photo 85: Gray threadfin seabass, *Cratinus agassizi*

Photo 86: Bacalao, *Mycteroperca olfax* (yellow phase)

Photo 87: Bacalao, Yellow grouper, *Mycteroperca olfax*

94

Photo 88: White-spotted rock seabass, *Paralabrax albomaculatus*

Photo 89: Barred serrano, *Serranus fasciatus*

Photo 90: Creolefish, *Paranthias colonus*

Photo 91: Creolefish, *Paranthias colonus* (night-time)

Photo 92: Cortez soapfish, *Rypticus bicolor*

Photo 93: Grey grunt, *Haemulon scudderi*

96

Photo 94: Yellowtail grunt, *Anisotremus interruptus*

Photo 95: Galápagos grunt, Forbes grunt, *Orthopristis forbesi*

Photo 96: Greybar grunt, *Haemulon sexfasciatum*

CORTEZ CHUB *(Kyphosus elegans)*
Silver-gray body with dark spines along sides. Faint dark stripe under the eye. Around shallow reefs, not very common. Length 40 centimeters (*see* photo 107, p.116).
Pacific range: Gulf of California to Panama, Ecuador, Revillagigedos, Cocos and Galápagos.

BLUE-BRONZE CHUB *(Kyphosus analogus)*
Brassy stripes on sides. Prominent stripe under eye. In shallow reefs down to 30 meters. Found in greater frequencies during El Niño 1982–83.
Pacific range: California to Peru.

RAINBOW CHUB *(Sectator ocyurus)*
Olive color above, whitish below, with wide blue and golden stripes along sides. Fins are yellow. Caudal fin forked. A schoolgoing pelagic fish, uncommon in Galápagos, near deepwater drop-offs. Seen at Wolf, Gordon Rocks. Length up to 40 centimeters (*see* photo 108, p.116).
Pacific range: Eastern Pacific, from Cabo san Lucas, Mexico, Panama to Galápagos.

Surfperches (Embiotocidae)

SHINER PERCH *(Cymatogaster aggregata)*
Maybe related to the Island Perch (*C. gracilis*). Translucid fish, elongate, compressed. In bays around piers, sandy bottoms and mangrove areas (eg. Puerto Villamil, Isabela). Length 25 centimeters.
Pacific range: Baja California.

Fishes with spiny rays or tapering bodies:
Squirrelfish, Bigeyes, Scorpionfishes, Hawkfishes, Goatfishes, Searobins, Lizardfishes, Cardinalfishes

Squirrelfishes (Holocentridae)

Elongate, compressed fishes. Basic color is red. Large black eyes and large mouth. Opercle and preopercle with spines. Pelvic fin consist of one spine and seven rays. Spinuous dorsal fin and anal spines. Squirrelfishes live in shallow waters usually hiding away from the light under rocks or in crevices around tropical coral reefs. Mostly seen at night, when they wander around. Three species recorded in Galápagos.

SUN SQUIRRELFISH *(Sargocentron suborbitalis)*
Color silver-pink, with two diagonal dark bars on the sides. Conspicuous mostly at night. Slender body with marked ctenoïd scales and three spines on the opercle. Hides during the day. Nocturnal, in shallow waters, among rocks, corals and caves. Length 25 centimeters.
Pacific range: Tropical Pacific. Eastern Pacific, Baja California to Ecuador, Revillagigedos, Clipperton, Cocos, Galápagos.

CRIMSON SOLDIERFISH *(Myripristis leiognathos)*
Also known as the Panamic soldierfish. Bright red color with big black eye circled in red. Nocturnal reef feeder. Hides during the day under rocks. Length 15 centimeters (*see* photo 109, p.117).
Pacific range: Gulf of California to Ecuador, Cocos, Galápagos.

BIG-SCALE SOLDIERFISH *(Myripristis berndti)*
Color uniformly reddish with dark red scale margins. Black margin on opercular membrane and all fin edges. One enlarged spine on the operculum. Lower jaw slightly protruding. An elongate blackish bar along hind edge of operculum. Spinous dorsal fin is red, outer rays of caudal fin are white. Living in groups in crevices during the day. Nocturnal planktivore, feeding on small crustaceans and larvae. Depth of one to 50 meters. Length about 15 centimeters.
Pacific range: Indo-West pacific.

TINSEL SQUIRRELFISH *(Adyorix suborbitalis)*
Color red to silvery-pink. Conspicuous spines on the opercule. Hides in cracks, caves and overlays during the day. Nocturnal feeder. Found at depths of five to 15 meters. Length up to 25 centimeters (*see* photo 110, p.117).
Pacific range: Central Baja California to Ecuador.

Bigeyes (Priacanthidae)

Small to medium size fish. Deep body with distinctive big eyes. Mouth large and slanting, with lower jaw ahead of the upper jaw. Single continuous dorsal fin. Anal fin has three spines. Body covered with ctenoïd scales. Two species recorded in Galápagos.

GLASSEYE *(Priacanthus cruentatus)*
Red body with silver bars. Black eye circled in red. Nocturnal fish in caves and crevices. In the related species *Heteropriacanthus cruentatus*, the silver body has yellow fins and tail, with the same round black eye circled in red. A school of ten individuals of the latter species was seen in the daytime in open water above the rocky bottom on the east coast of Wolf Island (personal observation, January 1992) Length up to 30 centimeters (*see* photo 111, p.117).
Pacific range: Gulf of California, Revillagigeds, Galápagos.

POPEYE CATALUFA *(Pseudopriacanthus serrula)*
Looking like a bigeye, with a big head and a characteristic slanted mouth, this crimson-colored fish is very compressed, unlike the former species. Serrated opercle. Ten dorsal spines can be erected. Shy nocturnal fish, which can develop silvery blotches when frightened. Seen on a night dive at Tagus Cove, on a volcanic sandy bottom at 17 meters (February 1992). Down to depth of 76 meters. Length about 15 centimeters (*see* photo 112, p.118). Pacific range: California to Peru, Galápagos.

Scorpionfishes (Scorpaenidae)

Fusiform, compressed fishes. Head with ridges and spines. Opercle with two spines, preopercle with five. Single dorsal fin with 11 to 17 spines. Spines of pelvic, orsal and anal fins contain venom gland, which may cause severe, painful injuries. Ten species have been recorded in Galápagos, including the Sailfin leaffish.

BANDFIN SCORPION (Scorpaena histrio)
Red to brown, ventrally pale. Large circular dark spot behind opercle. Pectoral and caudal fins with two broad bands. Cycloid scales. Fleshy appendages on scales and spines above eyes. Dorsal fin single and continuous with 12 spines. Found on reef and rocky habitats (Tagus, Baltra, Española, Isabela, Seymour).
Pacific range: Eastern Pacific, Gulf of California to Chile, Galápagos.

STONE SCORPIONFISH (Scorpaena plumieri mystes)
Robust body, rock color, hard to describe. Like an old piece of brown lava covered with white and orange lichens. Distinct orange-red at the base of pectoral fins. Occurs in shallow waters from sandy areas to rock and lava substrates. Length up to 40 centimeters. Conspicuous barbels under chin (skin flaps). Changes color with substratum (see photos 117, 118, pp.119–20). Pacific range: Gulf of California to Ecuador, Galápagos.

RAINBOW SCORPIONFISH (Scorpaenodes xyris)
Smaller than the previous species, it does not have any barbels under the chin. Color brownish-red to reddish-white mottled, with a black eye. A large dark spot on the lower rear edge of the gill cover. Thirteen spines in the dorsal fin. Rows of spines under the eye. Nocturnal, hides during the day in caves and crevices to depth of at least 27 meters. Seen at Santa Fé and west Isabela. Length to 15 centimeters (see photos 119, 120, p.120).
Pacific range: California, Gulf of California to Peru, Galápagos.

RED SCORPIONFISH (Pontinus furcirhinus)
Locally known as Brujo. Flame-red in color. Four species of Pontinus are found in the Galápagos, one is endemic, Pontinus strigatus. Usually found on sandy bottoms.

STALKEYE SCORPIONFISH (Pontinus strigatus)
Bright red, streaked and spotted with olive brown dots. Irregular size blotches on head. Three dorsal spines larger than others. Head and body with ctenoid scales. Locally known as Brujo (see photo 121, p.121).

SPOTTED SCORPIONFISH (Pontinus clemensi)
Rose-pink to red-orange. Distinct dark brown spots everywhere except underparts. Yellow-orange patches on head. Unique pigmented pattern. Length up to 28 centimeters.
Pacific range: Endemic to eastern Pacific.

SAILFIN LEAFFISH *(Taenianotus triacanthus)*
Color variation from pink to black, brown, white, orange, golden. Compressed body, sail-like dorsal fin. Piscivore, enjoys areas affected by surge with coral and algal development. Uncommon to Galápagos. Found to depth of 100 meters. One record at Santiago (Wellington, 1978). Length up to 15 centimeters.
Pacific range: Indo-West Pacific.

Searobins (Triglidae)

Bottom dwelling fishes. Small to medium size, large head covered with spines and ridges. Broad flat snout. Large wing-like pectoral fin with the first three rays free, non-attached to the fin. In the genus Prionotus, triangular, spiny dorsal fin with ten spines. Second dorsal fin and anal fin, soft, long and continuous. Searobins are inhabitants of continental and insular shelves of tropical and temperate seas, to a depth of about 95 fathoms (roughly 180 meters). Two species recorded in Galápagos, one of which, *Prionotus miles*, is endemic. The other species is the White margin searobin, *Prionotus albirostris*.

GALÁPAGOS SEAROBIN *(Prionotus miles)*
Also known as the Orange throat searobin. Color tan to dark tan, to grayish-pink. Throat and gill area bright orange. Dorsal and pectoral fins black. Uncommon. Usually found at depth of 20 to 30 meters over sandy bottom (Rabida, Floreana, Cristobal, North Seymour Channel). Omnivore. Length 30 centimeters (*see* photo 117, p.119).
Pacific range: Endemic to the Galápagos islands.

Goatfishes (Mullidae)

Elongated fishes with two separated dorsal fins. Two conspicuous barbels under the chin. Goatfish are bottom dwelling fishes. Color usually red or yellow, but can be white, with numerous variations. One species recorded in Galápagos.

MEXICAN GOATFISH *(Mulloidichthys dentatus)*
Body white with conspicuous yellow band extending from eye to caudal fin. Head slightly blunt, bigger than rest of body which tapers towards the tail. Two barbs under the chin are a very distinctive trait. Usually found in schools. Favors sandy bottoms and warm waters. Common in the northern islands. Length up to 30 centimeters (*see* photo 129, p.123).
Pacific range: Baja California to Peru, Galápagos.

Hawkfishes (Cirrhitidae)

Body oblong, distinctive dorsal spines, large mouth. Three species of Panamic origin recorded in Galápagos.

HIEROGLYPHIC HAWKFISH *(Cirrhitus rivulatus)*
Also known as the Giant Hawkfish. Beautiful fish, color brown, with darker brown bands and markings, fringed with turquoise blue lines on the sides and head. Gives the impression of a complicated map. Blue lines radiate from head. Commonly observed on reefs, perched on rocks, ledges, edge of crevices or drop-offs. Usually a solitary species, but can be found gregarious, in rock pools. Length 35 centimeters (*see* photos 122, 123, p.121). Pacific range: Gulf of California to Colombia, Revillagigedos, Cocos and Galápagos.

CORAL HAWKFISH *(Cirrhitichthys oxycephalus)*
Dorsally red with large spots. Ventrally white with light red spots. Common in black coral. Around coral heads, rocks and crevices. Length seven centimeters (*see* photos 124, 125, p.122).
Pacific range: Tropical Indo-Pacific, Gulf of California to Colombia and Galápagos.

LONGNOSE HAWKFISH *(Oxycirrhites typus)*
Distinctive pointed snout, tube like. Color white with square pattern of vertical and horizontal red lines on the sides of the body. Deep water hawkfish (27 to 30 meters). Uncommon in Galápagos. Perched on seafans and in branches of black coral (ex: at Cousin's Rock) Length eight centimeters (*see* photo 126, p.122).
Pacific range: Tropical Pacific, Galápagos.

Lizardfishes (Synodontidae)

Bottom dwelling fishes, elongate, cigar shaped. Almost round cross-section. Mouth wide, slightly oblique, maxilla extending beyond eyes. Jaws bear needle-like teeth, as does the tongue and the roof of the mouth. Dorsal fin short, caudal fin forked. Usually found over sand or mud. Three species in Galápagos, one endemic (from Marchena Island), *Synodus marchenae*.

SAURO LIZARDFISH *(Synodus lacertinus)*
Dark brown on back, ventrally white. Sides of the body striped with five dark bars. Caudal and dorsal fins speckled with dark spots. Solitary species on sand bottoms. Length 20 centimeters (*see* photos 127, 128, p.123).
Pacific range: California to Peru, Galápagos.

SPOTTED LIZARDFISH *(Synodus scituliceps)*
Color pale yellow with a thin dark bar across base of caudal fin. A row of six round brownish spots ventrally along sides. Length about 4.5 centimeters.
Pacific range: Mexico to Peru, Colombia, Galápagos.

Jawfish (Opistognathidae)

Small to medium-sized fish with narrow, tapering body and conspicuous, enlarged head and mouth. Usually in warm seas, where 70 species occur. Burrows by scooping sand or small stones with its mouth. Habit of oral egg incubation. Feeds on benthic and planktonic invertebrates.

GALÁPAGOS JAWFISH *(Opistognathus galapagensis)*
Whitish or pale tan, with six irregular brown bars, looking like longitudinal stripes. Six large brown blotches on back and onto dorsal fin. A prominent black spot on the first three dorsal spines. Dorsal anal fin yellowish with white spots. Found on sand and areas of rubble. Length up to 16 centimeters (see photo 166, p.152).
Pacific range: Endemic to Galápagos.

Cardinalfishes (Apogonidae)

Small fishes to be found hiding away from the light, around tropical coral reefs. Large eyes and big oblique mouth. Two separated dorsal fins. Anal fin with two spines. Five species in Galápagos; one recorded as endemic.

BLACKTIP CARDINALFISH *(Apogon atradorsatus)*
Color pink or red. Large black eyes. Dark pigmentation on first dorsal fin; second dorsal fin is black tipped. Hides in the daytime in caves and crevices. Nocturnal feeder on reef. Length eight centimeters (see photo 114, 115, pp.118–9).
Pacific range: Cocos, Malpelo and Galápagos (insular endemic).

TAILSPOT CARDINALFISH *(Apogon dovii)*
Small, red or pink. Recognized by a black spot on the caudal peduncle. In rocks, caves, under rocky ledges to depths of three to five meters. Not to be mistaken for the Pink cardinalfish, *Apogon pacificus*. Length up to 7.5 centimeters (see photo 116, p.119).
Pacific range: Mexico to Peru, Cocos, Malpelo, Galápagos.

PINK CARDINALFISH *(Apogon pacificus)*
Color red-orange to translucent. A black bar on back on sides behind dorsal fin reaching down to mid-body. Uncommon. Length up to five centimeters (see photo 113, p.118).
Pacific range: Gulf of California to Peru, Cocos, Revillagigedos, Galápagos.

Spindle-shaped and large fishes:
Anchovies, Herrings, Jacks, Mackerels, Tunas, Silversides, Barracudas, Porgies, Remoras, Bonefishes, Dolphins, Tilefishes, Sunfish, Marlins

Anchovies (Engraulidae)

Small, silver-colored fishes with a brighter band along sides. Mouth is large, maxilla extending beyond the eyes. Conical snout. Move in large schools in tropical and subtropical waters. Important industry on the South American coast due to the nutrient-rich Humboldt current. Only one species in Galápagos: *Anchoa naso*. Used as baitfish by the local fisheries.

Herrings (Clupeidae)

Large family with variable body shapes. Lower jaw projects beyond the upper. Anal fin larger than dorsal. Herrings belong to the order of the Clupeiformes, where the fish are small delicate and silver-colored. Distinctive schooling behavior displayed by this species that feeds by filtering plankton. Three species in Galápagos, one endemic.

GALÁPAGOS THREAD HERRING *(Opisthonema berlangai)*
Derives its name from a long filament extending after the last ray of the dorsal fin. Color dark blue dorsally, ventrally silver. Black spots noticeable on upper park of sides from opercle to middle body. Juveniles school close to shore, adults off-shore. Used as main baitfish in Galápagos coastal fisheries. Length 16 centimeters (*see* photo 130, p.124). Pacific range: Endemic to Galápagos (Grove, 1984).

PERUVIAN PACIFIC SARDINE *(Sardinops sagax sagax)*
Color gray-blue on back, silver ventrally. Numerous black spots on the sides of body. Juveniles school around beach areas and adults in open waters. Length up to 27 centimeters. Pacific range: Colombia to Peru, Galápagos.

Silversides (Atherinidae)

Small, delicate, elongate, slightly compressed fishes. Silver stripe between pectoral and caudal fins. Two well-developed separated dorsal fins. Spine precedes pelvic and anal fins. Brackish and marine water habitats. Two species in Galápagos: *Eurystole eriarcha* and *Nectarges nesiotes*, the latter being endemic.

Barracudas (Sphyraenidae)

Elongate with two separated dorsal fins, the first with five spines, the second with one spine only at the front. Pelvic and pectoral fins are small. Barracudas are recognized by their dark bars, chevrons or stripes on the upper sides. Known to be voracious predators, solitary or gregarious, feeding on fish. Man should be cautious of them. One species in Galápagos.

PELICAN BARRACUDA *(Sphyraena idiastes)*
Dorsally gray, with distinctive bars above lateral line. Ventrally silver. Juveniles in schools near coast, adults in deeper waters around rocks. Length about 55 centimeters (*see* photo 132, p.124). Pacific range: Peru and Galápagos.

Jacks (Carangidae)

Family with variable body shapes, elongate, fusiform, deep or strongly compressed. Caudal fins are noticeable forked. Usually in schools in deeper water around isolated rocks or drop-offs. Jacks are fast swimmers and highly sought-after by fishermen. Twenty-three species recorded in Galápagos (Grove & Lavenberg, 1997).

GAFFTOPSAIL POMPANO *(Trachinotus rhodopus)*
Usually a small jack. Short, deep, moderately compressed body. Silver color with about five thin, black vertical stripes along sides of the body. Tail forked like a pair of scissors, yellow. Soft dorsal and anal fin rays that reach beyond caudal fin base, color yellow. In schools around reefs. Seen at Gordon rocks. Length up to 60 centimeters.
Pacific range: California to Peru, Galápagos.

PALOMA POMPANO *(Trachinotus paitensis)*
Deep, strong compressed body. Bluish with orange reflections dorsally, silver ventrally. Dorsal fin slightly falcate with first rays black. Black stripe on pectoral fin. Anal and caudal fins pale, with black spots (Grove, 1984). Found in small numbers around shallow sandy areas, in central and northern islands. Length 15 centimeters.
Pacific range: Baja California to Chile, Galápagos.

STEEL POMPANO *(Trachinotus stilbe)*
Silver color, becoming bluish on back. Fins dark with pale margins. Dorsal and anal fins not falcate as in Paloma pompano. Usually found in large schools under the surface. In deeper waters, around isolated rocks and drop-offs (e.g. Gordon Rocks, Cousin's Rock). Length up to 40 centimeters (*see* photo 133, p.125).
Pacific range: Mexico to Peru, Revillagigedos, Cocos, Galápagos.

AFRICAN POMPANO *(Alectis ciliaris)*
Metallic blue-green above, silvery below. Blunt snout. Pectoral fins falcate. Juveniles have four bars on the sides and long thread-like extensions on dorsal and anal fins, like hairs. Adults usually near bottom to 54 meters. Length up to 90 centimeters (*see* photo 135, p.125).
Pacific range: Gulf of Mexico, Caribbean, Galápagos.

GREEN JACK *(Caranx caballus)*
Dorsally green, pale yellow ventrally. Elongate body with a dark spot on the opercle. Differs from other Caranx-type jack by its longer, more slender body. Pelagic species around reefs. Length up to 40 centimeters *(see* photo 136, p.126).
Pacific range: Gulf of California to Peru, Galápagos.

PACIFIC CREVALLE JACK *(Caranx caninus)*
Deep fusiform body, steep rounded head, a black eye circled in silver. Color of body, silvery. Lateral line, curved above mid-body, extends from above the eye to the caudal fin. Conspicuous keel on the caudal peduncle. A black spot on the upper edge of the opercle, and a dark spot on base of pectoral fin. Similar to the Green jack, but with a blunter nose. Usually seen in schools, moving fast. Length up to 76 centimeters.
Pacific range: South California, Tropical East Pacific, Galápagos.

BLACK JACK *(Caranx lugubris)*
Otherwise known as Brown jack. Pelagic fish. Sharp, slanting head profile. Color black to brown with a marked keel. Around reefs and islands. Length up to 90 centimeters *(see* photo 137, p.126).
Pacific range: World wide in tropical waters, Revillagigedos, Easter Island, Galápagos.

GOLD-SPOTTED JACK *(Carangoïdes orthogrammus)*
Gold spots above and below the lateral line and behind dorsal fin. Length up to 60 centimeters.
Pacific range: Tropical Indo-Pacific, Hawaï, Revillagigedos, Galápagos.

BIGEYE JACK *(Caranx sexfasciatus)*
Slender body with curved head and large eyes. Completely scaled breast. Dorsal fin white-tipped. Black spot on rear upper edge of gill cover. Different from the Pacific crevalle jack which has a deeper body, lacks scales on breast (except for a small patch), and has a dark blotch at the base of the pectoral fin. Usually found in schools around reefs, open waters over flat coral bottom (eg. Punta Espejo, Marchena). Length to 76 centimeters *(see* photo 138, p.126).
Pacific range: Indian and Pacific oceans, Gulf of California to Ecuador, Galápagos.

HORSE EYE JACK *(Caranx latus)*
Dorsally blue-gray, ventrally silver. Black spot on opercle and pectoral fin. Caudal fin yellow. Conspicuous black line from caudal peduncle towards middle of body on sides. Eye diameter black and large. Found in schools around northern islands like Marchena (Wellington, 1978). Length up to 65 centimeters.
Pacific range: Gulf of Mexico, Caribbean, Galápagos.

BLUEFIN JACK *(Caranx melampygus)*
Also known as Blue-spotted jack. Resembles the Amberjack but with a blunter head. Silvery-bluish body with blue and black spots on the sides, mainly above lateral line. Pelagic around reefs. Length up to 90 centimeters *(see photo 139, p.127)*.
Pacific range: Tropical Indo-Pacific, Baja California to Panama, Revillagigedos, Galápagos.

TILLE JACK *(Caranx tille)*
Dorsally bluish-green to silvery on sides and ventrally. Developed gelatinous membrane over the eye. Conspicuous black spot on the upper corner of gill cover. Slender shape. Yellow fins. A rare species, seen at Gordon Rocks. Length up to 80 centimeters *(see photo 140, p.127)*.
Pacific range: Indo-Pacific, Galápagos.

RAINBOW RUNNER *(Elagatis bipinnulatus)*
Blue dorsally, silvery ventrally. Yellow stripe between two blue stripes, extending from snout to caudal fin. Tail yellow. Elongate, slender, fusiform fish with pointed head. On or near surface of deep waters, around reefs (Gordon Rocks). Often seen in company of sharks. Length up to 70 centimeters *(see photo 141, p.127)*.
Pacific range: California to Peru, Galápagos.

ALMACO AMBERJACK *(Seriola rivoliana)*
Formerly known as Pacific amberjack. Elongate, fusiform, slightly compressed. Color bluish dorsally to brownish on the sides. Ventrally silvery. Olive band from eye to dorsal fin. Dorsal and anal fins short and falcate. Open sea species, small schools around reefs and drop-offs (Devil's Crown, Gordon Rocks). Length 1.5 meters *(see photo 142, p.128)*.
Pacific range: From California to Peru, Galápagos.

YELLOW TAIL AMBERJACK *(Seriola lalandei)*
Elongate, fusiform fish. Color olive brown above, whitish ventrally. A conspicuous brown-orange stripe runs across the sides from snout to tail. Caudal fin forked and yellow, all fins yellowish. Near surface around reefs, islets. Length up to one meter *(see photo 143, p.128)*.
Pacific range: British Columbia to Chile, Galápagos.

PACIFIC MOONFISH *(Selene peruviana)*
Silver with golden hue. Pectoral and caudal fins yellowish. Body extremely compressed, steep head profile very conspicuous. Pectoral fins long. Pelagic species, in close association with the bottom. Forms large schools. Coastal waters to a depth of 50 meters. Rare inshore species in the Galápagos (Cousin's Rock). Length from 27 to 60 centimeters.
Pacific range: Eastern Pacific, California to Peru, offshore islands, Galápagos.

BIGEYE SCAD *(Selar crumenophthalmus)*
Metallic blue to dark green above. White on sides, sometimes with a yellow stripe from opercle to base of tail. Dusky spot on opercle. Elongate, mackerel like. Eyes large. Feeds on plankton and benthic invertebrates, shrimps, crabs. A schooling species. Records from Floreana to Isabela. Length up to 27 centimeters.
Pacific range: Tropical and subtropical. Eastern Pacific from Cabo san Lucas, Mexico, Gulf of California, Panama, offshore islands, Galápagos.

SHORTFIN SCAD *(Decapterus macrosoma)*
Metallic blue above, silver below. Black blotch on opercle. Elongate, up to 30 centimeters.
Pacific range: Eastern Pacific, Gulf of California to Peru, Galápagos.

YELLOWTAIL SCAD *(Decapterus santae helenae)*
Similar to the former species. A conspicuous yellow tail. Food of bottlenosed dolphins. Length up to 30 centimeters (*see* photo 144, p.128).

MEXICAN SCAD *(Decapterus muroadsi)*
Dark green on back to pale green ventrally. Sides with faint orange or red stripe. Fins dusky yellow. The most elongate of Galápagos jacks. Large scutes on posterior portion of lateral line. Length up to 46 centimeters.
Pacific range: Eastern Pacific, central California to Ecuador, Galápagos.

Tilefishes (Malacanthidae)

Bass-like fishes with very long dorsal and anal fins, consisting of soft rays. Body rubust to elongate. A single, flat spine on the opercle. One species in Galápagos.

OCEAN WHITEFISH *(Caulolatilus princeps)*
Some authors put this species in the family Branchiostegidae. Fusiform compressed, head profile blunt. Gray-brown dorsally, white ventrally. Conspicuous blue lines on dorsal and anal fins. All fins are yellow. Similar to the Yellowtail, but the caudal fin is more truncate (Yellowtail has it forked). Over soft bottoms and reefs to a depth of ten to 40 meters. Length about 36 centimeters (*see* photo 145, p.145).
Pacific range: From Vancouver Island to Chile, Galápagos.

Dolphins (Coryphaenidae)

Elongate, compressed fishes. Long continuous dorsal fin like a sail, being above the eye. Anal fin from the middle of the body to tail. Caudal fin long and forked. Dolpins are noticeable for their iridescent colors, which fade out of the water, when dying and soon after death. One species in Galápagos.

DOLPHINFISH *(Coryphaena hippurus)*
Dorsally iridescent blue-green. Ventrally yellow-gold with dark spots. Dorsal fin black. Caudal fin deeply forked, also black. Color changes to silver-gray after death. Found on surface of open seas, deep waters. Abundant in the islands during the warm season, especially during the Niño year 1982–83. Locally known as Dorado. Length up to 105 centimeters (Niño, Dec. 1997, off Urvina Bay) (*see* photo 146, p.145).
Pacific range: Baja California to Chile, Galápagos.

Mackerels (Scombridae)

This large family of fishes includes Mackerels and Tunas, which have a high dispersal ability. Torpedo-shaped fishes, fast swimmers usually found in large schools in open oceans. Recognized by two dorsal fins and a series of finlets from the second dorsal and anal fins towards the tail. Two or three pairs of keels are found on the caudal peduncle. Small cycloid scales cover the body. At least eight species are recorded in the Galápagos.

WAHOO *(Acanthocybium solanderi)*
Also known as Spanish mackerel. Long, slender, slightly compressed fish. Dorsally dark green to steel blue. Ventrally pale. Narrow dark bars on sides. Head pointed. Dorsal fins hardly separated. Distinctive nine dorsal and anal finlets. Three keels on caudal peduncle. Offshore feeder on fish and squid on the ocean surface. One of the main resources of the Galápagos coastal fisheries. Length up to 1.8 meters (*see* photo 147, p.145).
Pacific range: California to tropical South America, Galápagos.

SIERRA MACKEREL *(Scomberomorus sierra)*
Elongate and fusiform. Dorsally bluish-green to iron gray, ventrally silver. Yellow spots along sides. Pale spiny dorsal fin, followed by eight to nine dorsal finlets. Nine to ten anal finlets. Resource of the Galápagos fisheries. Locally known as Sierra. Length up to 1.5 meters, but average is 80 centimeters (*see* photo 148, p.146).
Pacific range: Indo-West Pacific, California to Ecuador, Galápagos, Caribbean.

ORIENTAL BONITO *(Sarda orientalis)*
Also known as Striped bonito. Elongate and fusiform. Dorsally steel blue, ventrally silver. Horizontal lines on back. No stripes on belly. Often found in schools near surface of open waters. Commercially exploited in Galápagos. Length up to 90 centimeters (*see* photo 150, p.146).
Pacific range: Alaska to Chile, Galápagos.

SKIPJACK TUNA *(Katsuwonis pelamis)*
Also known as Black tuna. Robust and fusiform. Dorsally dark metallic blue. Fat, dark lines on upper back, fading on belly. Conspicuous black spots behind the pectoral fin. Ventrally silver. Four to six horizontal bands below laterally on belly. First and second anal

fins barely separated. Seven to nine finlets on the back and seven to eight after anal fin. Three keels on caudal peduncle. Schooling fish in tropical and subtropical open seas. One of the resources of the Galápagos coastal fisheries. Favorite food of the False killer whale. Length up to one meter (*see* photo 149, p.146).
Pacific range: British Columbia to Peru, Galápagos.

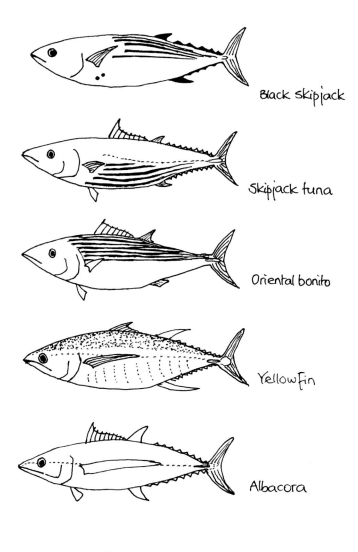

Black skipjack

Skipjack tuna

Oriental bonito

Yellowfin

Albacora

Tunas

© Piroco 2002

BLACK SKIPJACK *(Euthynnus lineatus)*
Irridescent blue on back, belly pale. Three to five narrow black bands on back behind corselet. Two black circular marks above pelvic fins. Fusiform, robust. Two dorsal fins, eight finlets behind dorsal fin. Large central keel on caudal peduncle. Opportunistic feeder on small surface fish, squid, crustaceans. Pelagic species, schooling, migratory. Open ocean near shore. Heterotypic schools, with yellowfin and skipjack tunas. Maximum size 99 centimeters.
Pacific range: Eastern Pacific, California to Peru, oceanic islands, Galápagos.

YELLOWFIN TUNA *(Thunnus albacares)*
Fusiform and compressed. Dorsally dark blue, ventrally gray. Fins and finlets yellow. Dorsal fin distinctively sharp and pointed. Caudal fin slender with lunate profile. Found in schools on surface in open waters. Favorite food of the Spotted dolphin. Length up to 1.8 meters, but usually 80 centimeters *(see photo 151, p.147)*.
Pacific range: California to Chile, Galápagos.

ALBACORA *(Thunnus alalunga)*
Dark blue to violet above, belly silver-white. Faint irridescent blue band on sides. Very long pectoral fins are conspicuous. Dorsal and anal fins yellow. Caudal fin white-edged. Oceanic schooling fish. Length up to 1.37 meters.
Pacific range: Tropical and subtropical Pacific, seasonal in Galápagos during the cool periods.

BIGEYE TUNA *(Thunnus obesus)*
Dark blue above, sides and belly silver-white. Fins light yellow, dorsal fin dark yellow. Pectoral fin long. Pelagic and oceanic. Ventral surface of liver striated. Length up to 2.3 meters. Pacific range: Tropical and subtropical.

CHUB MACKEREL *(Scomber japonicus)*
Elongate, fusiform. Dorsally green to blue-black, with wavy dark streaks on upper back and sides. Ventrally silver with dusky blotches. Dorsal and caudal fins dark. Five dorsal and anal finlets. Two distinct dorsal fins. Usually found in schools, pelagic. Length up to 65 centimeters.
Pacific range: Alaska to Chile, Galápagos.

Remoras (Echeneidae)

This family of fishes possesses an oval-shaped sucking disc on the top of the head. Remoras, or Sharksuckers as they are often known, are perfect hitchhikers, fixing themselves to a variety of large animals, including sharks, marine mammals, turtles, even ships at times or on the tank of a scuba diver! They feed on scraps of food left by their means of transport. One species in Galápagos: *Remora remora*. Color usually gray. Seen in pairs on the head of the giant manta. Can reach a length of 50 centimeters *(see photo 131, p.124)*.

Bonefish (Albulidae)

Elongate fusiform body with single dorsal fin and large caudal fin. In large seas around the world. One species in Galápagos: *Albula vulpes*. Color bluish to silvery, with distinctive cycloid scales and dusky stripes on sides. In shallow waters over soft bottoms. Length up to 90 centimeters. Pacific range: from California to Peru, Galápagos.

Tarpons (Elopidae)

Tarpons and their relatives occur in shallow warm seas and in estuaries. About seven species are found in the world; one on the Pacific coast.

TARPON *(Elops affinis)*
Also known as Machete. Belong to the family *Elopidae*, or Tarpons, distinguished by a slender, silvery body, with a large mouth. Caudal fin deeply forked. One dorsal fin with soft rays. Pelvic fins are abdominal. Color from blue above, to silver below. Usually in school, a very unusual occurrence in Galápagos. Seen by the author at Darwin Arc (Dec. 2004). Length up to 90 centimeters (*see* photo 156, p.148).
Pacific range: South California to Peru.

Porgies (Sparidae)

Oblong, compressed body. Head is large with steep profile. Mouth small. Opercle is scaled. Single dorsal fin. Pectoral fins long. Inshore fish over hard bottoms or over mud. Four species in Galápagos, one is endemic.

PACIFIC PORGY *(Calamus brachysomus)*
Overall silver color. Slope of the head profile steep. Lips and chin white. Long pectoral fins. Feeds over sandy substrates to a depth of 30 meters. Length up to 44 centimeters.
Pacific range: Baja California to Peru, Galápagos.

GALÁPAGOS PORGY *(Calamus taurinus)*
Color silver on back, ventrally white. Less deep bodied than the Pacific porgy, and smooth convex dorsal profile. Short pectoral fins. Rear edge of gill cover blackish. Dark spots or blotches on the sides of the body. Same sandy habitat as the previous species, but to depth greater than ten to 40 meters (Grove, 1984). Length about 37 centimeters (*see* photo 152, p.147).
Pacific range: Peru, Ecuador, Galápagos.

GALÁPAGOS SEABRIM *(Archosargus pourtalesi)*
Also known as the Blue-striped porgy (Peter Scott, 1976). Oval-shaped body. Dorsally light blue to silver ventrally. Seven golden-yellow stripes run longitudinally from head to caudal peduncle. A conspicuous black spot above pectoral fin makes it distinctive from

the similar Blue and gold snapper. Habitat usually in protected areas, in bays over sand and in cracks with sandy bottoms (eg. Franklin's Crack at Puerto Ayora, Santa Cruz, which holds a resident population). Length about 26 centimeters (see photo 153, p.147).
Pacific range: Endemic to Galápagos.

Molas (Molidae)

Unusual and weird looking fishes. Body is very deep and compressed. From the profile one would say that Molas look like a large blunt snout with two sail-like wings in a vertical axis (one sticking up, the other down), and the posterior part of the body just cut off. The mouth is small with teeth forming a parrot-like beak hidden inside mouth. The gill opening reduced to a round-oblong pore. No scales on the body, silvery and leathery looking. Short base dorsal fin, with very long rays.Three genera and four species known worldwide. At least two genera and two species recorded in Galápagos: *Mola mola*, the ocean sunfish and *Ranzania levis*, the slender mola. Feed on planktonic organisms and soft bodied jellies; not seaweed as formerly reported. Juveniles have prominent spines on head and body. Two species of Molas in the eastern Pacific, the second being *Mola ramsayi* (Chile and Easter Island). Latest research conducted in Bali, shows that the sunfish spends 30 percent of its time at depths below 200 meters and 30 percent of the time in depths of ten meters. In Galápagos, frequent sightings of concentrations off Punta Vicente Roca (1998–2000), also found at North Seymour, Gordon Rocks, Española, south Isabela (personal observation underwater, July 2001).

OCEAN SUNFISH *(Mola mola)*
Oval shape almost round. Dorsally blue-gray, ventrally metallic silver. Dorsal and anal fins very long, placed far back. Caudal fin reduced, flap-like. Body covered with thick mucus. On the surface in open waters, sometimes close to shore. Often seen on the west side of the archipelago, between the islands of Isabela and Fernandina (Punta Vincente Roca). Dorsal fin sticking upright out of the water, and moving laterally in a distinctive manner, rocking side to side. No possible mistake of identification with sharks or even manta ray fins. Feed on drifting ctenarian, salps, jellyfishes and animals on the seafloor. Seen basking in the sun, laying on the surface. Sometimes jumps out of the water to get rid of parasites. Length up to four meters. Weigh up to 2,000 kg (see photos 154, 155, p.148).
Pacific range: British Columbia to Chile, rare in Galápagos.

SLENDER MOLA *(Ranzania levis)*
Long, slender body with no caudal fin. Dark blue above, silver below. Several silver-white, black-edged bands and spots posteriorly between dorsal and anal fins. Body elongate, oval. Eighteen dorsal fin rays, 20 anal fin rays. Skin thin, smooth, formed of hard, fused hexagonal scales. Lips prominent in front of teeth. Oval mouth rather than wide (Grove & Lavenberg, 1997). Feeds on planktonic crustaceans, mollusks, fish.
Pacific range: California to Chile.

Photo 97: 84 Greybar grunt, *Haemulon sexfasciatum* (juvenile)

Photo 98: Brassy grunt, *Orthopristis chalceus*

Photo 99: Peruvian grunt, *Anisotremus scapularis*

114

Photo 100: Black-striped salema, *Xenocys jessiae*

Photo 101: White salema, *Xenichthys agassizi*

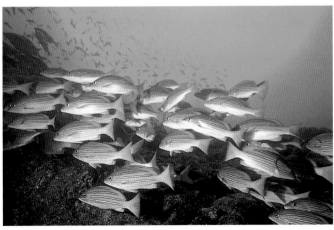
Photo 102: Blue and gold snapper, *Lutjanus viridis*

Photo 103: Yellowtail snapper, *Lutjanus argentiventris*

Photo 104: Mullet snapper, *Lutjanus aratus*

Photo 105: Spindle snapper, *Lutjanus inermis*

116

Photo 106: Dusky chub, *Girella fremenvillei*

Photo 107: Cortez sea chub, *Kyphosus elegans*

Photo 108: Rainbow sea chub, *Sectator ocyurus*

Photo 109: Crimson soldierfish, *Myripristis leiognathos*

Photo 110: Tinsel squirrelfish, *Adyorix suborbitalis*

Photo 111: Glasseye, *Priacanthus cruentatus*

Photo 112: Popeye catalufa, *Pseudopriacanthus serrula*

Photo 113: Pink cardinalfish, *Apogon pacificus*

Photo 114: Blacktip cardinalfish, *Apogon atradorsatus*

Photo 115: Blacktip cardinalfish, *Apogon atradorsatus*

Photo 116: Tail spot cardinalfish, *Apogon dovii*

Photo 117: Galápagos searobin, *Prionotus miles* (Vivien Li)

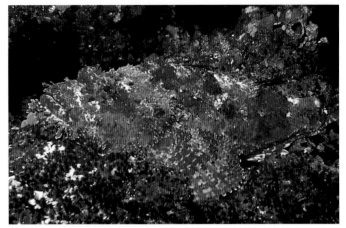

Photo 118: Stone scorpionfish, *Scorpaena plumieri mystes*

Photo 119: Rainbow scorpionfish, *Scorpaenodes xyris*

Photo 120: Rainbow scorpionfish, *Scorpaenodes xyris* (juvenile)

Photo 121: Stalkeye scorpionfish, *Pontinus strigatus*

Photo 122: Hieroglyphic hawkfish, *Cirrhitus rivulatus*

Photo 123: Hieroglyphic hawkfish, *Cirrhitus rivulatus* (juvenile)

Photo 124: Coral hawkfish, *Cirrhitichthys oxycephalus*

Photo 125: Coral hawkfish, *Cirrhitichthys oxycephalus*

Photo 126: Longnose hawkfish, *Oxycirrhites typus*

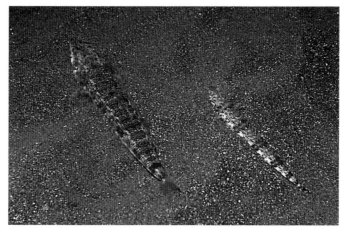

Photo 127: Sauro lizardfish, *Synodus lacertinus*

Photo 128: Sauro lizardfish, *Synodus lacertinus*

Photo 129: Mexican goatfish, *Mulloïdichthys dentatus*

Photo 130: Galápagos thread herring, *Opisthonema berlangai* (E)

Photo 131: Remora, Sharksucker, *Remora remora*

Photo 132: Pelican barracuda, *Sphyraena idiastes*

Photo 133: Steel Pompano, *Trachinotus stilbe*

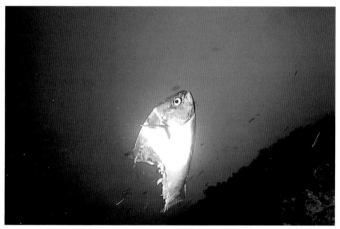

Photo 134: Pompano, *chomp chomp!*

Photo 135: African pompano, *Alectis ciliaris*

126

Photo 136: Green jack, *Caranx caballus*

Photo 137: Black jack, *Caranx lugubris*

Photo 138: Big eye jack, *Caranx sexfasciatus*

Photo 139: Bluefin jack, *Caranx melampygus*

Photo 140: Tille jack, *Caranx tille*

Photo 141: Rainbow runner, *Elagatis bipinnulatus*

128

Photo 142: Almaco jack, *Seriola rivoliana*

Photo 143: Yellowtail amberjack, *Seriola lalandi*

Photo 144: Yellowtail scad, *Decapterus santae helenae*

Swordfishes (Xiphiidae)

SWORDFISH *(Xiphias gladius)*
Very dark blue to blue-black dorsally. Light brown to white below. Very long upper jaw, flat, sword-like. No pelvic fins. Strong keel on the caudal peduncle. Local name Pez Espada. Found at depths down to 650 meters. Length up to five meters.
Pacific range: Tropical and subtropical, Oregon to Chile, Galápagos.

Billfishes, Marlins (Istiophoridae)

PACIFIC SAILFISH *(Istiophorus platypterus)*
Dark blue above, light brown spots laterally. Silver-white ventrally. Twenty lateral stripes. Sail-shaped dark blue dorsal fin, with longest rays near the middle. Open ocean near surface. Migrates into nearshore waters. Length up to 3.4 meters.
Pacific range: Tropical and subtropical, California to Chile.

BLACK MARLIN *(Makaira indica)* Jordan and Hill.
Color black-blue on back, sides silver-white. No spots on sides. Pectoral fin rigid in position, pointing downward. Dorsal fin blue-black, other fins brown. Oceanic, near surface. Solitary species, in warm waters, near coast.
Pacific range: Western Pacific, northeast Australia, Polynesia, Central America to Peru, Chile, Ecuador, Galápagos.

STRIPED MARLIN *(Makaira mazara)* Jordan and Snyder.
Also known as Indo-Pacific blue marlin. Color dark blue dorsally, silver ventrally. A sail-like dorsal fin. Elongated body with a circular cross-section, and characteristic sword protruding from the upper jaw. Tail like a thin half moon. Conspicuous vertical cobalt-blue stripes on sides of body, as circular spots and narrow bars. Can reach a racing speed of 120 kilometers per hour. Oceanic, near surface. Inhabits warm waters. Length up to 4.5 meters.
Pacific range: Indian and Pacific oceans, Japan, Philippines, Hawaii, California to Chile, Galápagos.

(*See* sketches of Swordfish, Sailfish and Marlins on p.131).

Croakers, Drums, Mullets, Snooks

Drums, Croakers (Scianidae)

Elongate, slightly compressed fishes, living mainly close to the bottom. Chin barbels and rostral pores are frequent. Two dorsal fins separated by a distinct notch. Two spines on the anal fin. Body covered with ctenoid scales. Seven genus and seven species recorded in Galápagos, two are endemic: the Galápagos rock croaker, *Pareques perissa* and the

Galápagos croaker, *Umbrina galapagorum*. One is insular endemic to Cocos and Galápagos, the Wide eye croaker, *Odontoscion eurymesops*. Other species include the Corvina drum, *Cilus gilberti*; the Large eye drum, *Corvula macrops*; the Cachema weakfish, *Cynoscion phoxocephalus*; the Pacific drum, *Larimus pacificus*.

GALÁPAGOS ROCK CROAKER *(Pareques perissa)*
Also known as Gungo drum. Oblong body, color dark brown to purple, ventrally pale. Iris golden-brown. Lips flesh-colored. Rough cycloid head scales. An Eastern Pacific genus with two distinct body markings. One uniform, one with six to nine black stripes horizontally, in juveniles or adults, on a cream white background and a vertical black band from the dorsal fin to the pelvin fin. Margin of pectoral fin white. No barbels on chin. Nocturnal species, hiding during the day in crevices and under rocks (Grove, 1984). Length 23 centimeters. Pacific range: Endemic to Galápagos.

WIDE EYE CROAKER *(Odontoscion eurymesops)*
Also known as Yellow-eyed croaker. Elongate body. No barbel on chin. Dorsally silver-gray, ventrally silver. Dark horizontal bands along sides. Yellow iris. Inshore, shallow waters on sandy bottoms. Often found in schools. Feeds on plankton and nekton. Length up to 25 centimeters.
Pacific range: Insular endemic to Cocos, Galápagos.

GALÁPAGOS CROAKER *(Umbrina galapagorum)*
Elongate body, with short barbel on tip of chin. Mouth horizontal, underslung. Color gray-silver on back, white ventrally. Oblique gold streaks along sides. Dorsal fins dark. Pelvic, anal and caudal fins yellow. Shallow waters above algae covered rock or near sandy beaches. Umbrina are striped drums with stout, rigid barbell at tip of lower jaw, rounded and pierced with pore (Grove, 1997). Length 41 centimeters.
Pacific range: Endemic to Galápagos.

Mullets (Mugilidae)

Elongate fishes, head nearly cylindrical. Snout blunt, mouth small, premaxilla protractile. Two well-separated dorsal fins. Body covered with cycloid scales. No laternal line. Six species recorded in Galápagos, one is endemic: *Mugil galapagensis*, known locally as Lisa.

STRIPED MULLET *(Mugil cephalus)*
Also known as Blacktail mullet. Silvery color to bluish-green on back. Six to seven dark stripes on sides from opercle margin to tail. Caudal fin is forked. First dorsal fin with four weak spines. Fins dark, except pectoral fins which are white. Occur in schools, feeding on small algae and detritus in mud, near coast. Open waters and inshore. Length up to 60 centimeters (*see* photo 157, p.149).
Pacific range: California to Chile, Galápagos.

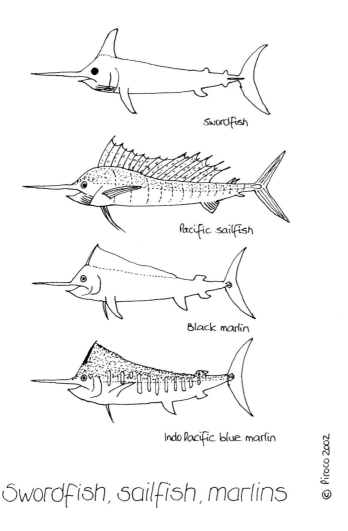

Swordfish

Pacific sailfish

Black marlin

Indo Pacific blue marlin

© Piroco 2002

Swordfish, sailfish, marlins

ORANGE-EYED MULLET *(Xenomugil thoburni)*
Color dark blue dorsally, silver ventrally. No stripes along sides. All fins dark, except pectoral fins which are white. Orange iris. In schools near coast. Length 31 centimeters.
Pacific range: Baja California to Chile, Galápagos.

GALÁPAGOS MULLET *(Mugil galapagensis)*
Locally known as Lisa. Dorsally olive-green, silvery on sides, ventrally white. Five to six indistinct stripes along sides. Rows of scales. Caudal fin black. Upper head dark, lower head and cheeks silver. Small schools in shallow waters and protected bays, faults, on sandy bottoms. A yellowtail morph of *M. galapagensis* exists: olive-green dorsally, pelvic fins white, pectorals with dark blue blotch at base (Grove 1997). Length 35 centimeters (*see* photo 158, p.149).
Pacific range: Endemic to Galápagos.

Snooks (Centropomidae)

Rather large fish, elongate, compressed, dorsal fins well separated. Snout pointed, mouth large. Three spines on the anal fin. Lateral line extends to rear edge of caudal fin. One species recorded in Galápagos: *Centropomus nigrescens*. Tropical coastal waters and lagoons.

Batfishes, Frogfishes

"Eighteen meters down, we encountered the weird batfish: *Ogcocephalus darwinii*, perched on the coarse brown lava sand. With its elongated snout, flaring fins and bright red lips, this Galápagos native belongs to an old group that has become completely adapted to bottom dwelling. Propped off the sea floor by stilt like fins, it hops about lethargically, aided by an occasional swish of the tail." (after G. Wellington, 1978, in Tagus Cove, Isabela Island.)

Batfishes (Ogcocephalidae)

Four genera and 12 species known from the Eastern Pacific. Great color variation, often with reticulated pattern on back, spots or ocelli. Ventrally white. Fishes with a disk-shaped body when seen from above, flattened ventrally. Pectoral fins look like limbs. Distict tail. Snout projects like a spine in front of the eyes. Gill opening reduced to a hole behind limb like pectoral fins. Batfishes feed on snails, clams, crustaceans and small fishes. Two genera and two species recorded in Galápagos, one endemic: *Dibranchus species*.

RED-LIPPED BATFISH *(Ogcocephalus darwinii)*
Also known as Red lips batfish. Color light brown, to blue-gray, emerald-green; or cream-beige color with two dark longitudinal stripes along the back. A black protuberance on the forehead. Light ventrally with white blotches under the mouth. Bright red lips. Habitat in sandy and volcanic areas. Usually still on the sandy bottom, hops lethargically like a frog, and when forced to flee it swims like a snake with a shark like motion of the tail, using its spread 'wings' as stabilizers. Active at night, attracted by light (seen at Tagus Cove, Isabela; Punta Mejia, Marchena). Originally an endemic species (Hubbs, 1958), but recent records found it in Peru and Ecuador (Chirichigno 1974, Massay, 1983). Shallow waters to greater depths, from three meters to 73.5 meters (Grove, 1984). Length 15 centimeters (*see* photos 159, 160, pp.149–50).
Pacific range: Ecuador to Peru, Galápagos.

GALÁPAGOS BATFISH *(Dibranchus species)*
Species of this genus are usually in deep waters on shelf below 200 meters. One record in shallow water, in Tagus Cove (J. M. McCosker, 1978).
Pacific range: Endemic to the Galápagos.

Frogfishes (Antennariidae)

Small, globulate fishes, slightly compressed bodies. Camouflage needed against predators. Poor swimmers. Long dorsal fin; the first spine acts as a lure to attract prey. Pectoral fins limb-like, but not as pronounced as in batfishes. Fleshy flaps are often found on a prickly or smooth skin. Feeding techniques includes ambush, waiting and enticing potential victims with wiggling action of the lure-spine, located above mouth and anterior to eyes. Frogfishes are fast gulpers. Three species recorded in Galápagos: *Antennarius sanguineus*, *Antennarius strigatus* (Gill) and the Roughjaw frogfish, *Antennarius avalonis*. Length about 15 centimeters.

SANGUINE FROGFISH *(Antennarius sanguineus)*
Color purple-pink to gray, mottled, showing an adaptation for camouflage, according to the rocky substrate. Appears red mottled in flash light. Black-green irridescent eye with a whitish eye ring and 'sunrays' around it. Absolutely motionless, it waits for its prey, mouth open under the wriggling lure. Does not mind to be bothered. In cracks, crevices, under rocks and ledges in shallow waters to a depth of 13 meters. Seen at Cousin's Rock, and Punta Albemarle, Isabela. Length ten to 15 centimeters *(see* photo 161, p.150).
Pacific range: Central Gulf of California to Peru, Galápagos.

BANDTAIL FROGFISH *(Antennarius strigatus)*
Differs from the former species by a clear band followed by a dark band around the caudal peduncle.
Pacific range: Central Gulf of California to Colombia, Galápagos.

Lefteye Flounders, Flounders, Soles

Lefteye flounders (Bothidae)

Highly compressed fishes. Eyes and color on the left side of the body, pigmented, usually brownish. Markings are frequent. Blind side is white. Capacity to change color like chameleons, depending on the substratum. Edge of opercle visible, not hidden by skin. Dorsal and anal fins long, not connected to the caudal fin. Sexual dimorphism occurs in a few species. Two species recorded in Galápagos: Bigmouth sanddab, *Citharichthys gilberti* and Blue-eyed flounder, *Bothus mancus*. None is endemic.

BLUE-EYED FLOUNDER *(Bothus mancus)*
Belongs to the family Bothidae. Color bluish to brownish with 'eyes' all over the exposed left side, speckled with blue dots and a few black spots—usually two large ones—behind the pectoral fin. The pectoral fin is long, sometimes half the size of the body, black rays with blue dots. Able to adapt color to the substrate, with perfect camouflage. This flatfish is found over sandy bottoms, coral bottoms, and eventually forages over rocks. Seen at

Punta Espejo, Marchena, Wolf Island and North Seymour. Length up to 45 centimeters. (*see* photo 162, p.150).
Pacific range: South Africa to eastern Pacific, Japan, Easter Island, Polynesia, Galápagos.

LEOPARD FLOUNDER *(Bothus leopardinus)*
Oval-shaped body. Light brown with numerous dark brown blotches and white spots, with central mark surrounded by brown ring. Diet of small fish, crustaceans, polychaetes, mollusks. Found on sandy bottoms, near sandy beaches to a depth of 20 meters. Length up to 15 centimeters (*see* photo 163, p.151).
Pacific range: Eastern Pacific, California to Columbia, Cocos, Galápagos.

Flounders (Paralichthyidae)

Three genera and three species in the Galápagos, none is endemic. Flatfishes differ from the Bothidae by having ribs extended ventrally from their vertebrae and intermuscular bones (Grove, 1997). Bottom dwelling, rapid color changes to match substrate. Bury into the mud or sand. Benthic marine species in all oceans.

BIGMOUTH SANDDAB *(Citharichthys gilberti)*
Extremely compressed, deep body with eyes on left side. Color brown with mottling, dull orange spots may be seen on body and fins. Blind side white or light brown. Ridge between eyes. Usually found on soft bottoms to a great depth, 300 fathoms. Length 22 centimeters.
Pacific range: Gulf of California to Peru, Galápagos.

Soles (Soleidae)

Flatfishes. Eyes on the right side of the body. Color blackish-brown with blotches or bars. Edge of opercle hidden by skin (different from flounders). Body shape round to oval. Lips fleshy, fringed with dermal flaps. Eyes are small and close together. Usually found in shallow coastal waters as deep as 100 Fathoms (180 meters). Two species recorded in Galápagos: *Trinectes fonsecensis* and *Aseraggodes herrei*.

STRIPED SOLE *(Trinectes fonsecensis)*
Right-eyed, bottom dwelling fish. Cream color with 12 to 13 dark bars across the body from gill to tail. Anal and dorsal fins along the whole length of the sides. On sandy bottoms. Length 15 to 23 centimeters.
Pacific range: Mexico, Panama, Peru, Galápagos.

RETICULATED SOLE *(Aseraggodes herrei)*
A right-eyed flounder with mouth on the right side. Body with brown and white reticulations and small black spots. Fins black and white with spots. Tongued-shaped with a rounded head, small eyes are close together. Snout like a hook with curved jaws. Feeds on invertebrates: crustaceans, mollusks. Found on sand and gravel bottons where it can change color to match the substratum. Throughout the archipelago, from Darwin to Floreana (*see* photo 164, p.151).
Pacific range: Eastern Pacific, Gulf of California to Peru, Revillagigedos, Cocos, Galápagos.

Tonguefishes (Cynoglossidae)

Three species recorded in Galápagos, one endemic: the Small scale tonguefish, *Symphurus diabolicus*, pale to straw yellow in color.

RAINBOW TONGUEFISH *(Symphurus atramentatus)*
Small, teardrop-shaped flatfish with a pointed tail end. Round head, small black eyes close together on the left side of the body, with twisted mouth. Color brownish (in flash), or bluish, red in transversal bands across the body. No pectoral fin, but a single pelvic fin. No lateral line. Anal and dorsal fins are joined at the tail, with rays alternating black and white, forming nice stripes. Bottom dwelling fish, on volcanic sandy bottoms or in bays over mud to a depth of 20 meters. Length about five to seven centimeters. Active at night. Feed on invertebrates, crustaceans and polychaete worms. Related to the California tonguefish, *Symphurus atricauda* (*see* photo 165, p.151).
Pacific range: Galápagos.

FRECKLED TONGUEFISH *(Symphurus varius)*
Pale yellow to tan. Numerous dark brown and white speckles. Posterior third of dorsal and anal fins spotted. Uncommon. Length up to five centimeters.
Pacific range: Equatorial eastern Pacific, Cocos, Malpelo, Galápagos.

Morays, Snake Eels, Conger Eels, Cusk Eels

Includes four families of fish: the Muraenidae (Morays), the Congridae (Conger eels), the Ophichthyidae (Snake eels) and the Ophidiidae (Cusk eels). Only the last two families have endemic species.

Morays (Muraenidae)

Heavy and more compressed than eels. Dorsal fin present and very long. No pectoral fins. Thick leathery skin. Small, round gill opening. Jaws are powerful and armed with knife-like or molar-like teeth. Habitat usually restricted to shallow coral reefs, rocky areas. Hides during the day in holes and crevices. Active at night. A moray bite can inflict serious deep wounds. Thus this animal is considered as dangerous and should not be disturbed on purpose. Twenty-one species recorded in Galápagos. None is endemic.

Main genera represented are: Anarchias (1 species), Gymnothorax (6 species), Muraena (4 species), Gymnomuraena (1 species), Echidna (2 species), Siderea (1 species), Enchelycore (2 species), Uropterygius (4 species). List of the 21 species (Jordan and Evermann, 1896; McCosker and Rosenblatt, 1975; Grove and Lavenberg, 1997).

HARDTAIL MORAY *(Anarchias galapagensis)*
Color brown or reticulated yellow-brown. Dorsal and anal fins absent. Tip of tail is hard and pointed. Prominent interorbital pore over the eye. One of the smallest morays which has a maximum length of 12.5 centimeters.
Pacific range: Central Gulf of California, Panama, Galápagos.

BLACK MORAY *(Gymnothorax buroensis)* Bleeker
Color dark brown to black, overlain with wavy irregular mottling. Two rows of teeth on the maxillary, five rows longitudinally on the upper jaw. Length ten to 46 centimeters.
Pacific range: Indo-West Pacific, Hawaii, Clipperton, Panama, Cocos and Galápagos (specimen from Darwin Bay, Tower Island).

PANAMIC GREEN MORAY *(Muraena castaneus)* Jordan and Gilbert
Color greenish-brown, sometimes with small white spots. Dorsal fin well developed. Mainly foraging at night over reef or sandy bottoms. Hides during the day in holes and crevices. Length up to 1.2 meters *(see photo 168, p.152)*.
Pacific range: Gulf of California to Colombia, Malpelo, Galápagos.

MAGNIFICENT MORAY *(Muraena argus)* Steindachner
Also known as White-spotted moray. Body with three rows of large, irregular yellow blotches, and many scattered, small white spots. Black spot at corner of mouth. Yellow eye. Posterior nostril tubular. Dorsal and anal margins white (McCosker and Rosenblatt, 1975). Length about 90 centimeters (specimen from James Bay, Santiago; Gordon Rocks) *(see* photo 172, p.154). Pacific range: Baja California to Peru, Galápagos.

BLACKSPOT MORAY *(Muraena clepsydra)* Gilbert
Also known as Hourglass moray. Color gray, speckled with white. A large black spot around gill opening, circled with white. Adult speckled with small irregular spots on body and fins. Length 30 to 90 centimeters *(see photo 167, p.152)*.
Pacific range: Baja California to Peru, Galápagos.

JEWEL MORAY *(Muraena lentiginosa)* Jenyns
Also known as Lentil moray. Color brown to light brown. Network of yellowish-cream spots of same diameter as eye. Dorsal fin starts from head and is continuous with the anal fin. Teeth conical. Nocturnal predator on shallow rocky substrates and reefs. Length 50 centimeters *(see photos 170, 171, p.153)*.
Pacific range: Baja California to Peru, Galápagos.

ZEBRA MORAY *(Gymnomuraena zebra)* Shaw
Color dark brown to black, purple-red at times. Body encircled by numerous narrow white or bluish rings. Blunt, molar-like teeth (instead of canines). Specimen seen at Gordon Rocks and Wolf Island. Length 80 centimeters (*see* photo 174, p.154).
Pacific range: Indo-West Pacific, Gulf of California to Panama, Galápagos.

YELLOWMARGIN MORAY *(Gymnothorax flavimarginatus)*
Color yellowish-brown, densely mottled with small dark brown spots. Gill opening in a black blotch. Origin of dorsal fin slightly anterior to gill opening, edged with yellow-green posteriorly. Depth of body 11 to 18 centimeters along total length. Short snout. Teeth in front of jaw long and fang like. Maximum size 120 centimeters.
Pacific range: Indo-Pacific and east Pacific, Galápagos.

FINE-SPOTTED MORAY *(Gymnothorax dovii)*
Also known as Speckled moray. Color dark green to olive. Numerous fine white dots all over the body. In holes, crevices in rocky areas and at times seen foraging on open ground. Rather common in the archipelago, it is unafraid of divers. Length up to 1.2 meters (*see* photo 169, p.153).
Pacific range: Panama, Colombia, Galápagos.

WHITE MOUTH MORAY *(Gymnothorax meleagris)*
Also known as Guineafowl moray. Easily distinguished by a network of round white spots all over a brown body. Interior of mouth is white. An Indo-Pacific species, found in warm waters. Inhabits coral reef crevices. Seen at Wolf Island. Length up to 120 centimeters (*see* photo 173, p.154).
Pacific range: Indian Ocean, southeast Asia, Great Barrier Reef, Indo-Pacific.

PAINT-SPOTTED MORAY *(Siderea picta)*
Also known as White-speckled moray, formerly *Gymnothorax pictus*. Color white, mottled with brown, from head to tail. Uniformly white on belly. In shallow waters, on coral reefs. One row of sharp conical teeth on each jaw. Feeds during the day on fish and crabs, forages across exposed reef flats. Can travel long distances in the water. Length one to two meters.
Pacific range: Indo-West Pacific, French Polynesia, Galápagos (rare).

SLENDERJAW MORAY *(Enchelycore octaviana)*
Grayish-brown, with curved slender jaws, and apparent fang-like teeth when the mouth is closed. Uncommon. Personal observation at Guy Fawkes Island (Jan. 1992) (*see* photo 175, p.155).
Pacific range: Upper Gulf of California to Colombia, Galápagos.

MOSAIC MORAY *(Enchelycore lichenosa)*
Also know as Reticulate hookjaw moray. Color dark brown. Numerous light spots on head and throat. Series of large light blotches along sides. Length 55 centimeters.
Pacific range: Indo-Pacific, Galápagos (Punta Espinosa, Fernandina).

RUSTY MORAY *(Uropterygius necturus)* Jordan & Gilbert
Dark color with rusty mottlings. Head and trunk shorter than tail. Posterior nostril with a raised rim located behind center of eye (McCosker and Rosenblatt, 1975). Length 23 to 28 centimeters.
Pacific range: Gulf of California to Panama, Galápagos.

MORAYS IN THE GALÁPAGOS (21 SPECIES)

Anarchias galapágensis (Seale, 1940)	Hardtail moray
Echidna nocturna (Cope, 1872)	Night moray, freckled moray
Echidna nebulosa	Snowflake moray
Muraena castaneus (Jordan & Gilbert, 1882)	Panamic green moray
Muraena lentiginosa (Jenyns, 1843)	Jewel moray
Muraena clepsydra (Gilbert, 1888)	Blackspot moray
Muraena argus (Steindachner, 1870)	Magnificent moray
Gymnomuraena zebra (Shaw, 1797)	Zebra moray
Gymnothorax flavimarginatus (Rüppell, 1830)	Yellowmargin moray
Gymnothorax funebris (Herre, 1936)	Olive moray
Gymnothorax dovii (Günter, 1870)	Fine-spotted moray
Gymnothorax buroensis (Bleeker)	Black moray
Gymnothorax panamensis (Steindachner, 1876)	Masked moray
Gymnothorax meleagris	White mouth moray
Siderea picta (Ahl, 1789)	Paint-spotted moray
Enchelycore octaviana (Myers & Wade, 1941)	Slenderjaw moray
Enchelycore lichenosa (Jordan & Snyder)	Mosaic moray
Uropterygius polysticus (Myers & Wade, 1941)	Peppered moray
Uropterygius necturus (Jordan & Gilber, 1882)	Rusty moray
Uropterygius versutus	Blackeye moray
Uropterygius macrocephalus (Bleeker, 1864)	Longhead moray

Snake Eels (Ophichthyidae)

Distinctive snake-like shape of this family of eels. Pointed snouts, often with tubular anterior nostrils. Dorsal and anal fin sometimes continuous around the tail, but may be totally absent in certain species. Color varies from striking to drab. Snake eels should not be touched for they are able to inflict painful wounds with their fang-like teeth. Nine species recorded in Galápagos, of which three are endemic: the Burrowing Galápagos snake eel *Callechelys galapágensis* (McCosker and Rosenblatt), the Pouch snake eel, *Paraletharchus opercularis* (Myers and Wade) and the Thread snake eel, *Apterichtus equatorialis* (Myers and Wade).

TIGER SNAKE EEL *(Myrichthys tigrinus or M. maculosus)*
Color light brown to cream. Many large and black spots along sides. Anterior nostrils tubular, hanging vertically from side of upper lip. Body long and slender, slightly compressed. Anal fin behind anus. Two rows of large dark spots on sides and back. Few smaller spots on top and sides of head. Snout is pointed. Small pectoral fins. Caudal and ventral fins absent. Lives among rocks and reefs. Mostly a nocturnal species. Length 42 centimeters (*see* photo 177, p.155).
Pacific range: Trans-Pacific species. Gulf of California to Peru Galápagos.

PACIFIC SNAKE EEL *(Ophichtus triserialis)*
Color whitish-cream with small brown dots over body. Spots vary in size. Conspicuous large mouth. Usually found on shallow sandy bottoms. Active at night. Burrows in sand, with head sticking out, to a depth of 23 meters. Common on shrimp grounds. Easily mistaken for the Tiger snake eel, which also has spots but arranged in about four rows, not at random like this species. Length up to 1.1 meters (*see* photo 178, p.156).
Pacific range: California to Peru, Galápagos.

Conger Eels (Congridae)

Two species in Galápagos: *Paraconger californiensis* (Kanazawa, 1961) and *Heteroconger klausewitzi* (McCosker and Taylor, 1978), the latter being endemic.

GALÁPAGOS GARDEN EEL *(Heteroconger klausewitzi)*
Snake-like body with a blunt snout. Color light to dark brown. A line of white spots along the lateral line on sides of body. Black pectoral fins, transparent dorsal fin. Burrows itself in sandy bottoms, or in broken shells in areas of strong current (narrow water channels). Garden eels make important colonies of up to 50 individuals, from which their name derives. When disturbed they disappear slowly in their holes like timid periscopes, to reappear a while later. Records to a depth of 30 meters (north and south of Baltra Island, Plazas Island and around Devils's Crown, Floreana; Grove, 1984). Length 55 centimeters (*see* photo 176, p.155).
Pacific range: Endemic to Galápagos.

BLACKFIN CONGER *(Paraconger californiensis)*
Congrid eel, flesh color. Silvery-pink body with a long dorsal fin fringed with black. Head with a black eye and nose almost translucid. Pectoral fins developed. Nocturnal species foraging on volcanic sandy bottoms to a depth of 20 meters. When scared burrows itself tail first, leaving the head sticking out. Shallow water between 15 to 80 meters. Personal observation at Tagus Cove, night dive (March 1991, February 1992) Length about 40 centimeters *(see* photo 179, p.156).
Pacific range: Tropical and subtropical waters of the new world. Gulf of California to Peru, Cocos, Galápagos.

Cusk Eels, Brotulas (Ophidiidae)

Not to be mistaken with Viviparous brotulas (Bythitidae). There are 49 genera and 183 described species of ophidiids worldwide. Brotulas and cusk eels are bottom living creatures, elongate, eel-like with two pairs of whiskers on the chin (pelvic fins). The body is laterally compressed or cylindrical towards head. Dorsal and anal fins are confluent. Ophidiids are divided into four groups (subfamilies) with representatives in the eastern Pacific. Brotulinae: two species in eastern Pacific, one species in Galápagos: the Spotted brotula, *Brotula ordwayi*. Brotulotaeniinae: one species in eastern Pacific, also in Galápagos, the Brownspot cusk eel, *Otophidium indefatigable*. Neobythitinae: 37 genera, 120 species in deepwater, along continental slope. One shallow water species in Galápagos, the Velvetnose brotula, *Petrotyx hopkinsi*. Ophidiinae: eight genera, 47 species worldwide; six genera and 15 species in eastern Pacific; six undescribed species, including one in the Galápagos, the Galápagos brotula (endemic), *Ophidion* species.

GALÁPAGOS BROTULA *(Ophidion species)*
Body elongate, eel like, color silvery to gray. Dorsal and anal fins confluent. Tail rounded. Pelvic fins below eyes, each being two filamentous rays joined at base. No scales on head. Cycloid body scales. Outer edge of dorsal and anal fins, blackish. Length up to 13 centimeters. On sandy bottoms near reefs. Undescribed species. Nocturnal, seen on night dives at Tagus Cove *(see* photo 180, p.156), where it buries into the sand easily. Uncommon. Pacific range: Endemic to Galápagos.

Freshwater Eels

For a number of years, so-called 'freshwater eels' have been occasionally sighted in the brackish water lagoons and waterholes in the lava flows of Punta Moreno (Julian Fitter, 1996) and of Puerto Villamil, on Isabela Island. Scientists were never able to catch any for identification. The first specimen was captured by Jacinto Gordillo at 'Laguna las Diablas', in Puerto Villamil in June 1997, but sightings had been made by locals since the 1960s. This was the first record of a freshwater eel in the Eastern Pacific region.

GALÁPAGOS FRESHWATER EEL *(Anguilla marmorata)*

Also known as Giant mottled freshwater eel. It belongs to the Anguillidae family.   On 7 February 2006, the author managed to get into the water of one of his ponds, and took an underwater photo of an adult individual, attracted by curiosity, but eventually frightened away! The eel is grey to light-brown, speckled, with a large mouth and rounded head. A long dorsal fin extends from mid-back to tip of tail, joined to a similar anal fin. Two conspicuous rounded pectoral fins. The pupil of the eye is like a pin point. *Anguilla marmorata* usually feeds at night on crabs, frogs and fish. Eels are catadromous, whereby juveniles and adults live in estuaries and freshwater, and the semelparous adults return to oceanic gyres to spawn and die. The larvae, called 'leptocephali', return via surface currents to the estuaries, transform into juvenile elvers and then enter the freshwater habitat as an adult.

Recent studies have demonstrated that extreme El Niño events may increase the likelihood of larval transport of the freshwater eel to the Galápagos from the Central Pacific (Grove, 1989). Slow growing and long lived, it can reach a length of 2 meters and weigh up to 21 kg. The European species may live up to 50 years; the New Zealand long-finned eel may live up to 60 years (see photo 183, p.157).

Pacific range: widely distributed in the tropical Indo-west Pacific from East Africa to the Society Islands, up north to southern Japan. Galápagos.

PART III: RAYS

Six families and 15 species are recorded in the Galápagos (Grove and Lavenberg, 1997). Rays, like Skates, belong to the orders of the Rajiformes and the Myliobatiformes. They consist of a group of fish having the gills confined to the ventral surface of the body.

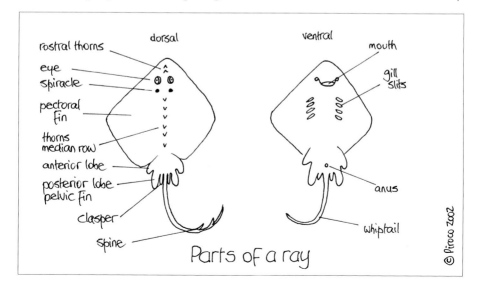

Parts of a ray

© Piroco 2002

Elongate, depressed, the body is almost elliptical in cross section. Pectoral fins have large bases, greatly extended and attached to the sides of the body from the tip of the snout to the anterior margin of pelvic fins (see drawing on p.143). Anal fin is absent.

RAYS IN THE GALÁPAGOS

Family	common name	scientific name	size
Order Rajiformes			
Rhinobatidae (Guitarfishes)	Pacific guitarfish	*Rhinobatos planiceps*	< 0.76m
Rajidae (Skates)	Witch skate	*Raja velezi*	< 0.56m
Pseudorajidae (False skates)	Southern false skate	*Gurgesiella furvescens*	< 0.52m
Order Myliobatiformes			
Dasyatidae (Stingrays)	Whiptail stingray	*Dasyatis brevis*	< 2m
	Longtail stingray	*Dasyatis longus*	< 2.57m
	Pelagic stingray	*Dasyatis violacea*	
	Black-blotched stingray	*Taeniura meyeri*	< 3m
Myliobatidae (Eagle and Cownose rays)			
	Spotted eagle ray	*Aetobatus narinari*	< 1.2m
	Barred eagle ray	*Pteromylaeus asperrimus*	< 0.8m
	Golden cownose ray	*Rhinoptera steindachneri*	< 0.9m
	Bat eagle ray	*Myliobatis californica*	
Mobulidae (Mantas, Devil rays)			
	Giant manta	*Manta birostris*	< 6.1m
	Smoothtail mobula	*Mobula munkiana*	< 2.2m

Stingrays (Dasyatidae)

Greatly depressed disc and distinct tail. Pectoral fins extend forward beyond the mouth. Dorsal fin absent. The genera *Dasyatis* and *Urotrygon* have a poisonous spine in the tail, which may cause severe wounds and extreme pain to swimmers and waders. An encounter with such a dangerous creature may be prevented by shuffling feet when entering shallow waters on sandy bottoms to frighten it away. Stingrays stir the bottom with their pectoral fins, to search for worms, mussels and small crustaceans on which they feed. Three species are recorded in Galápagos: Whiptail stingray, *Dasyatis brevis*, Longtail stingray, *Dasyatis longus* and Round stingray *Urotrygon species.*

WHIPTAIL STINGRAY (Dasyatis brevis)
Shape of the disc subquadrangular, wider than length. Tail more or less same length as the disc. Three rows of tubercules are clearly distinguished on the back of the body. Well developed caudal fin. Dorsally gray, ventrally cream colored. The most common ray in Galápagos. Usually found in shallow waters, covered with sand (White beach, Punta Cormorant, Floreana; North East Lagoon, Santa Fé; South Beach, Bartolomé) or to a greater

depth of ten to 40 meters, under rocks or at the entrance of caves (Devil's Crown, Floreana; Bartolomé; Punta Estrada, Academy Bay, Santa Cruz). Feeds on worms and crustaceans buried in the mud, which they dislodge with their pectoral fins. The powerful muscular armed tail makes the stingray a potentially dangerous species. The injected venom may cause paralysis in the legs, or may be fatal if in the stomach. See medical aspect, treatment and prevention of stingray wounds on p.161. Ovoviviparous reproduction (i.e. giving birth to live young that have hatched from eggs held inside the body without receiving nutrients from the mother). Length up to two meters (*see* photo 181, p.157). Pacific range: California to Peru, Galápagos.

LONGTAIL STINGRAY *(Dasyatis longus)*
Shape of disc subquadrangular, wider than length. Tail twice as long as the disc, with small spines. Color brownish dorsally, light ventrally. Feeds on clams, crabs, occasionally small fish, on sandy substrates to moderate depth. Teeth are molar-like (J. Armas, 1984). Ovoviviparous reproduction. Length up to 1.2 meters.

BLACK-BLOTCHED STINGRAY *(Taeniura meyeri)*
Distinguished from other stingrays by it conspicuous black color with gray blotches on the back. Ventrally white. Grows to very large size. Rests on rocky bottoms in areas of current, sometimes hides under rocks and overhangs, in pairs. Rather common in the Galápagos, central and northern islands (*see* photo 182, p.157). Pacific range: Tropical Indo-Pacific, Galápagos.

Eagle Rays (Myliobatidae)

Robust body and rather falcate pectoral fins. Disc is wider than length. Anterior part of pectoral fins from one or two lobes (subrostral lobes) under snout. The head is distinctively separated from the disc and the eyes are on the sides. Tail longer than disc, has a dorsal fin and a venomous spine.

SPOTTED EAGLE RAY *(Aetobatus narinari)*
Color dorsally black, with white spots (juveniles) or black spots circled in white (adults). Ventrally white. Tail very long, whip-like, two spines at base of tail. Differ from the Mobulids (Mantas) in that the anterior subdivision of the pectorals form either one soft fleshy lobe extending forward below the front of the head, or two such lobes joined together basally. Single subrostral lobe or fin. Eagle rays prefer warm temperate or tropical waters. Spend their time cruising over the bottom or near the surface, with a flying like motion (Halstead, 1970). Mostly found in shallow waters, where they feed on crustaceans and molluscs, which they excavate from sand or mud with their large pectoral fins. Distribution in the northern and central islands. These graceful swimmers have, when pursued, the habit of making spectacular leaps in the air. Ovoviviparous. Length up to 2.8 meters, average 1.5 meters (*see* photos 186, 187, 188, pp.158–9). Pacific range: Gulf of California to Peru, Galápagos.

BAT EAGLE RAY *(Myliobatis californica)*
A diamond shaped disc, with long wings. Unlike the spotted eagle ray, the head is rounded and extends beyond the front of disc. Colour olive brown to sooty grey. The tail is long and whiplike. Habitat is in sandy areas and bays. Seen at the northern exit of Tagus Cove, over rocks (Nov. 2002) and in Puerto Villamil, southern Isabela Is. over sand (Jan. 2006). Width up to 1,8m.
Pacific range: West coast of North America, from Oregon to Gulf of California, Galápagos.

GOLDEN COWNOSE RAY *(Rhinoptera steindachheri)*
Dorsally golden-brown, ventrally white, tail black. Distinctive fleshly lobe in front of disc divided into two sections. Tail is slender and whip-like, longer than disc. Differs from the Eagle rays by possessing a pair of subrostral lobes or fins (B. W. Halstead, 1970). Feeding habits similar to the Myliobatidae, largely on bivalve molluscs and crustaceans. Usually found in mangrove areas and protected lagoons (Tortuga Negra, Santa Cruz; Elizabeth Bay, Isabela), gliding at the surface of the water, often in schools. Sometimes in deeper waters around rocks, drop-offs (Daphné Mayor). Ovoviviparous reproduction. Length up to two meters, average one meter or less in the Galápagos *(see photos 184, 185, p.158)*.
Pacific range: Gulf of California to Peru, Galápagos.

Mantas (Mobulidae)

The name Manta comes from the Spanish word for blanket. Conspicuous cephalic fins make these rays very different from the Eagle rays (anterior subdivision of the pectoral fins modified as two separate fins located on the head). Posterior edges of pectoral fins falcate. Small dorsal fin on the tail. Most members of the Mobulidae family are without a sting. Devil rays (another name for the Mantas) are similar to the Myliobatids in their swimming motions, flapping their pectoral fins as if they were flying. They often leap out of the water or somersault in the air, falling back with a noisy splash. The reason why they leap is subject to speculation: to get rid of parasites, as defensive tactics, in pure play (Gail Crampton, 1977). Usually found in warm tropical waters of coastal areas and offshore islands, feeding on small pelagic organisms, schooling fishes, which they scoop in their mouths with the help of the cephalic fins. Ovoviviparous reproduction.

GIANT MANTA *(Manta birostris)*
Dorsally black, ventrally white. Wing span may reach more than six meters. Tail as long as body. Weight as much as 1,400 kilograms. Rather frequent in the Galápagos. Seen at Punta Cormorant and Devil's Crown, Floreana; Darwin Bay, Tower; Academy Bay, Santa Cruz, Gordon Rocks, Isabela and Fernandina *(see photos 189, 190, pp.159–60)*.
Pacific range: Pan-tropical, California to Peru, Galápagos.

Photo 145: Ocean whitefish, *Caulolatilus princeps*

Photo 146: Dolphinfish, *Coryphaena hippurus*

Photo 147: Wahoo, *Acanthocybium solandri*

146

Photo 148: Sierra mackerel, *Scomberomorus sierra*

Photo 149: Skipjack tuna, *Katsuwonis pelamis*

Photo 150: Oriental bonito, Sarda orientalis

Photo 151: Yellowfin tuna, *Thunnus albacares*

Photo 152: Galápagos porgy, *Calamus taurinus*

Photo 153: Galápagos seabrim, *Archosargus pourtalesi*

Photo 154: Ocean sunfish, *Mola mola*

Photo 155: Ocean sunfish, *Mola mola*

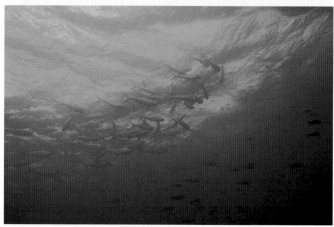

Photo 156: School of Tarpon, *Elops affinis*

149

Photo 157: Striped mullet, Blacktail mullet, *Mugil cephalus*

Photo 158: Galápagos mullet, *Mugil galapagensis*

Photo 159: Red-lipped batfish, *Ogcocephalus darwinii*

Photo 160: Red-lipped batfish, *Ogcocephalus darwinii* (front)

Photo 161: Sanguine frogfish, *Antennarius sanguineus*

Photo 162: Blue-eyed flounder, *Bothus mancus*

Photo 163: Leopard flounder, *Bothus leopardinus*

Photo 164: Reticulated sole, *Aseraggodes herrei*

Photo 165: Rainbow tonguefish, *Symphurus atramentatus*

Photo 166: Galápagos jawfish, *Opistognathus galapagensis*

Photo 167: Blackspot moray, *Muraena clepsydra*

Photo 168: Panamic green moray, *Muraena castaneus*

Photo 169: Fine-spotted moray, *Gymnothorax dovii*

Photo 170: Jewel moray, *Muraena lentiginosa*

Photo 171: Unidentified moray (Vivien Li)

Photo 172: Magnificent moray, White-spotted moray, *Muraena argus*

Photo 173: White mouth moray, *Gymnothorax meleagris*

Photo 174: Zebra moray, *Gymnomuraena zebra (Lionel Pozzoli)*

Photo 175: Slenderjaw moray, *Enchelycore octaviana (Lionel Pozzoli)*

Photo 176: Galápagos garden eel, *Heteroconger klausewitzi*

Photo 177: Tiger snake eel, *Myrichthys tigrinus*

156

Photo 178: Pacific snake eel, *Ophichthus triserialis*

Photo 179: Blackfin conger, *Paraconger californiensis*

Photo 180: Galápagos brotula, *Ophidion sp.* (E)

Photo 181: Whiptail stingray, *Dasyatis brevis*

Photo 182: Black-blotched stingray, *Taeniura meyeri*

Photo 183: Galápagos Freshwater Eel, *Anguilla marmorata*

Photo 184: Golden cownose ray, *Rhinoptera steindachneri*

Photo 185: Golden cownose ray, *Rhinoptera steindachneri*

Photo 186: Spotted eagle ray, *Aetobatus narinari*

Photo 187: Spotted eagle ray, *Aetobatus narinari*

Photo 188: Spotted eagle ray, *Aetobatus narinari*

Photo 189: Giant manta, *Manta birostris*

160

Photo 190: Giant manta, *Manta birostris*

Photo 191: Whitetip reef shark, *Triaenodon obesus*

Photo 192: Whitetip reef shark, *Triaenodon obesus*

SMOOTHTAIL MOBULA *(Mobula munkiana)*
A smaller version of the manta ray, very conspicuous in size, with a very long whip-like tail. Black dorsally, white ventrally. Moves fast, in areas of current and channels. Often found in large schools at the arrival of the warm season. Length up to two meters.
Pacific range: Indo-Pacific, Galápagos.

Sting Anatomy, Medical Aspect, Symptoms

"Though this fish is greatly feared by bathers, in the aquarium it proved very reluctant to sting." (Campbell, 1951). It has been suggested by various authors that the spine is replaced yearly, but there is no evidence to support this idea. Actually, multiple spines may be present. When this is the case, the oldest is the most posterior one on the tail. But it may vary from one specimen to the next.

The stinging is always directed to the side by a bending of the tail towards the evoking stimulus. The tip of the tail takes no part in the stinging action. The sting is an organ producing venom. The venom is produced in the glandular tissue lying along the ventral groves of the spine, and is released into the wound when the integumentary sheath is torn in the process of stinging or cutting (Crampton, 1977). The stingray venom depresses respiration, occasionally produces convulsive seizures, maybe due to cardiovascular failure.

MEDICAL ASPECT AND SYMPTOMS:
The pain symptoms quickly develop within ten minutes of the attack. The wound is surrounded by an inflamed area of ten centimeters in diameter. The pain becomes severe in the first half an hour, progressively reaching its maximum intensity within 90 minutes. The pain effect gradually diminishes from six to 48 hours. The symptoms are variable and diversified. It may start with a fall in blood pressure, then vomiting, diarrhea, sweating and may lead to muscular paralysis and even death. Nausea, vertigo, faintness may occur within ten minutes of attack, resulting from pain shock. The initial lesion is a laceration or a puncture wound, which soon becomes necrotic or ulcerated.

The treatment should follow as soon as possible after the attack.

1) Immediately irrigate the wound with cold salt water. It facilitates the removal of venom, acts as a vasoconstrictor and mild anesthetic agent.
2) Apply tourniquet and release every three minutes. Clean the wound of pieces of sting.
3) Put the leg in hot water, soaking for 30 to 90 minutes, adding magnesium sulfate if possible.
4) The use of anti-tetanus agents is recommended. Antibiotics may be required (Halstead, 1970).

Prevention: Always shuffle feet in the sand when entering the water to frighten any rays away. A stick is convenient probe to use along the bottom in order to rid area of lurking rays.

PART IV: SHARKS

> *"From the moment we touched the water, sharks as long as four meters surrounded us. Five solid gray Galápagos sharks headed for me out in the distant haze. I pressed my back against the coral as one swam directly over my head, its belly passing within half a meter of my face mask. Moments after we were all sequestered in coral foxholes, more sharks appeared and still more. We counted 16 at one time, circling and passing around us. Fortunately the sharks showed no sign of aggressive behavior and slowly swam away.*
>
> *A sudden uneasy calm prevailed. Where were all the fish? Looking up we saw 24 massive Scalloped hammerhead sharks cruising scarcely ten meters away. Eyes mounted at the end of strange cartilaginous protuberances, these beasts formed an echelon from top to bottom in the water column. Big hammerheads have been known to attack man, and we shared uncomfortable visions of being the entrée in a shark feeding frenzy. Yet, at the same time, we were captivated by their gracefulness."*
>
> from *Diving at Darwin Island* by Gerard Wellington (1978)

Of the recently known 344 species of sharks in the world today (Reader's Digest, 1986), about 35 would be potentially dangerous to man (Gilbert, 1968), and 27 species have been implicated definitely in attacks on man or boats (Garrick and Schultz, 1975). From these figures we may conclude that roughly ten percent of the world's sharks are dangerous to man. Furthermore, fewer than 100 shark attacks occur every year in the world and only 50 percent are considered to be fatal. But this is only data, probably only of use to specialists, and does not remove the fear that human beings have for the beast, the 'jaws' of the ocean.

Nevertheless, coming from the darkness of the origins of time, the shark is an impressive, if not amazing, living underwater machine, and for sure a breathtaking wonder of the ocean depths. It possesses a hydrodynamic shape, acoustic perfection, long-ranging olfactive senses, a muscular body capable of high speed, and a gracefulness of motion that inspires both a disconcerting mixture of seduction—attraction and striking fear of death.

Sharks, like ratfishes, sawfishes, skates and rays, and cartilaginous fishes belong to the class of Chondrichthyes. They possess well-developed jaws, five to seven pairs of gill openings, and paired fins supported by pectoral and pelvic girdles. Each pelvic fin on the male has a clasper, that is, a finger-like appendage that facilitates internal fertilization (the sex organ). Unlike most bony fishes, cartilaginous fishes lack a swim bladder and must move constantly or sink to the bottom.

Among other sophisticated particularities, the visual apparatus of sharks deserves some attention. While all sharks have relatively immobile upper and lower lids, several species possess a third eyelid or nictitans. The so-called nictitating membrane is conspicuously developed in Hammerhead sharks and Requiem sharks (Carcharhinids). It moves freely upward and backward from the lower nasal corner of the eye, between the lower eyelid and the cornea. Thus, it may cover totally the exposed portion of the eye (Gilbert, 1968).

According to Franz (1931), the visual acuity of a shark is about five percent that of a fish. Lacking cones, the majority of sharks rely on their sensitive rods for the perception of movement. Their capacity to distinguish details and colors of either preys or predators is extremely poor if not non-existent. Practically, at distances over 50 feet, depending on direction and strength of the current, clarity of the water and amount of light, vision increases in importance. At close range, three to four meters or less, vision seems to be the principle sense involved in directing sharks to food (experiences made on Lemon sharks at Lerner Marine Lab. by Gilbert, 1961–62).

The former phenomenon has been confirmed by Eibl-Eibesfeldt and Hass (1959) who believe that, if vibrations alert sharks and attract them from a distance, at closer quarters "the rush at living prey is mainly optically oriented."

From further experiments, Gilbert noted that even though the elasmobranch eye is poorly adapted for distinguishing details and colors, it is well equipped for differentiating an object from its background, especially a moving one; a good reason, under any circumstances, for humans to keep cool in the presence of sharks and avoid quick motion.

If You Meet a Shark

First of all, one of the most famous sentences on the subject: "sharks are unpredictable."

This further advice is always useful:
1) Always swim with a companion.
2) If dangerous sharks are known to be in the area, stay out of the water.
3) Since blood attracts and excites sharks, do not enter or remain in the water with a bleeding wound.
4) Avoid swimming in turbid or dirty waters where visibility is very poor.
5) Do not provoke sharks.
6) Shark will circle many times before it makes an aggressive 'pass'. In case of attack, hit shark snout with club or 'shark billy'.
7) Remain calm when shark is sighted. Leave water as quickly as possible.
8) Adopt a sensible attitude towards sharks. Remember that the likelihood of attack is less than of being struck by lightning.
9) Attack is almost assured if one deliberately grabs, injures, or in some way provokes even a small and seemingly harmless shark. (from "Advice to those who frequent or find themselves in shark-infested waters" by Perry W. Gilbert in *Sharks and Survival*, chapter 21, Oct. 1968)
10) My personal advice to you: Show no fear; sharks sense it, just like dogs.

Sharks in the Galápagos

Nobody knows for sure how many species of sharks are in the islands. However, one thing is certain, there was not any real attack of a shark on man in the Galápagos islands until 1989. The first credible record of a shark attack was reported in December 1989 on the south of Pinzon Island, where a park guard, standing in shallow water near shore, was attacked by a "three-meter-long gray shark," that came straight for him and bit off a piece of his leg. A second shark attack was reported at Playa Miedo, south Santa Fé Island in November 1989; then again between January and March 1990, attributed to a Galápagos shark (Patrick Wheelan, marine biologist, CDRS, Darwin Station).

A report of a two-meter-long Great white shark was made at Playa Escondido, north east Pinzon Island, in March 1991, when naturalist guide Jonathan Green was visited in the water while snorkelling. No injury was caused and in fact the shark swam away after being kicked. Jonathan said he recognized the long pectoral fins, the deep body, pointed nose and black eyes of the Great white. Unfortunately no picture was taken. The feared Great white shark has also been reported once at Baltra, Aeolean Cove, when "it jumped out of the water with a manta ray in its jaws" in 1995 (Gundi Schreyer, personal communication). Otherwise unknown to the archipelago, it is believed to inhabit the deeper waters far to the west or possibly to the north around Darwin and Wolf, the isolated satellite islands of the Galápagos group. Finally, bullsharks were identified for the first time at the northeast lagoon of Santa Fé in 2001, causing serious concern to SPNG and CDRS.

Of the eight orders of sharks in the world, six are represented in the Galápagos Islands: the Carcharhiniformes, Heterodontiformes, Lamniformes, Orectolobiformes, Pristiophoriformes, Squaliformes. Nine families and 30 species of sharks have now been recorded and are known to frequent Galápagos waters. The best represented family is the Carcharhinidae (Requiem sharks), with at least ten species; followed by the Sphyrnidae (Hammerhead sharks) with three species; Heterodontidae (Bullhead sharks) one species; Rhincodontidae (Whale sharks) one species; Lamnidae (Mackerel sharks) three species; Triakidae (Houndsharks) three species; Scyliorhinidae (Catsharks) two species; Alopidae (Thresher sharks) three species; Squalidae (Dogfish sharks) two species.

Some unknown species have been reported from the west of Isabela Island, off Punta Moreno (David Day, 1986 personal communication: possibly Taurus shark).

SHARKS IN THE GALÁPAGOS (32 SPECIES)

Carcharhinidae (Requiem sharks) 13 species
Carcharhinus galapágensis	Galápagos shark
Carcharhinus amblyrhynchos	Gray reef shark
Carcharhinus limbatus	Black tip shark
Carcharhinus albimarginatus	Silvertip shark
Carcharhinus falciformis	Silky shark
Carcharhinus altimus	Bignose shark (deepwater)
Carcharhinus plumbeus	Sandbar shark
Carcharhinus longimanus	Oceanic whitetip
Carcharhinus leucas	Bull shark
Triaenodon obesus	White tip reef shark
Galeocerdo cuvieri	Tiger shark
Prionace glauca	Blue shark
Nasolamia velox	White nose shark

Sphyrnidae (Hammerhead sharks)
Sphyrna zygaena	Smooth hammerhead
Sphyrna lewini	Scalloped hammerhead
Sphyrna mokarran	Great hammerhead

Heterodontidae (Bullhead sharks)
Heterodontus quoyi	Hornshark
Heterodontus mexicanus	Mexican hornshark

Triakidae (Houndsharks)
Mustelus mento	Speckled smoothhound (bottom)
Mustelus species	Broadnose smoothound (bottom)
Triakis maculata	Spotted houndshark (bottom)

Scyliorhinidae (Catsharks)
Apristurus campae	Longnosed catshark (deepwater)
Apristurus stenseni	Panama ghost catshark (deepwater)

Alopidae (Thresher sharks)
Alopias superciliosus	Bigeye thresher (oceanic)
Alopias vulpinus	Thresher shark (oceanic)
Alopias pelagicus	Pelagic thresher (oceanic)

Squalidae (Dogfish sharks)
Centroscyllium nigrum	Combtooth dogfish (deepwater)
Isistius brasiliensis	Cookie cutter shark (deepwater)

Rhincodontidae (Whale sharks)
Rhincodon typus	Whale shark

Lamnidae (Mackerel sharks)
Isurus paucus	Longfin mako
Isurus oxyrhinchus	Shortfin mako
Carcharodon carcharias	Great white shark

Carcharhinidae (Requiem sharks)

The family of Requiem sharks are often hard to identify because of their similarity. Of the two dorsal fins, the first is larger, and none of the two has spines. The upper lobe of caudal fin is elongate and pointed. Teeth are blade-like, with smooth or serrate cutting edges. Carcharhinidae is the largest family of sharks in the world with 48 species. Only 12 species are represented in the Galápagos.

BLACKTIP SHARK *(Carcharhinus limbatus)*
Dorsally gray to ashy-blue, ventrally white. All fins are conspicuously tipped with black. Pectoral fins falcate. Snout is long and pointed. Teeth in the front are erect, sharp pointed and serrate. Habitat in coastal waters and offshore. Usually found in schools at the surface. Juveniles often congregate in protected areas (eg. Academy Bay, Santa Cruz; Stephens Bay and Wreck Bay, San Cristobal). Feed on squid and herrings. Known for leaping and spinning in the air in pursuit of food. Distinctive from Galápagos shark by its arched back. Length 1.8 to 2.4 meters.
Pacific range: Baja California to Peru, Revillagigedos, Cocos, Galápagos, Hawaii and Indo-West Pacific.

SILVERTIP SHARK *(Carcharhinus albimarginatus)*
Dorsally gray to blue-gray on sides. Ventrally white. Dorsal, pectoral and caudal fins white tipped. First dorsal fin high and pointed. Differs from the common White tip reef shark by the presence of white markings on the pectoral fins. Active around shallow reefs, inshore waters. Large silvertips are pelagic. Not too common in Galápagos. Length 2.2 to three meters (*see* photo 195, p.177).
Pacific range: Baja California to Ecuador, Galápagos. Tropical waters distribution.

GALÁPAGOS REQUIEM SHARK *(Carcharhinus galapágensis)*
Discovered by Heller and Snodgrass in 1905. Dorsally gray-brown with greenish hue. Ventrally white to yellowish. Pectoral fins long with a wide base and slender tips. Iris of eye silver-gray (Grove, 1984). Lower rows of teeth on jaw smooth and pointed like nails, upper jaw with serrate triangular teeth. Common species in the Galápagos, abundant on the west side of Isabela and Fernandina. Curious of man, but indifferent. Often seen in schools. Length two to 3.7 meters (*see* photo 194, p.177).
Pacific range: Galápagos, Cocos, Clipperton, Revillagigedos, Colombia to Peru, Hawaii, French Polynesia.

GRAY REEF SHARK *(Carcharhinus amblyrhynchos)*
A black vertical band on the fringe of the caudal fin, second dorsal fin black, and black tips under pectoral fins, are key identification marks which permit the differentiation between the Gray reef and the Galápagos requiem shark. Color is gray dorsally, fading to white ventrally. A newly reported species which is easily mistaken for the Galápagos

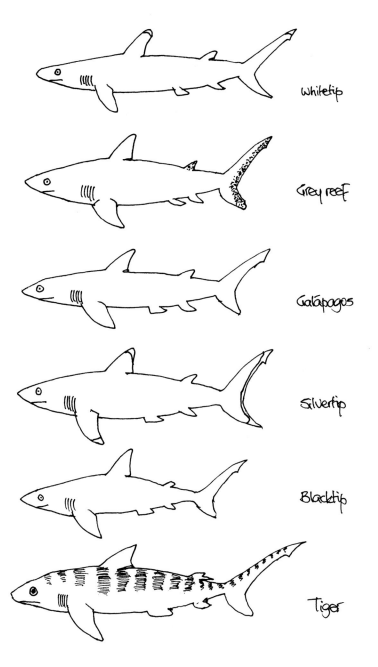

Whitetip

Grey reef

Galápagos

Silvertip

Blacktip

Tiger

Sharks

© Piroco 2002

requiem shark, also gray in color. I witnessed this shark once while skin diving at Tortuga Island, near Isabela (May 1986), an isolated young individual of small size, about three feet long, and secondly, when scuba diving off the east of Champion Island (Oct. 1986), where we were surrounded by an impressive school of about 12 highly curious adults, eight feet long. In both occasions pictures were taken, decisive in the final identification of the Gray reef, although first thought to be regular Galápagos sharks. In conditions of stimulation, may be aggressive (Johnson, 1978). Length up to 2.35 meters. Pacific range: Known in French Polynesia as the Raira, in the east Pacific from Hawaii to Easter Island, Galápagos.

BULL SHARK *(Carcharhinus leucas)*
Also known as Shovel nose and Square nose shark. Dorsally grayish, ventrally white. Snout short and rounded. Teeth strongly serrate, triangular in upper jaw, slender in lower jaw. Pectoral fins are conspicuously broad with pointed tips. Inhabits inshore waters, never far from land. Feeds on other sharks and rays, including hammerheads, stingrays and even young of its kind. Possibly the most dangerous tropical shark, responsible for attacks on people (observed by David Day, off Punta Moreno, 1986, west Isabela). The bullshark was again possibly identified in the northeast lagoon of Santa Fé in 1999, where it attacked the head of a snorkeller (who fortunately escaped). Other individuals were

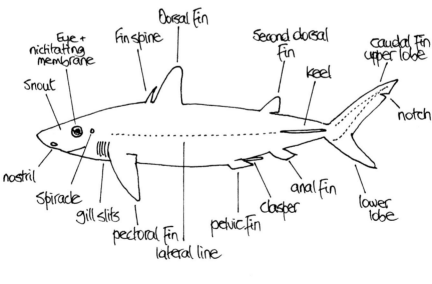

Parts of a shark

© Piroco 2002

seen and are likely to hang around because of the sea lion colony. Reported in July 2000 by Benjamin Ruttenberg (CDRS), less than one meter away, outside the bay in ten meters visibility. He pushed the square nose with his bare hand. Length up to 3.4 meters.
Pacific range: Indian Ocean, Baja California to Peru, Nicaragua, Galápagos.

WHITETIP REEF SHARK *(Triaenodon obesus)*
Dorsally gray to light brown, ventrally white. Tips of dorsal and upper lobe of caudal fin white. Body thinner than Silvertip shark, smaller in size. Very common around the islands, coastal areas. Curious of man, but not aggresive in the Galápagos. Length two to 2.5 meters *(see* photos 191, 192, 193, pp.160, 177).
Pacific range: Tropical and subtropical seas. From Costa Rica to Ecuador, Cocos and Galápagos, Indo-West Pacific.

TIGER SHARK *(Galeocerdo cuvieri)*
Color gray to grayish-brown, paler on sides. Conspicuous dark spots like bars for specimens less than two meters. These seem to fade with age. Snout is short, bluntly rounded. Teeth deeply notched and serrate; show no difference from upper to lower jaw. Small distinct spiracle behind eyes. Dermal ridge is noticeable on caudal peduncle. Caudal fin falcate. Usually found in coastal waters near surface, but do occur offshore. Not so common in Galápagos. Omnivorous and varacious predator of other sharks, fishes, porpoises, turtles, beef bones, dogs, tin cans, garbage. Dangerous to people, the Tiger shark should not be approached deliberately. Best advice would be to leave the water upon sight. Length up to four to 5.5 meters.
Pacific range: Tropical and subtropical seas, Panama to Peru, Chile, Cocos, Revillagigedos, Galápagos.

Hammerhead Sharks (Sphyrnidae)

A unique family with greatly depressed and laterally expanded head. The eyes positioned at the extreme ends of the 'hammer', gives the shark an inconceivable 360° vision, and a more perfect depth perception. Larger species are mostly oceanic, juveniles more confined to coastal areas. Of the four species of existing Hammerheads, the Bonnethead *(Sphyrna tiburo)*, the Great hammerhead *(Sphyrna mokarran)*, the Smooth hammerhead *(Sphyrna zygaena)* and the Scalloped hammerhead *(Sphyrna lewini)*, only the last three species have been recorded in the Galápagos.

The Great hammerhead (five meters) is circumtropical in distribution, common in the tropical Indo-Pacific and Australia, but rare in the eastern Pacific along the shores of North and South America. The Bonnethead, the smallest of the four (1.4 meters) ranges from South Carolina to Peru in the east Pacific, and totally harmless to people. The Smooth and Scalloped hammerheads are common to the East Pacific coast of North and South America.

Hammerheads attacks have been recorded in the Pacific by Garrick and Schultz (1975), who give the following figures:
    434 unprovoked attacks in California.
    448 unprovoked attacks in Australia.
    937 provoked attacks in Australia.

Only one attack of a Hammerhead has been reported in the Galápagos (1992), even though they are often met on the diving sites. Of course they do show a great curiosity towards man and may eventually approach them very close (as close as one meter), but then turn away with indifference.

SMOOTH HAMMERHEAD *(Sphyrna zygaena)*
Color olive-gray to brownish above, pale to whitish ventrally. The front margin of the 'hammer' is convex and lacks indentations, unlike the Scalloped hammerhead where three lobes may be seen. Tips of fins dusky to black. Teeth slightly saw edged. Found off-shore and inshore, often in small numbers (five to six). Common places would be around rocky islets and drop-offs (eg. Gordon Rocks, Devil's Crown, Floreana; Cousin's Rock; Kicker's Rocks; Darwin Bay; Tower; northern islands). Feeds on stingrays, smaller sharks, shrimp, crab and squid. Length up to 3.5 meters, usually 2.5 meters.
Pacific range: Southern California to Peru, Chile, Cocos, Galápagos.

SCALLOPED HAMMERHEAD *(Sphyrna lewini)*
Color light gray above, shading to white ventrally. Front margin of the 'hammer' is convex and indented in the midline. Teeth are smooth edged. Lower surface of pectoral fins tipped with black. Large eyes separated from nostrils by a distance equal to the diameter of the eye (which is a distinguishing mark, for the Smooth hammerhead has eye and nostril closer together). Usually found on the surface with its dorsal fin sticking out, feeding on fish and squid. Favors deep waters and drop-offs, feeding also close to the bottom for stingrays, amberjacks and bottom fishes. May be seen in small groups around Santiago Island, Macgowen and Hancock Banks (Grove, 1984). Length 2.5 meters up to four meters (*see* photos 196, 197, p.178).
Pacific range: Indo-Pacific, Philippines, southern Australia, Hawaii, South California to Ecuador, Cocos, Galápagos.

Bullhead Sharks (Heterodontidae)

Bottom dwelling sharks, with large blunt heads and elongate bodies. In tropical and semi-tropical waters. Two recorded species in the Galápagos islands.

GALÁPAGOS HORNSHARK *(Heterodontus quoyi)*
Known to be related to the Port Jackson shark from Australia. Color light brown with dark blotches all over the body. Short distinctive spine anterior to the two dorsal fins. No nictitating membrane. Horn sharks deposit their eggs in grenade-shaped horny cases. A

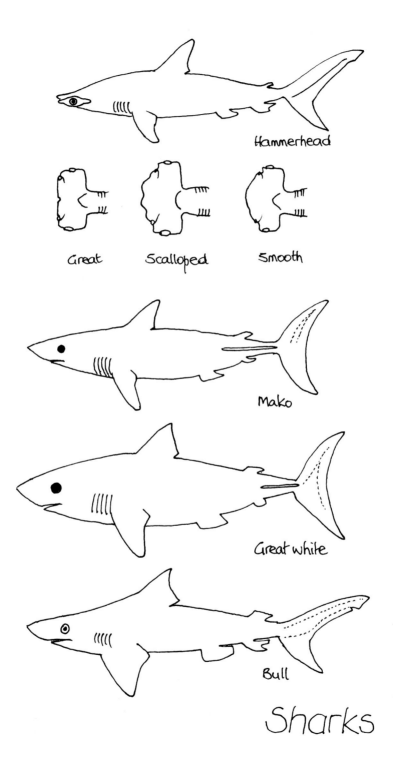

Hammerhead

Great   Scalloped   Smooth

Mako

Great white

Bull

Sharks

© Piroco 2002

poor swimmer, it is a sedentary species found on sandy substrates and around shallow reefs at depths of two to 12 meters. Frequent on the west side of the archipelago: Tagus Cove (west Isabela), Punta Espinosa (Fernandina). Length of 45 centimeters up to one meter (*see* photos 198, 199, p.178–9).
Pacific range: Ecuador to Peru, Galápagos.

MEXICAN HORNSHARK *(Heterodontus mexicanus)*
Very similar to the former species, it is nevertheless bigger in size, with a conspicuous stripe beween the eyes. Color cream to white, with dark spots all over the body. Likes to hide under rocky ledges during the day; forages at night over sandy bottoms. Grinds shellfish between teeth. Seen both during the day and night at the exit of Tagus Cove. Length up to 70 centimeters.
Pacific range: California to Peru, Galápagos.

Houndsharks (Triakidae)

Locally known as Cazones and Tollos. Thirty-four species of Triakids are known world-wide, three genera and ten species are found in the eastern Pacific. Only two genera and three species are found in the Galápagos. Horizontal, oval eyes, sharply pointed snouts. Nictitating eyelids. Anterior nasal flaps usually not barbel-like. Diorsal fins lack spines. Live close to the bottom on the continental shelf and around oceanic islands. Some deep-water species are found are 2,000 meters. Triakids prefer sandy, muddy and rocky coastal areas and enclosed bays. Active at night, near the bottom, they feed on pelagic inverte-brates (cephalopods, crustaceans) and bony fish. None is dangerous to humans.

SPECKLED SMOOTHHOUND *(Mustelus mento)*
Locally known as Tollo Fino. Gray with conspicuous small white spots. New borns have several dark bars across dorsal surface and disappear at lengths greater than 35 centimeters. No barbels with nostrils. Pavement-like teeth for crushing crustaceans, mollusks, hard-bodied invertebrates. Small in size, less than two meters. Viviparous, they lay between six to 13 pups per litter. A female (92.5 centimeters) was caught at Punta Espinosa in April 1984. Maximum size up to 1.5 meters.
Pacific range: Eastern Pacific from Gulf of California to Mexico, Ecuador and the Galápagos.

SPOTTED HOUNDSHARK *(Triakis maculata)*
Differs from *Mustelus species* by the short arcuate mouth, rather than a long pointed snout. Light gray or brown, sides with black spots and flecks. Lobate anterior nasal flaps fail to reach the mouth. All fins are rounded except for broad falcate pectoral fins. Feed on ben-thic invertebrates, in coastal waters of continental shelf. Ovoviviparous, they lay 14 pups per litter. A photo was taken by McCosker off Fernandina in 1980. Seen at Academy Bay in 1984 (David Day). Maximum size 2.4 meters, on average 1.8 meters (Grove, 1997).
Pacific range: Eastern Pacific, North Peru to Chile, Galápagos.

Whale Sharks (Rhincondontidae)

A monster of its kind, usually seen on the surface, the whale shark is nevertheless a quite harmless species to man, only filter feeding offshore. Distinctive checkered color pattern, humpback and lunate tail. Unmistakably different from any other shark.

WHALE SHARK *(Rhincodon typus)*
Color dark gray to brown with a checkerboard pattern of white lines and white spots. Three ridges on the sides running from upper head to caudal peduncle. Gill openings long and wide. Usually found in open sea feeding on small crustaceans and fishes that it gulps in mouthfuls and strains with its branchial sieve. Most likely to be seen around areas of upwelling. Very rare in Galápagos. First seen by William Beebe's Acturus Expedition on June 9, 1925; then one species was captured by Mr. Astor in Elizabeth Bay in spring 1933 (reported by E. W. Gudger, 1933). Recently filmed by Dieter Plage and Friedemann Köster of Anglia Productions, in 1983. Last seen at Gordon Rocks (Naranjo, 1984). Length 14 to 18 meters (*see* photo 200, p.179).
Pacific range: Baja California to Chile, Galápagos.

Mackerel Sharks (Lamnidae)

Sharks with torpedo-shaped bodies, a distinct keel on the caudal peduncle, almost equal lobes in caudal fin and large teeth. The fifth gill slit is located in front of the insertion of the pectoral fin. The Great white shark belongs to the Lamnidae family. The distinct lunar shape of the tail is like that of the Mackerel family of fishes. Three species recorded in Galápagos: the Shortfin mako, the Longfin mako and the Great white shark.

SHORTFIN MAKO *(Isurus oxyrinchus)*
Dorsally grayish-blue to deep blue, ventrally white. Fusiform and slender, pointed snout, conspicuous lunate or crescent 'new-moon-shaped' caudal fin, and extensive keel on the caudal peduncle. Teeth large and smooth. A very active shark. Found on surface of open seas, often near shore (One personal observation, in Darwin Bay, Tower, 1984). Also known as the Bonito shark. Rarely seen in Galápagos. Length up to 3.8 meters.
Pacific range: From Columbia River, Gulf of California to Chile, Easter Island, Galápagos, tropical and temperate oceans.

GREAT WHITE SHARK *(Carcharodon carcharias)*
Large deep-bodied shark, color slate-blue to gray or brownish-black above. Ventrally white. Often with black spot at base of pectoral fin. Nose pointed, protruding jaws, large triangular teeth with serrated edges. Large black eye. Long pectoral fins. Lunate tail and a conspicuous keel on caudal peduncle. Will eat anything, including turtles, sea lions,

other sharks, sea birds. Habitat, offshore and coastal, down to depths of 1,280 meters. Seen at Playa Escondido (Pinzon Island, 1989), Aeolean Cove (Baltra, 1995). May grow up to nine meters.

Pacific range: Worldwide, temperate and tropical seas, Alaska, Gulf of California, Panama to Chile.

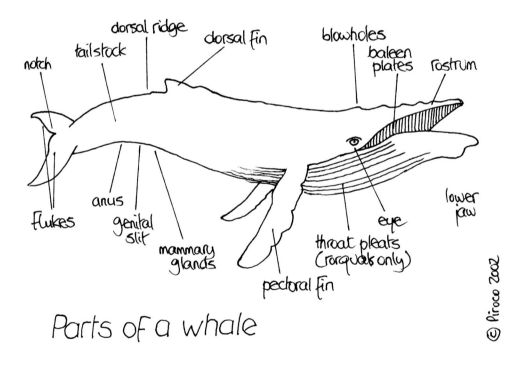

Parts of a whale

WHALES AND DOLPHINS

The mammalian order of Cetacea comprises whales, dolphins and porpoises. Even though the marine environment has imposed on this group a fish-like form, they are in fact mammals.

All mammals are air breathing animals. They are warm blooded (endothermic) and therefore must maintain a constant body temperature. At some stage in their life they have hair on their body. The body covering is made of a smooth leathery skin on top of a thick insulating layer of oil-impregnated fibrous tissues. The blubber (whale's fat) as it is called, maintains a body temperature similar to that of man. This layer of fat is approximately 30 centimeters thick. Another characteristic of mammals is that they bear their young alive and nurse them. The young are developed in the uterus of the female. A pair of nipples, located on either side of the genital slit, allows nursing after birth. The mother's milk is forced into the mouth of the young after the contraction of muscles covering the mammary glands. The gestation period is between 11 to 12 months in most of the species. Twin or multiple births do occur, even though one offspring is more usual. Two years will be the average interval between pregnancies.

The fusiform body with paddle-shaped anterior flippers and the movements of cetaceans are obviously related to their feeding habits. These carnivorous aquatic animals, like Baleen whales (eg. Fin, Sei, Humpback whales), feed by filtering water and collecting organisms—mainly small fish and shrimp-like planctonic crustaceans—which are abundant in northern latitudes during the summer months.

Well known as migratory species, Baleen whales return to warm waters to breed and give birth to their young during fall and winter months. It has been suggested that the waters around the Galápagos may be a birthing area, as many species in the islands have been reported with young.

With their long, narrow jaws, equipped with numerous sharp teeth, the dolphins feed mostly on small surface-swimming fish in the open waters. Despite being very active, they lack the capacity for prolonged deep diving possessed by other toothed whales, such as the Beaked whale and the Sperm whale, which feed primarily on squid.

The Orca, or Killer whale, is a fierce predator on warm-blooded marine animals and other animals such as fish, cephalopods, birds and sea turtles. Exceptionally strong teeth and jaws and a powerful body, make this whale a perfect killer, which in Galápagos is known to prey on sea lions and other whales.

To breathe air is a must for cetaceans. Periodically, they are seen breaching (ie. to leap above the water surface) or most commonly coming up to the surface to refresh their body tissues following submergence. The nostrils, or blowholes, are situated on the back of the head at some distance from the tip of the snout—to facilitate breathing while swimming. These blowholes, which may be single in Toothed whales or double in Baleen whales, open up immediately after surfacing, and the warm moisture charged breath is violently discharged. This distinctive phenomenon by which we recognize whales at a distance, follows a dive which may last from five to 15 minutes or less in Baleen whales, to one hour in sperm whales. Many people mistakenly believe that the conspicuous 'blow' of the whale is a fountain of water, but this is not the case. No air or water can enter the lungs through the mouth, for there is a continuous passage between the blowholes and the lungs.

The breaching technique still is not fully understood. It may serve to dislodge parasites stuck to the skin, or as a signal to other whales; or maybe it is just playful exercise.

Unlike the tail fins of fishes, the horizontally disposed set of broad flukes, terminating the streamlined body, provides propulsion. The flukes lack internal bony supporting structures. They are separated on the tail by a distinct notch. The tail stock is the long, thin section that connects the tail and the body (see Parts of a Whale, p.174). Tail lobbing is a frequent sight in a few Baleen whales (Humpback whales) and in Sperm whales. This is when the tail is raised upright above the water surface and then slaps down loudly. This action may play a role in feeding (especially for Dolphins and Killer whales). Just like the tail, the dorsal fin, present in most species, is composed of skin and fibrous tissues and lacks bony support.

In Baleen whales, also known as Whalebone whales, teeth are present in the foetal stage, but disappear before birth. They are instead replaced by parallel horny plates of whalebone suspended from the roof of the mouth. The inner edge of these plates are frayed to form a sieve used to strain small animals from the water (Gordon C. Pike, 1956). Toothed whales, dolphins and porpoises have from one to 250 teeth, which are sometimes concealed under the gums.

Whales, especially Toothed whales have astonishing acoustic talents, which have been developed in response to the physical demands of the water environment. Below depths of 150 meters darkness prevails in the ocean. Since sound travels at great speed underwater, the emission of sounds developed as an excellent means to detect objects or food, evaluate distances, and to distinguish between various kinds of fish or sea-wandering animals. This process of sensing the environment (using sonar in a similar way to bats) is called echolocation. It may be simply understood as a physical effect of sound reflection, but in fact it appears to be much more complex when considering the bending or refracting of sound waves within water. Boundaries between layers of water caused by temperature and pressure changes, variations in salinity, shifts in the frequency of the echo perceived due to a moving target, are just some of the many factors which can influence the echolocation technique. Dealing with such variables brings man to believe that whales have "an exquisite working awareness of the physics of sound in water" (Minasian, Balcomb III and Foster, 1984). The social gathering of whales proves to be an excellent example of their loquaciousness on given occasions. Computer tests on cetacean abilities are now underway to understand about signals discrimination and communication.

Photo 193: Whitetip reef shark, *Triaenodon obesus* (resting in group)

Photo 194: Galápagos shark, *Carcharhinus galapagensis*

Photo 195: Silvertip shark, *Carcharhinus albimarginatus*

Photo 196: Scalloped hammerhead, *Sphyrna lewini*

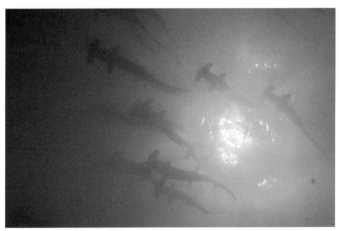

Photo 197: School of Scalloped hammerheads

Photo 198: Galápagos hornshark, *Heterodontus quoyi* (night-time)

Photo 199: Mexican hornshark, Heterodontus mexicanus

Photo 200: Whale shark, *Rhiniodon typus*

Photo 201: Mexican anemone, *Bunodactis mexicana*

Photo 202: Mexican anemone, *Bunodactis mexicana*

Photo 203: Leopard-spotted anemone, *Antiparactis sp.*

Photo 204: Orange anemone

Photo 205: Pacific tube anemone, *Pachycerianthus fimbriatus*

Photo 206: Cerianthid anemone

Photo 207: Anemone

182

Photo 208: Orange cup coral, *Tubastrea coccinea*

Photo 209: Orange cup coral, *Tubastrea coccinea* (night-time)

Photo 210: Pink cup coral

183

Photo 211: Galápagos black coral, *Antipathes galapagensis*

Photo 212: Stinging hydroids

Photo 213: Coral

184

Photo 214: Coral

Photo 215: Red gorgonian

Photo 216: Gorgonians

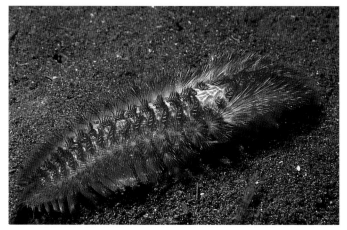

Photo 217: Common fireworm, *Eurythoe complanata*

Photo 218: Ornate fireworm, *Chloeia viridis*

Photo 219: Panamic horse conch, *Pleuroploca princeps*

Photo 220: Chief rock snail, *Hexaplex princeps*

Photo 221: Grinning tun, *Malea ringens*

Photo 222: Starry flatworm, *Pseudobiceros species* 6 (E), Santiago Island

Photo 223: Orange spotted nudibranch, unidentified (Vivien Li)

Photo 224: Panama aglaja, *Navanax aenigmaticus*

Photo 225: Carolyn doris, *Platydoris carolinae* (E), Tortuga Island

Photo 226: Apricot slug, *Berthellina engeli*

Photo 227: Blue-striped sea slug, *Tambja mullineri* (E)

Photo 228: Warty sea slug, *Pleurobranchus areolatus*

Photo 229: Galápagos discodoris, *Discodoris species* (E), Piedra Blanca

Photo 230: *Roboastra* nudibranch preying upon *Tambja mullineri*

Photo 231: Starry night nudibranch, *Hypselodoris lapizlazuli* (E)

Photo 232: Spanish shawl, *Flabellina sp.*

Photo 233: Blunthead seahare, *Dolabella auricularia*

Photo 234: Walking seahare, *Aplysia cedrosensis*

Photo 235: Galápagos twin-spot octopus, *Octopus oculifer*

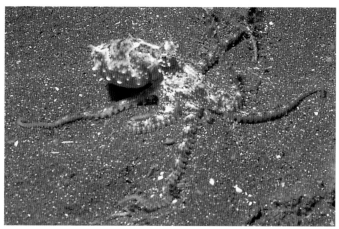

Photo 236: Dwarf octopus

Photo 237: Purpleback flying squid, *Sthenoteuthis oualaniensis*

192

Photo 238: Giant hermit crab, *Petrochirus californiensis*

Photo 239: Hairy hermit crab, *Aniculus elegans*

Photo 240: Bar-eyed hermit crab, *Dardanus fucosus*

Social activity includes various aspects beyond simple feeding techniques and includes mating and rearing of young. Whales may have many mates in a life time. Males are believed to assist each other when one individual is trying to copulate with a female which is trying to escape. In the rearing of the off-spring the young may accompany their mothers for six months to a year, while they nurse. In some species, the parental care may last for many years after weaning. Mothers are known to show great tenderness to the young, but are able to display legendary ferocity to protect their offspring in times of danger.

Two Suborders of Cetaceans:

Cetaceans are divided in the suborders of Mysticeti (Baleen whales) and Odontoceti (Toothed whales).

Mysticeti: Instead of teeth, Baleen or Whalebone whales have several hundred plates of horny baleen, suspended from the upper jaw. These enable them to strain food which consist of krill, or primary crustaceans and small schooling fish. Salt water is gulped into the mouth, then forced out through fringes of overlapping baleen plates. Baleen are modified mucous membranes, not bones.

Mysticetes have paired blowholes, producing a visible spout or blow. This suborder includes three families, of which only the Balaenopteridae (Rorquals) are represented in the Galápagos waters up to this date.

Odontoceti: Toothed whales are endowed with teeth from birth. The number may vary from one to 250 teeth. Odontocetes have a single blowhole, but only the Sperm whale emits a visible spout or blow. Other toothed whales will only produce a light puff.

This suborder includes six families of which three are commonly represented in the Galápagos: the Physeteridae (Sperm whales), the Ziphiidae (Beaked whales) and the Delphinidae (Ocean dolphins). The suborder of Odontoceti is better represented in number of species, both in the Galápagos and in the eastern Pacific.

DESCRIPTION OF FAMILIES AND SPECIES

Rorquals (Balaenopteridae)

Balaenopteridae are the largest creatures on earth. Among the cetaceans they are simply referred to as the large whales. The record in length is held by the Blue whale (30 meters), which has been reported in Galápagos waters. This species has been heavily hunted by whalers and its number reduced to less than 25,000 individuals (Minasian, Balcomb III and Foster. 1984). The writer Herman Melville was one of these whale-hunters who came to the Galápagos many times.

Whales & Dolphins in the Galápagos

MYSTYCETI: BALEEN WHALES
Rorquals (Balaenopteridae) 6 species

Blue whale	*Balaenoptera musculus*
Fin whale, Finback or Common rorqual	*Balaenoptera physalus*
Sei whale	*Balaenoptera borealis*
Bryde's whale	*Balaenoptera edeni*
Minke whale	*Balaenoptera acutorostrata*
Humpback whale	*Megaptera novaeangliae*

ODONTOCETI: TOOTHED WHALES
Sperm whales (Physeteridae) 3species

Sperm whale, Cachalot	*Physeter catodon* or *macrocephalus*
Pygmy sperm whale	*Kogia breviceps*
Dwarf sperm whale	*Kogia simus*

Beaked whales (Ziphiidae) 5 species

Cuvier's beaked whale	*Ziphius cavirostris*
Southern bottle-nosed whale	*Hyperodon planifrons*
Blainville's beaked whale	*Mesoplodon densirostris*
Lesser beaked whale	*Mesoplodon peruvianus*
Gingko-toothed whale	*Mesoplodon gingkodens*

Ocean dolphins
Subfamily Globicephalidae (6 species)

Killer whale	*Orcinus orca*
Pygmy orca	*Feresa attenuata*
False killer whale	*Pseudorca crassidens*
Melon-headed whale	*Peponocephala electra*
Short-finned pilot whale	*Globicephala macrorhynchus*
Long-finned pilot whale	*Globicephala melas*

Subfamily Stenidae (1species)

Rough-toothed dolphin	*Steno bredanensis*

Subfamily Delphinidae (7 species)

Risso's dolphin, Gray grampus	*Grampus griseus*
Common dolphin	*Delphinus delphis*
Bottle-nosed dolphin	*Tursiops truncatus*
Fraser's dolphin	*Lagenodelphis hosei*
Spotted dolphin	*Stenella attenuata*
Spinner dolphin	*Stenella longirostris*
Stripped dolphin	*Stenella coeruleoalba*

Rorquals are long, slender and very streamlined whales. The snout is pointed, they have two blowholes and a broad flat rostrum. Baleen plates are broad and short. Falcate dorsal fin. Grooves of varying length are seen on the throat and chest. At least six species have been recorded in the Galápagos: Blue, Fin, Sei, Bryde's, Minke and Humpback whales.

BLUE WHALE *(Balaenoptera musculus)*
The largest of all whales, it is found in the Galápagos but probably only as large as *B. physalus*. Pale coloration with pale blotches all over the body. Dorsal fin very small. Seen near islands, it may belong to a population of Pygmy blue whales, *B. musculus brevicauda* resident in Costa Rica. Dorsal fin located one third forward of tail. A rare species in the Galápagos. Seen on north-west Fernandina, off Punta Moreno and south-west Isabela. Length up to 26 meters.

FIN WHALE *(Balaenoptera physalus)*
Fin whales may reach 27 meters, but the average length is about 20 meters. Weighs up to 73 tons. Color dark gray to brown dorsally, ventrally white. Undersides of flukes and flippers white. Inside and outside of the right lower lip is also white-yellow. Dorsal fin prominent and falcate, about 60 centimeters high, located one third forward from tail. Ventral grooves extend to navel. Head sharply shaped. The Fin whale is also called Razorback, because of ridges between dorsal fin and tail.
- Feeds on small crustaceans, small pelagic fish such as mackerel, herring and squid.
- When breathing and diving, Fin whales take five to six breaths at intervals of several minutes. The dive lasts up to 15 minutes, to a depth of at least 230 meters. The blow is like an inverted cone, 4.5 to six meters high. Flukes are seldom raised prior to diving.
- Fin whales may live to between 75 and 100 years.
- May be mistaken for Minke, Sei and Bryde's whales.

SEI WHALE *(Balaenoptera borealis)*
Name derives from *seje*, the Norwegian word for 'pollack' (codfish), on which Sei whales feed around Norway. May reach 19 meters in length and weigh as much as 24 to 26 tons. The body appears shiny. Dorsally steel gray, front of belly white. Right lower lip gray. Baleen plates grayish-black. Undersides of flippers and flukes are dark. Snout is slightly arched and not very pointed. Rostrum with single median dorsal ridge. Two blowholes on head. Dorsal fin strongly falcate, about 25 to 61 centimeters, located one third forward from tail. Ventral grooves extend from midway between base cf pectoral fins and navel.
- Feeds on small crustaceans, anchovies, herrings, sardines, cod.
- Blows two to three times every 17 seconds before diving for five to ten minutes. The blow is an inverted cone of maximum 4.5 meters in height. Does not expose flukes prior to dive. Rises to the surface in a horizontal position.
- Sei live up to 70 years at least.
- May be mistaken for Minke, Bryde's and Fin whales.

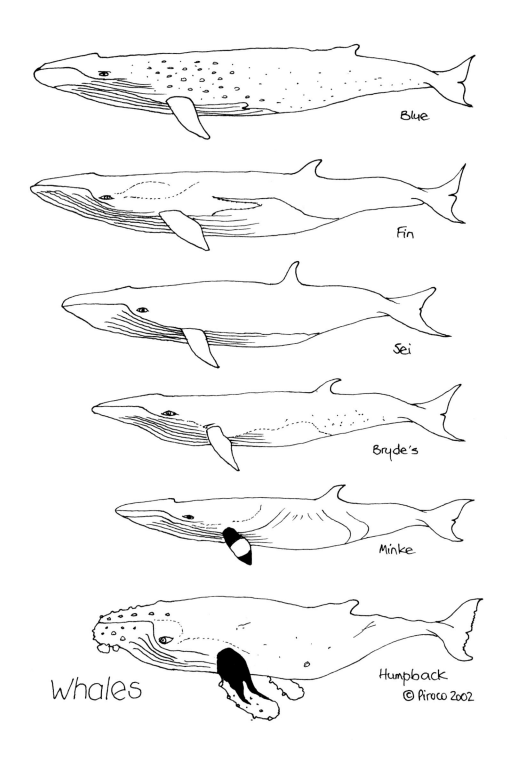

Blue

Fin

Sei

Bryde's

Minke

Humpback

Whales

© Piroco 2002

Sperm

Orca

False killer

Long finned pilot whale

Pygmy orca

Toothed
whales

© Piroco 2002

BRYDE'S WHALE *(Balaenoptera edeni)*
Grows up to 14.6 meters, and weighs up to 22 tons. Color dorsally gray, ventrally lighter. Often with small dark oval white scars, which may be due to shark bites. Right lower lip dark gray. Baleen plates slate gray. Undersides and front edges of flippers grayish-white. Snout slightly arched and rostrum shows three medium dorsal ridges. Dorsal fin extremely falcate but small (45 centimeters), one third forward from tail. Ventral grooves extend to navel.
- Feeds on schooling fish, sardines, crustaceans and squid.
- When breathing and diving, several average 3.5 meters high blows, followed by an eight to ten minute dive. Shallow dives down to 15 to 30 meters can be spotted by slicks of turbulence at the surface. They are deep divers. Due to the steep angle of rising, blowholes appear first, then the dorsal fin.
- Bryde's are known to breach and may live to about 40 years.
- May be mistaken for Sei or Fin whales.

MINKE WHALE *(Balaenoptera acutorostrata)*
Grows up to ten meters and may weigh ten tons. The smallest of the rorquals. Dorsally dark gray to black, ventrally white. Flippers black with a conspicuous white diagonal band. Undersides of flippers white. Baleen plates yellowish anteriorly, fringed with brown. Single median dorsal ridge on flat rostrum (narrow and pointed). Dorsal fin tall and falcate, one third forward from tail. Ventral grooves extend from chin to navel.
- Feeds on small shoaling fish, herring, cod, krill.
- When breathing and diving, a shallow dive is follow by five to ten breaths, then the Minke whale goes for a deeper dive lasting ten minutes. Arches its back when diving. Quick, inconspicuous blow.
- Also known as the Little piked whale, Lesser rorqual and Little finner, the Minke whale may be seen breaching, often approachs boats and swims around them. May live as long as 50 years.
- Minke whales may be confused with Sei, Fin whales and Baird's beaked whale.

HUMPBACK WHALE *(Megaptera novaeangliae)*
Grows up to 19 meters, and may weigh up to 53 tons. Color black. Undersides vary from dark gray to white. Flippers may be all white; undersides of flukes nearly white. Baleen plates black with dark olive bristles. Fleshly knobs are distinctive on the top of the head and lower jaw. Two blowholes. Very long flippers (one third of body length) with scalloped front edges. Dorsal fin small, on distinct bump on the back, placed one third forward from tail. Flukes are deeply notched. Ventral grooves extend beyond navel.
- Feeds on krill, plankton, sardines, mackerel, anchovies and small schooling fish.
- When breathing and diving, Humpback remains on surface three to six minutes breathing at 15 to 30 seconds intervals. A longer dive lasts up to 30 minutes, with raising of the tail high into the air. The blow is tall, thin and conspicuous.

- Humpback whales are known to engage in severe fights in mating areas to determine which male will be mate and/or accompany females. Humpbacks 'sing' specific vocal patterns, more so than other species of whales.
- Not to be confused with any other whale. The Humpback has been reported in Punta Cormorant, Floreana (Chris McFarling, 1984, personal communication), Roca Redonda (northwest Isabela, 1990).

Sperm Whales (Physeteridae)

An almost unchanged group for 30 million years. This family is comprised of two genera: the genus *Physeter*, with huge heads and the genus *Kogia*, which is much smaller overall and lacks the huge head. Sperm whales belong to the suborder of the Toothed whales, and therefore possess only a single blowhole. Three species so far have been recognized in Galápagos waters: *Physeter catodon*, belonging to the 'huge head' genus; *Kogia breviceps*, the Pygmy sperm and *Kogia simus*, the Dwarf sperm whale.

SPERM WHALE *(Physeter catodon or macrocephalus)*
Also known as Cachalot. Grows up to 21 meters and weighs about 35 to 50 tons. Color light brown to blue-gray. Lips are marbled outside the white mouth. Huge head, reaching almost one third of the body length. Snout squarish and blunt. Single blowhole located on the left of the midline. Large teeth on the lower jaw, small teeth buried in the upper jaw. Dorsal fin almost inexistant looks more like a triangular bump (one third forward from tail), followed by a series of smaller ones. Flippers small and stubby, to the rear of the eyes. Eyes located above convergence of upper and lower jaw. Flukes separated by median notch, have rounded tips and are serrate along the trailing edge. Distinct ventral keel.
- Feeds primarily on squid (including giant species) and on a variety of fish.
- When breathing and diving Sperms may remain on the surface for ten minutes with blows every ten to 30 seconds, then submerges with flukes high out of the water. The Cachalot may dive to a 1,000 meters and stay in the water for up to one hour. The blow, like a bushy spout, is directed forward to the left.
- Sperm whales are often seen breaching and tail lobbing, and live up to 70 years.
- Sperms are known to produce intense clicking sounds using their box-shaped head as a resonating chamber. "Listening to a herd of Sperm whales is a little like listening to a score of carpenters nailing up a wall," (Minasian, Balcomb III and Foster, 1984). These monotonously repetitive clicks are still a mystery to man. The sophisticated echolocation technique used by Sperm whales has brought investigators to believe that the whale's brain creates an acoustic hologram from the echoes of all those clicks. In other words an 'ear-picture' to Sperms is what an 'eye-picture' would be to man. Amazing.
- Sperm whales have been heavily hunted in the past and during the 19th century Galápagos whaling industry (1793–1870). Herman Melville came to Galápagos to

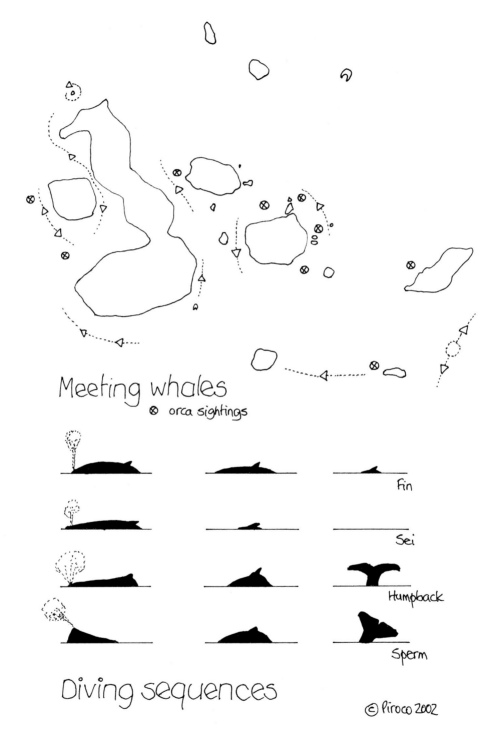

Meeting whales

⊗ orca sightings

Diving sequences

Fin

Sei

Humpback

Sperm

© Piroco 2002

track these whales. His famous novel *Moby Dick*, was written because of the Great White Sperm whale. In Galápagos waters, Sperms have been reported to the west of Floreana, Isabela and Fernandia, often in groups of three to 50 females with one or two males and a few young (Godfrey Merlen, 1985). The feared predator of the Sperm is the Orca, which is always trying to get the young from the herd and usually attacks fiercely in small numbers.
- Not to be confused with any other whale.

PYGMY SPERM WHALE *(Kogia breviceps)*

DWARF SPERM WHALE *(Kogia simus)*
It is similar to the Pygmy sperm whale and considered to have a northerly distribution above the Tropic of Cancer. Dorsally black, pale on sides. Dorsal fin like that of dolphins. Rostrum extends forward with mouth below and behind it, like a shark. Crescent shape behind the eye, looking like a gill. Not active on the surface, may rise with little movement of water. Seen as single individual or in small groups, two to five individuals. Maximum length 2.7 meters. The Pygmy sperm is larger in size (3.4 meters), but has a smaller dorsal fin. Rare sightings, north and south of Fernandina. Feeds on squid, fish and crustaceans.

Beaked Whales (Ziphiidae)

Ziphiids are poorly known. They belong to the suborder of the Toothed whales or Odontoceti and may reach between 3.7 and 12 meters in length. These shy creatures inhabit remote offshore waters. A single blowhole. Flukes lack the median notch on tail. A distinct snout with a few teeth often visible. Functional teeth in adult males only (lower jaw).

A few Beaked whales are present in Galápagos waters, five species including the Cuvier's beaked whale (or Goose beaked whale) have been reported. All these whales are deep divers and rarely seen. The genus Mesoplodon is poorly known and identification difficult. Concave forehead and tapering snout. Three species are likely in the Galápagos: Blainville's, Lesser and Gingko-toothed whales.

CUVIER'S BEAKED WHALE *(Ziphius cavirostris)*
Considered to be the rarest whale, known partly from stranding on beaches. Grows up to seven meters and weighs up to five tons. Color rusty red-brown dorsally to black ventrally. Body splotched with white. Scars are visible and result from fights with older males. Head is small with concave upper profile. White head on large whales. In large individuals the beak is indistinct. Males have a pair of teeth at the tip of the lower jaw. Dorsal fin falcate and tail (up to 38 centimeters) on the rear of the midback region. Flippers small and rounded. Flukes are rounded at tips.
- Feeds on squid and deep-dwelling oceanic fish.
- When breathing and diving may remain underwater for 30 minutes. Two or three breaths at ten to 20 seconds intervals, raising flukes at 45° angle prior to lengthy

dives. Forehead, back and dorsal fin usually seen. Blow not distinct. Breaching is
rare. Cautious with boats.
- In March 1983, six of these whales entered Aeolean cove in Baltra (Airforce base)
and tried mysteriously to beach themselves. The incident was attributed to a
probable attack of Killer whales. Two whales died on the beach, the other made it
back to the sea. Also reported to the north of Isabela (Merlen, 1985).
- May live 35 years.

BLAINVILLE'S BEAKED WHALE *(Mesoplodon densirostris)*
Body black or dark gray above, white underneath. Scarring and blotching of pink and
gray. High arching mouth line and protruding tooth are noticeable in each lower jaw.
Cuvier's beaked whale is light-colored and larger, with no distinctive teeth. Temperate and
tropical waters distribution. Length up to 4.5 meters.

LESSER BEAKED WHALE *(Mesoplodon peruvianus)*
Color dark gray with a short beak. Described in 1991. May occur in Galápagos
(G.Merlen, 1997). Length up to 3.5 meters.

OTHER BEAKED WHALE
Another unidentified beaked whale, rather frequent in the eastern tropical Pacific, shows
visible saddle forward of dorsal fin (Wade and Gerrodette, 1993).
    The skull of the Gingko-toothed whale *(Mesoplodon gingkodens)* was found by Tjitte
de Vries (CDRS museum) on Genovesa Island in 1970. The only evidence of its presence
in Galápagos waters. Similar to the Blainville's beaked whale, except for two flat lower
teeth, resembling gingko leaves.

Ocean Dolphins (Delphinidae)

This huge family comprises 32 well-known species and maybe up to 50 species
(Minasian, Balcomb III and Foster, 1984). The ocean dolphins are medium-sized whales,
with a spindle-shaped cylindrical body. Prominent beaks are usual, but bulbous head with
short beak is also found (Risso's dolphin, Pilot whale). Both jaws are dotted with conical
teeth. Echolocation abilities are well developed. Conspicuous dorsal fin. The main distinction from Beaked whales is the size. Ocean dolphins are gregarious with elaborate
social structures. At least eight or nine species have been reported in Galápagos.

KILLER WHALE *(Orcinus orca)*
Hyenas of the sea, technically like dolphins, the Killer whales are the largest members of
the Delphinidae. Grows up to 9.6 meters and weighs from 4.5 tons (females) to nine tons
(males). Color is deep black with snow-white areas on undersides from chin to anus. Oval
white patch is seen above and behind the eye. Undersides of flukes white. Gray saddle
behind dorsal fin, the latter being two meters in height (six feet) for males, and 91 cen-

timeters (three feet) for females (falcate). Flukes are broad and possess a definite median notch. Flippers are rounded and paddle shaped. Teeth are conical, slightly curved back, found on upper and lower jaws. Head is broad and rounded.

- Feeds on fish, cephalopods, birds, sea turtles and marine mammals.
- When breathing and diving, takes a series of a dozen short dives, breathing every ten to 30 seconds. A longer dive follows.
- Orcas are active on the surface, ferocious in their feeding habits, frequently attacking Baleen whales and pinnipeds (sea lions and fur seal lions). No recorded attack on humans, but caution should be taken. They are known to be inquisitive and come close to small boats. Breaching is common. Swims at times in very shallow water, less than four meters.
- In Galápagos waters, they have been reported at Baltra, Plazas, Mosquera, James Bay (Santiago), Española, Floreana, Genovesa and to the west of Fernandina (G. Merlen, 1985).

Godfrey Merlen's monitoring program started in 1992 and reported 135 sightings in an article published in 1999 (Noticias de Galápagos). It states that Orcas are regular visitors to Galápagos waters, with pod size averaging three individuals (on June 15, 1981 an exceptional pod of 48 individuals was seen). Orcas roam around sea lion colonies on which they prey (Plazas, Gardner, Punta Cormorant, Puerto Egas, Bolivar Channel). Species attacked by Orcas include sharks, hammerheads, mantas, stingrays, sunfish (mola mola), turtles, sperm whales, dolphins, rorquals and pilot whales. In 1985, an Orca beached itself on the north shore of South Plaza in order to catch a sea lion pup. Sperm whales were seen chasing Orcas (April 1991). A question remains: is there a resident population in Galápagos?

PYGMY ORCA *(Feresa attenuata)*
Similar in looks to the Melon-headed whale, *Peponocephala electra*. Dorsal fin like that of Bottle-nosed dolphins. Often swim together. Overall coloration dark gray. Pygmy killer whale has white markings on the stomach and a white chin. Flippers have round tips, while Melon-headed whale has pointed tips. Both species are gregarious, found in shallow water as well as in pelagic conditions. Sightings north of Santiago. Length up to 2.7 meters.

FALSE KILLER WHALE *(Pseudorca crassidens)*
Another large dolphin, known to beach itself and strand in large numbers. The reason why is not known. Grows up to six meters (males) or five meters (females) and weighs about 2.2 tons to 2.6 tons for females. Color black to pale gray ventrally. Round bump on forehead. Head is narrow. Teeth are conical, large and strong. Flippers have a distinctive broad hump on the front edge. Dorsal fin tall and falcate, on midback (18 to 41 centimeters in height). Flukes thin and pointed at tips.

- Feeds on squid and fish. Known to attack dolphins in the Eastern Tropical Pacific (Minasian, Balcomb III and Foster, 1984). In Galápagos they prey on Black skipjack tuna.

- False Killer whales are fast swimmers and leap out of the water. Often approach boats and play in the waves formed by vessels (Merlen, 1985).
- Reported in Galápagos waters, near shore in Santa Fé (David Day, personal communication). Often swim in the company of the Bottle-nosed dolphins.
- May be confused with the Pilot whale and the Killer whale.

SHORT-FINNED PILOT WHALE *(Globicephala macrorhynchus)*
Easily recognized by the distinctive round and bulbous shape of the head. Grows to seven meters and weighs about three tons. Color overall black, with light gray areas on chest. Flippers are short. Dorsal fin low, falcate, with a large base forward of mid-back, rounded at the top. Large flukes with distinct median notch.
- Feeds on squid and small fish.
- When breathing and diving, Pilot whales may dive to 600 meters.
- Often seen in groups, associated with dolphins, or 'logging' on the surface when they remain stationary (exposing bulbous head and dorsal fin).
- Reported in Galápagos waters in the south, west and east of Isabela, around Marchena, south of Española, Cristobal.
- May be confused with the False Killer whale.

LONG-FINNED PILOT WHALE *(Globicephala melas)*
Head rounded in shape. Not easy to differentiate from the Short fin pilot whale. May occur in Galápagos waters, but found in colder waters of the Humboldt current to the south of Peru. Seen in groups of ten to 20 individuals, close together. Since 1984, a stranding of a total of 54 pilot whales has occurred over three separate occasions. Pilot whales have been seen around Isabela, the northern islands and southeast of the archipelago. Feeds on squid. Length up to 5.4 meters for males, four meters for females.

RISSO'S DOLPHIN, GRAY GRAMPUS *(Grampus griseus)*
Distinguished by robust body. Grows to 4.5 meters and weighs about 680 kilograms. Color dark gray, lightens with age. Head and chin often whitish. Numerous white scars on back and body due to confrontations with other Risso's dolphins. Large 'melon' of head divided by a vertical groove from forehead to mouth. Head is bulbous, V-shaped, snout blunt. Teeth absent from upper jaw, conical teeth on lower jaws. Prominent tall and falcate dorsal fin (38 centimeters) on mid-back, slightly rounded at the tip. Flippers and flukes long and pointed. Distinct median notch on tail.
- Feeds on cephalopods, small fish.
- Rapid swimmer, often make twisting and rolling leaps from the water. When accompanying small boats, they raise their heads above water surface, sometimes ride on the bow wave. Blow is undistinct. Risso's dolphins and Pilot whales are often seen together.
- May live up to 20 years at least.
- Risso's dolphin may be confused with Bottle-nosed dolphin.

COMMON DOLPHIN *(Delphinus delphis)*
Also known as the White-bellied dolphin. Reaches a length of 2.6 meters and weighs up to 135 kilograms. Dorsally black to gray on flanks from eye to tail. Belly white. Rostrum black with white tip. Thin dark line between beak and forehead, extending to dark eye patch. Dorsal fin triangular to falcate on mid-back, with rounded top. Flippers dark. Flukes with median notch, are pointed at tips.
- Feeds on schools of migrating fish, anchovies, herrings, sardines, also squid.
- Common dolphins dive as deep as 280 meters for a maximum of 8 minutes. Daily cycle of activity, feeding groups scatter in the late afternoon. Frequently leaping clear of the water.
- In Galápagos waters, the Common dolphin is not as frequent as the Bottle-nosed dolphin and will never be seen riding bow waves. They usually shy away from boats. May be witnessed feeding and leaping out of the water in herds at a fair distance (west Isabela and Fernandina.)
- Population in Eastern Tropical Pacific: 2,931,000.

BOTTLE-NOSED DOLPHIN *(Tursiops truncatus)*
The most frequently seen dolphin in Galápagos waters, between islands. Reachs four meters in length and a weight of 650 kilograms. Dorsally dark gray to pale gray on flanks, white or pinkish ventrally. The 'melon' is well defined where beak and forehead meet. Lower jaw extend beyond upper jaw and curves up. Dorsal fin prominent and falcate on mid-back, with a pointed tip. Flippers medium sized, rounded at tips. Flukes with median notch. Teeth sharp, conical on upper and lower jaws.
- Feeds on small fish, eels, mullet and squid.
- Usually seen riding bow waves of boats in Galápagos. May remain underwater several minutes. Breathes every 15 to 20 seconds when swimming.
- Excellent skills in echolocation.
- Bottle-nosed dolphins are known to display 'babysitter' behavior. An adult may attend the young when the female is away feeding.
- May living up to 35 years or more.
- Possible confusion with the Risso's dolphin.

SPOTTED DOLPHIN *(Stenella attenuata)*
Also known as the Eastern Tropical Pacific Spotted dolphin. A gregarious species often seen in the company of other dolphins. Reachs about 2.1 meters in length and a weight of about 127 kilograms. Dorsally steel gray to gray on flanks and belly. Extended stripe from leading margin of flippers to rostrum. Tip of rostrum white. Upper and lower lips often white. Whitish spots on the back, and lighter parts on the body. Calves may be purple-gray and ventrally white (in offshore populations) without spots. Ventral spots appear with maturity. Dorsal fin falcate on mid-back. Flippers small and pointed. Flukes pointed with median notch. Teeth conical in upper and lower jaws.

- Feed on Yellowfin tuna, squid and surface-dwelling fish, like flying fish. When swimming, the Spotted dolphin shows a distinctive porpoising behavior, ie. long, shallow leaps clear of the water.
- Rarely seen in Galápagos. Associates with Spinner dolphins. May be confused with the Bottle-nosed dolphin.
- Population in Eastern Tropical Pacific: 1,921,000 (Wade and Gerrodette, 1993).

SPINNER DOLPHIN *(Stenella longirostris)*
The species of Spinner dolphin found in Galápagos is probably related to the Costa Rica spinner dolphin, or the Eastern spinner dolphin. Reachs 2.1 meters in length and a weight of about 68 kilograms. Color is dark gray dorsally, ventrally lighter. Beak is extremely long and slender. Dorsal fin is conspicuously triangular and erect and slightly canted towards the front. Flippers are long, thin and pointed. Teeth are conical in upper and lower jaws. Long, black-tipped beak, black lips. Slim appearance.
- Feeds on Yellowfin tuna, small fish. Spinner dolphin herds may reach 1,000 individuals.
- May dive to 61 meters. Easily identified by its leaping and spinning habits when swimming.
- Rarely seen in Galápagos. May be confused with the Common dolphin. Godfrey Merlen recognizes it as the White-bellied spinner dolphin (1998).
- Cosmopolitan population in tropical and subtropical waters.

STRIPED DOLPHIN *(Stenella coeruleoalba)*
Of the five recognized Stenella species, this is the largest and most robust. Grows to 2.7 meters and a weight of 115 kilograms. Dorsally blue-black from tip of beak to mid-way between dorsal fin and tail. Lighter gray on flanks. Conspicuous black line extending from eye to near anus. Second black line from eye to flipper and beyond. Third black line to leading edge of flipper. Tall falcate dorsal fin at midback. Fippers small and curved, pointed at tips. Beak is black. Teeth on upper and lower jaws, conical.
- Feeds on small fish, shrimp, squid. Also known to associate with Yellowfin tuna, but in lesser importance when compared to the Spotted, Spinner and Common dolphins.
- Striped dolphins may live up to 50 years. Possible confusion with the Common dolphin and the Fraser dolphin, which has a shorter snout and wider stripe along sides.

FRASER'S DOLPHIN *(Lagenodelphis hosei)*
Poorly known since it was described in 1956. Cosmopolitan in oceanic tropical waters. Distinguished by a broad dark band running from the beak, the eye, to anal area on sides. Not as acrobatic as Common dolphins, but agitates the surface. Sightings west of Isabela, often associated with Striped dolphins, Spotted dolphins, cetaceans. Two observations of monotypic schools (Hal Whitehead). Feeds on squid and fish at depth. Grows to a maximum of 2.6 meters.

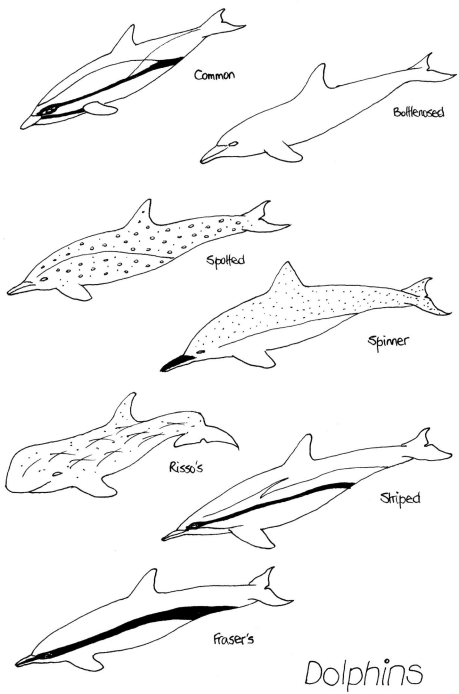

Common

Bottlenosed

Spotted

Spinner

Risso's

Striped

Fraser's

Dolphins

© Piroco 2002

CONFUSION BETWEEN WHALES

FIN WHALE		SEI WHALE
Slightly falcate	**Dorsal fin**	Sharply falcate
Head appears first Oblique rise Arches its back after blowing, rolls forward, showing dorsal fin.	**Surfacing**	Horizontal rise Head and dorsal fin visible at the same time. When diving starts does not arch back conspicuously.
Tall, inverted cone Blows 4–7 times	**Blow**	Small inverted cone Blows 1–3 times
Dives for 6–15 minutes Flukes rarely shown prior to diving.	**Diving**	Dives for 1–2 minutes or 5–10 minutes. Often swimming slightly submerged, leaving swirls on the surface. Flukes rarely shown prior to diving.
White	**Color of undersides**	Mostly gray
Right side white Left side gray	**Lower lip**	Gray

PILOT WHALE	FALSE KILLER WHALE	RISSO'S DOLPHIN
Bulbous, thick head	Gently tapering black head	Pointed head with a groove on the 'melon' May be all white.
Robust body	Long and slender	
Medium-low dorsal fin, rounded and wide on base, Forward on back.	Very tall, gently falcate dorsal fin.	Falcate and pointed (like Bottlenose D.) Midway on back.
Does not ride on bow waves of vessels	May ride on bow waves of vessels Not scarred	Frequently scarred
Color black Gray saddleback behind dorsal fin and gray region on chin.	All black	Young are gray Older ones may be all white.

(see p.225 for Confusion between Dolphins)   (after Steve Leatherwood, 1972)

Photo 241: Stanford swimmer crab, *Portunus stanfordi*

Photo 242: Sally lightfoot crab, *Grapsus grapsus*

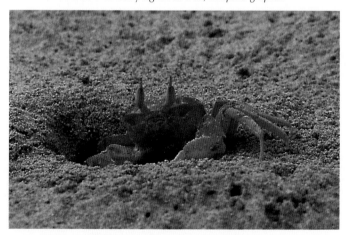

Photo 243: Ghost crab, *Ocypode sp.*

Photo 244: Panamic arrowhead crab, *Stenorhynchus debilis*

Photo 245: Shamed face box crab, *Calappa convexa*

Photo 246: Yellow snout red shrimp, *Rhynchocinetes typus*

Photo 247: Big eye shrimp, *Metapenaeopsis kishinouyei*

Photo 248: Giant khaki shrimp, *Litopenaeus stylirostrsis*

Photo 249: Red-banded shrimp, *Cinetorhynchus hiatti*

212

Photo 250: Gold-spotted shrimp, *Sicyonia aliaffinis*

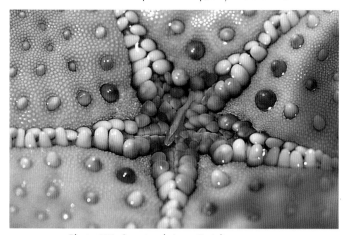

Photo 251: Sea star shrimp, *Periclimenes soror*

Photo 252: Red spiny lobster, *Panulirus penicillatus*

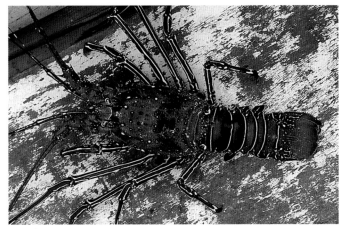

Photo 253: Blue lobster, *Panulirus gracilis*

Photo 254: Slipper lobster, *Scyllarides astori*

Photo 255: Armored sand star, *Astropecten armatus*

214

Photo 256: Sand star, *Luidia foliolata*

Photo 257: Variable sea star, *Linckia columbiae*

Photo 258: Panamic cushion star, *Pentaceraster cummingi*

Photo 259: Chocolate chip star, *Nidorellia armata*

Photo 260: Blue sea star, *Phataria unifascialis*

Photo 261: Pyramid sea star, *Pharia pyramidata*

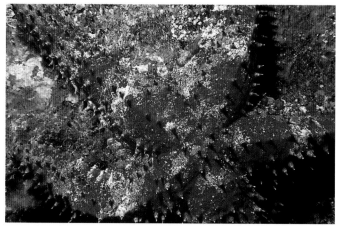

Photo 262: Keeled sea star, *Asteropsis carinifera*

Photo 263: Smooth seastar, *Leiaster teres*

Photo 264: Bradley sea star, *Mithrodia bradleyi*

Photo 265: Rathbun's seastar, *Rathbunaster californicus*

Photo 266: Prickly seastar, *Paulia horrida*

Photo 267: Giant seastar, *Tethyaster sp.*

Photo 268: Alexander's spiny brittle star, *Ophiocoma alexandri*

Photo 269: Pencil sea urchin, *Eucidaris thouarsii*

Photo 270: Needle sea urchin, *Diadema mexicanum*

Photo 271: Crowned sea urchin, *Centrostephanus coronatus*

Photo 272: Green sea urchin, *Lytechinus semituberculatus*

Photo 273: White sea urchin, *Tripneustes depressus*

Photo 274: Flower sea urchin, *Toxopneustes roseus*

Photo 275: Galápagos sand dollar, *Encope galapagensis*

Photo 276: Sea cucumber, pepino, *Stichopus fuscus*

Photo 277: Giant sea cucumber, *Stichopus horrens*

Photo 278: Giant sea cucumber, *Stichopus horrens* (night-time)

Photo 279: Warty sea cucumber, *Holothuria fuscocinerea*

222

Photo 280: Camouflaged sea cucumber, *Holothuria kefersteini*

Photo 281: Black turtle, *Chelonia agassizi* with Mexican hogfish (females)

Photo 282: Killer whale, *Orcinus orca*

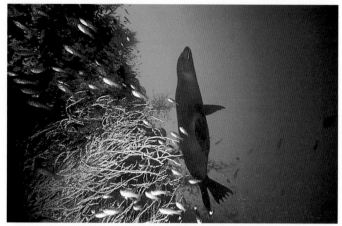

Photo 283: Sea lion missile and black coral

Photo 284: Sea lion chasing school of fish

Photo 285: Killer whale, *Orcinus orca*

Photo 286: Galápagos penguin, *Spheniscus mendiculus*

Photo 287: Pierre Constant before a dive (2004)

Photo 288: The author with dive guide Macarron (2001)

CONFUSION BETWEEN DOLPHINS

	SPOTTED	SPINNER	COMMON	STRIPED
Color	Gray with spots	Dark gray	Dorsally black Hourglass pattern on sides Belly white Black line from eye to arms.	Bluish-black Sides gray Belly gray or white.
Dorsal fin	Distinctly falcate erect, slight bent forward.	Triangular falcate	Distinctly	Falcate
Length	2.1m	2.1m	2.6m	2.7m
Weight	127 Kg	68 Kg	135 Kg	115 Kg
Behavior	Jumps, does not spin.	Leaps and spins on long axis.	Jumps	

226 of the animal kingdom

MARINE INVERTEBRATES

Marine invertebrates represent 98 percent of the animal kingdom and are composed of seven major groups (Phylum) which are: Protozoans, Cnidarians, Arthropods, Mollusks, Annelids, Echinoderms and Sponges.

Phylum Cnidaria

Class Anthozoa: Anemones, Corals, Gorgonians

PACIFIC TUBE ANEMONE *(Pachycerianthus fimbriatus)*
Color black or white with long, extended tentacles, worm-like. Burrows in volcanic sand at shallow depth, five to 30 meters. Seen at Rabida, red beach, and at Tagus Cove, Isabela *(see* photo 205, p.181).

MEXICAN ANEMONE *(Bunodactis mexicana)*
Purple in color. Forms large colonies on rocks *(see* photos 201, 202, pp.179–80).

LEOPARD-SPOTTED ANEMONE *(Antiparactis species)*
White with little brown spots. Found at depths of 30 to 40 meters, attached to black coral stems. Forms small colonies *(see* photo 203, p.180).

ZOANTHID *(Zoanthus species)*
Usually found in coastal lagoons, they look like anemones with a light brown to translucid color. Live in colonies, over rocky substrates, in shallow water.

ORANGE CUP CORAL *(Tubastrea coccinea)*
Bright yellow to orange, cylindrical. Colonies common on rocks, shaded areas, beneath overhangs and under ledges, from 0 to 20 meters. Food and habitat of the gastropod Coral wentletrap *(Epitonium billecanum)* (see photo 208, daytime; 209, night-time, p.182). Pacific range: Central and southern Gulf, to Ecuador, Galápagos. Circumtropical.

TAGUS CUP CORAL *(Tubastrea tagusensis)*
Similar to the species described above, but whitish tentacles surround a reddish oral disk. This species seen at Tagus Cove, west Isabela and Fernandina has apparently disappeared after the disastrous 1982–83 Niño.
Pacific range: Endemic to the Galápagos Islands.

YELLOW POLYP BLACK CORAL *(Antipathes galapagensis)*
Also known as Galápagos black coral. Yellow polyps on a black coral skeleton, form colonies with a diameter of 0.3 to two meters. Fixed on rocky reefs, drop offs and walls from three to 76 meters. Often found among the coral branches are the shrimp, *Periclimenes infraspinis*, the Pacific sea horse, *Hippocampus ingens* and the Long-nosed hawkfish, *Oxycirrhites typus*. Once thought endemic to the Galápagos (*see* photo 211, p.183).
Pacific range: Central and southern Gulf to Ecuador, Galápagos.

BLACK CORAL *(Antipathes panamensis)*
Most important species in the Galápagos, found on vertical rock faces. Development between three and 50 meters, optimum at 15 meters. Basic food is zooplankton. Exploitation for jewellery purposes has started due to the increase of tourism.
Pacific range: Panama to Colombia, Ecuador and Galápagos.

Other Types of Coral

PEBBLE CORAL
> *Cycloseris elegans*
> *Cycloseris mexicana*

REEF-BUILDING CORALS

Psammocora brighami	*Pocillopora capitata*	*Pavona clavus*
Psammocora stellata	*Pocillopora damicornis*	*Pavona gigantea*
Porites lobata	*Pocillopora elegans*	*Pavona varians*
Agaricella species	*Gardineroseris planulata*	

Phylum Annelida

Class Polychaeta: Segmented Worms, Bristleworms

Both species belong to genera of Amphinomids.

COMMON FIREWORM *(Eurythoe complanata)*
Light pink to pinkish-blue, with bluish spines, white venomous bristles on sides. Highly toxic, it can inflict painful stings with bristles. Deep reds gills. Body rectangular in cross-section, 60 to 350 segments present. In tide pools, infra and mid-littoral zones, under rocks on reef flats, to a depth of 61 meters. Length ten to 40 centimeters (*see* photo 217, p.185). Abundant in the Sea of Cortez.
Pacific range: Throughout the Gulf to Panama, Galápagos.

ORNATE FIREWORM *(Chloeia viridis)*
Also known as Red-tipped fireworm. Ornate feathery gills, greenish-white to brownish-pink, mottled, iridescent, dark stripe down middle of back. Each segment fringed with large tuft of white bristles with red tips. Dorsal surface has three longitudinal stripes on the anterior end of the body. Length seven to 12 centimeters. On sandy or mud bottoms, to depth of 91 meters. Highly toxic *(see* photo 218, p.185).
Pacific range: Gulf to Panama., Galápagos.

Phylum Mollusca

Class Polyplacophora: Chitons

RIPPLED CHITON *(Chiton sulcatus)*
Also known as Sculptured chiton. Color dark green to black. Flattened, oval shape, with a row of eight valves along back, each of them rippled in V-shapes. Found on rocky substrates in the mid-littoral zone (0.5 to 1.5 meters above low tide level).
Pacific range: Mexico, Revillagigedos, Galápagos.

CHITON *(Chiton goodalli)*
Similar, but more rounded than the former, with no ripples on the valves of the back. Found on rocky substrates of the low littoral zone, ie. low-tide level, tide pools, and in deeper water up to two meters. Endemic to the Galápagos.

Class Cephalopoda: Cephalopods

Family Octopodidae

GALÁPAGOS TWIN-SPOT OCTOPUS *(Octopus oculifer)* (Moynihan & Rodaniche, 1977)
Nobody knows how many species of octopus exist in the Galápagos. A similar species, *(Octopus bimaculeatus)* was described by Verril in 1883. One single species is actually recognized by the latest research of Kirstie L.Kaiser (1997). Found in rocky areas, rock faces (Gordon Rocks, Cousin's Rock). (see photo 235, p.191). A smaller individual was observed foraging on volcanic sand at night and could be a different species.
Pacific range: Tropical Eastern Pacific, California to Mexico, Galápagos.

Family Argonautidae (Argonauts)

Argonauts are open ocean pelagic octopuses. The female produces a brittle shell and they are often called the Paper nautilus for that reason. The male argonaut does not produce a shell. Found in temperate and tropical waters of the world.

PACIFIC ARGONAUT *(Argonauta pacificus)* (Dall, 1869)

Family Enoploteuthidae (Enope Squids)

Small squids in the open ocean, at mid-depths and over the continental shelf. Small chemical light organs are found on the undersides of body, head and arms. Have large eyes. Feed in shallow waters at night. Reach sizes of up to 13 centimeters in length.

ENOPE SQUID *(Abraliopsis affinis)* (Pfeffer, 1912)
Doubtful according to Finet 1985, not listed 1994.

ENOPE SQUID *(Pterygioteuthis giardi)* (Fisher, 1896)
Doubtful according to Finet 1985, not listed 1994.

Family Ommastrephidae (Flying Squids)

Muscular fast swimming squids, which can reach one meter in length. Eleven genera and more than 20 species occur in all the world's oceans. Resting in deep waters during the day, they come up at night to feed.

PURPLEBACK FLYING SQUID *(Sthenoteuthis ovalaniensis)* (Lesson, 1830)
Found in the Pacific and Indian oceans, down to depths of 100 meters. Recognized by a large yellow light organ under the skin of the back. Reaches a size of 35 centimeters.

Family Cranchidae (Glass Squids)

Occurs in surface and mid-water depths in the open ocean. Most species are transparent with swollen bodies and short arms. The arms bear two rows of suckers or hooks. Eyes have light organs on the undersides. Possesses a large fluid filled chamber containing ammonia to help buooancy. Grows from ten centimeters to two meters. Sixty species worldwide.

GLASS SQUID *(Liocranchia reinhardti)*

Class Bivalves

MAGNIFICENT SCALLOP *(Nodipecten magnificus)*
Typical scallop of the Pectinidae family. Flat shape, 13 to 15 radial ribs with red or purple-black flesh. Subtidal. Rocky areas, walls, cracks and crevices. Length up to 20 centimeters. Pacific range: Probably endemic to the Galápagos.

Class Gastropoda: Snails, Sea Slugs, Sea Hares, Nudibranchs

PANAMIC HORSE CONCH *(Pleuroploca princeps)*
Animal flesh brilliant red with blue spots. Nests in a snail-like pointed shell of 15 to 45 centimeters. Preys on Murex and Strombus gastropods. Harvested for food by commercial divers. Usually seen fixed on rocks at low depths (see photo 219, p.185).
Pacific range: Throughout the Gulf to Ecuador, Peru, Galápagos.

CHIEF ROCKSNAIL *(Hexaplex princeps)*
Formerly known as the Murex shell, of the Muricidae family. Conspicuous, massive rock shape. Shell is white and dented, often covered by red or blue sponges. Large brown operculum. Subtidal, feeds on barnacles. Very common in Galápagos, on rock walls, holes. Length up to 25 centimeters (*see* photo 220, p.186).
Pacific range: Gulf of California to Peru, Galápagos.

GRINNING TUN *(Malea ringens)*
A very large gasteropod of the Tonnidae family with a white, rounded shell. Shaped and lined with a spiral twist. Flesh of animal black. In tide pools and on sandy bottons down to 15 meters. Seen during a night dive at Punta Vicente Roca. Length up to 24 centimeters (*see* photo 221, p.186).
Pacific range: Gulf of California to Peru, Galápagos islands.

LITTLE DEER COWRIE *(Cyprae cervinetta)*
Little cowrie of the Cypraeidae family. Color light brown with white spots and markings. Elongated shape. Intertidal, on coral reefs but also on rocks or underneath. Length up to eight centimeters.
Pacific range: From Mexico (Sonora) to Peru, Galápagos Islands.

THIN-SHELLED HELMET *(Cypreacassis tenuis)*
Color mottled brown with white axial bars, spotted. Thick outer edges. Sandy tide pools, subtidal down to 15 meters. Seen foraging at night on volcanic sand in Tagus Cove. Feeds on the green sea urchin in Galápagos. Length up to 14 centimeters.
Pacific range: Gulf of California to Ecuador, Galápagos.

GALÁPAGOS ABALONE *(Haliotis dalli)*
Family Haliotidae. Ear-shaped with a red shell. Holes conspicuous on the edge. Offshore at depth from 30 to 70 meters. Rare in the islands. Length up to 2.5 centimeters (*see* photo 222, p.186).
Pacific range: Colombia to Galápagos.

GALÁPAGOS BLACK SEA SLUG *(Onchidella steindachneri)*
Oval-shaped, black sea slug. Found in the mid-littoral zone, 0.5 to 1.5 meters above low tide level, in rocks.
Pacific range: Endemic to the Galápagos.

BLUE-STRIPED SEA SLUG *(Tambja mullineri)*
Body black, with turquoise-blue stripes on back. Rhinophores and gills are deep blue-black. Intertidal and subtidal rocky substrates to 45 meters. Length two to three centimeters (*see* photos 227, 228, p.188).
Pacific range: Endemic to Galápagos.

STARRY NIGHT NUDIBRANCH *(Hypselodoris lapizlazuli)*
Body dark blue with yellowish dots, fringed with white, gills whitish, rhinophores blue-black with yellow dots. Length up to five centimeters. On rocky substrates, drop-offs, walls, down to 30 meters. Feeds on sponges. Personal observations at Cousin's Rock, Punta Vicente Roca (Isabela) *(see* photo 231, p.189).
Pacific range: Endemic to Galápagos.

CARNIVOROUS NUDIBRANCH *(Roboastra species)*
A large-sized nudibranch lined with blue, green and yellow. Blue mouth tube. Family Polyceridae. Preys on the smaller *Tambja mullineri*, and swallows it like a vacuum cleaner. Found at depth of 30 to 40 meters (Gordon Rocks, Cousin's Rock). Length up to five centimeters *(see* photo 229, p.189).
Pacific range: Gulf of California, Galápagos.

WALKING SEA HARE *(Aplysia cedrosensis)*
Humped body, with a large flap like parapodia that forms a spacious mantle cavity. Ground color is reddish-brown with lighter blotches speckled with white spots. Habitat in tide pools, shallow subtidal zone, but also seen in 20 meters depth on volcanic sandy bottoms foraging at night. Herbivorous, feeds on red and green algae. Length up to 15 centimeters *(see* photo 234, p.190).
Pacific range: Cedros Island on the Pacific coast of California, Galápagos.

SPANISH SHAWL *(Flabellina species)*
Belongs to the suborder Aeolidiacea or Aeolids. Red to pink color with cream-colored tipped fleshy appendages or finger like cerata all over the back. Carnivorous, it feeds on hydroids, sea anemones, bryozoaires and gorgonians. Stinging cells are located at the tip of the cerata. Intertidal and subtidal on rocky substrates. Length up to three centimeters *(see* photo 232, p.190).
Pacific range: East Pacific Coast, Galápagos.

PANAMA AGLAJA *(Navanax aenigmaticus)*
Belongs to the family *Aglajidae*, of the order *Cephalaspidea*, or 'head shield' slugs. The genus *Navanax* is restricted to the Eastern Pacific and possesses an internal shell. Adapted for burrowing, these carnivores feed on nudibranchs. The body is wrapped in its parapodia, that displays pearl-like spots along the edges. Rectangular head with earlike folds. Color from greenish to tan, speckled with whitish streaks. On sandy bottoms, intertidal and in tidal pools. Length up to 7.5 centimeters. Seen on a night dive in Santa Fe's north east lagoon *(see* photo 224, p.187).
Pacific range: South Mexico to Chile.

WARTY SEA SLUG *(Pleurobranchus areolatus)*
Belongs to the family *Pleurobranchidae*. A big-size species in Galápagos, seen during night dives on rocks or rubble. Color yellow orange. Dorsal surface covered with wart-like bumps. Intertidal and subtidal down to 30 meters. Seen on a night dive at Rabida island. Length up to 15 centimeters *(see* photo 228, p.188).
Pacific range: Sea of Cortez, Mexico to Ecuador, Cocos Is.

APRICOT SLUG *(Berthellina engeli)*
Belongs to the family Pleurobranchidae. A bright orange, soft, rounded body. Gill located on the right side. Found in tidepools, under rocks, on sandy bottoms down to ten meters. Observed at Urvina bay and Rabida (night dive). Length up to six centimeters *(see* photo 226, p.188).
Pacific range: Southern California to Ecuador, Galápagos.

CAROLYN DORIS *(Platydoris carolynae)*
Belongs to the family *Platydorididae*. Body is oval shaped, flattened and leathery. Color is reddish-brown with white markings on the edges and center. Underparts are white. Conspicuous gills on back. Rhinophores tan to dark. Feeds on sponges. Intertidal to subtidal. Endemic to Galápagos. Seen at Tortuga island (South Isabela). Length up to 8 centimeters *(see* photo 225, p.187).

GALÁPAGOS DISCODORIS *(Discodoris species)*
A beautiful yellow orange seaslug speckled with black or brown spots all over the body. Rhinophores and gills bright orange. Subtidal, found on rocks. Seen at Piedra Blanca on the west side of Santiago island, at depth of 32 meters. Length up to 8 centimeters. Endemic to Galápagos *(see* photo 229 , p.189).

OPISTOBRANCHS OF GALÁPAGOS

ORDER CEPHALASPIDEA (Fisher, 1863)
Family Aglajidae
Panama aglaja — *Navanax aenigmaticus* (Bergh, 1893)
Starry night — *Philinopsis* cf. *cyanea* (von Martens, 1879)
Family Bullidae
Bubble snail — *Bulla gouldiana* (Pilsbry, 1895)
Mottled bubble snail — *Bulla punctulata* (Adams in Sowerby, 1850)

ORDER ANASPIDEA (Fisher, 1883)
Family Aplysiidae
Blue-ringed seahare — *Stylocheilus longicauda* (Quoy & Gaimard, 1824)
Walking seahare — *Aplysia* cf. *cedrosensis* (Bartsch & Rehder, 1939)
Family Dolabriferidae
Warty seacat — *Dolabrifera dolabrifera* (Rang, 1828)
Bluntend seahare — *Dolabella auricularia* (Lightfoot, 1786)

ORDER NOTASPIDEA (Fisher, 1883)
Family Pleurobranchidae
Warty seaslug — *Pleurobranchus areolatus* (Mörch, 1863)
Orange blob, apricot slug — *Berthellina engeli* (Gardiner, 1936)
Starred seaslug — *Berthella stellata* (Risso, 1826)

ORDER ASCOGLOSSA (Bergh, 1876)
Family Juliidae
Green berthelinia — *Berthelinia chloris* (Dall, 1918)

ORDER NUDIBRANCHIA (Blainville, 1814)
SUBORDER DORIDACEA
Family Goniodorididae
Ancula letiginosa (Farmer & Sloan, 1964)
Family Polyceridae
Polycera atra (Mac Farland, 1905)
Limacia jansi (Bertsch & Ferreira, 1974)
Roboastra species
Carnivorous nudibranch
Blue-striped sea slug — *Tambja mullineri* (Farmer, 1978) (E)

Family Conualevidae
White smoothhorn doris — *Conualevia alba* (Collier & Farmer, 1964)
Family Chromodorididae
Dall doris — *Cadlina sparsa* (Odhner, 1921)
Baumann doris — *Chromodoris sphoni* (Marcus, 1971)
Chromodoris baumanni (Bertsch, 1970)
Ruzafa doris — *Chromodoris ruzafai* (Ortea, Bacallado, Valdez, 1992) (E)
Red-tipped sea goddess — *Glossodoris sedna* (Marcus & Marcus, 1967)
Banks glossodoris — *Glossodoris banksi* (Farmer, 1931)
Starry night nudibranch — *Hypselodoris lapizlazuli* (Bertsch & Ferreira, 1974) (E)
Family Platydorididae
Carolyn doris — *Platydoris carolinae* (Mulliner y Sphon, 1974) (E)
Family Dendrodorididae
Orange doris — *Dendrodoris krebssi* (Mörch, 1863)
Doriopsilla janaina (Marcus & Marcus, 1967)
Family Discodorididae
Mavis doris — *Geitodoris mavis* (Marcus & Marcus, 1967)
Galápagos discodoris — *Discodoris* species (E)
SUBORDER AEOLIDIACEA
Family Aeolidiidae
White aeolis — *Aeolidiella alba* (Risbec, 1928)
India aeolis — *Aeolidiella indica* (Bergh, 1867)
Spurilla chromosoma (Cockerell & Eliot, 1905)
Family Favorinidae
Phidiana lascrucensis (Bertsch & Ferreira, 1974)
Family Flabellinidae
Translucent aeolis — *Flabellina telja* (Marcus & Marcus, 1967)
Spanish shawl — *Flabellina* species
Marcus aeolis — *Flabellina marcusorum* (Gosliner & Kuzirian)
Family Facelinidae
Favorinus species

(courtesy of Dr. Jesus Ortea, 1992, Departamento de Biología de Organismos y Sistemas, Universidad de Oviedo, Spain).
Completed from: Field guide to marine mollusks of Galápagos, by C.Hickman Jr. and Yves Finet, 1999.

(E) = Endemic

Phylum Arthropoda

Class Crustacea: Crabs, Shrimps, Lobsters

GALÁPAGOS PEBBLESTONE CRAB *(Mithrax nodosus)*
Small greenish-brown or black, spider-like crab. Length about three centimeters. In the intertidal zone, among rocks, sometimes with Pocillopora corals.
Pacific range: Galápagos, Chile.

GIANT HERMIT CRAB *(Petrochirus californiensis)*
Rusty brown with pronounced knobs on the claws. Red and white banded antennae. Pincers red and white. On rocky and sandy volcanic bottoms down to 30 meters. Forages at night. Feeds on worms, polychaetes. Occupies various empty shells, of *Murex*, *Pleuroploca* or *Strombus*, which sometimes have a live anemone fixed on top. Carapace up to 13 centimeters, body size up to 35 centimeters *(see* photo 238, p.192).
Pacific range: Throughout the Gulf to Ecuador, Galápagos.

HAIRY HERMIT CRAB *(Aniculus elegans)*
Legs red and pink banded, with hairs. Hairs on top of head. Antennae with no color. This hermit crab is a coral browser. Carapace up to seven centimeters *(see* photo 239, p.192).
Pacific range: Gulf of California to Ecuador, Galápagos.

BAR-EYED HERMIT CRAB *(Dardanus fucosus)*
Reddish-tan. Black bar across blue eyes. Walking legs with bristles. On sand and mud bottoms. Frequently uses the shell of the tulip snail and various conchs. Forages at night (seen at Tagus Cove) *(see* photo 240, p.192).
Pacific range: Gulf of California to Peru, Galápagos.

STANFORD SWIMMER CRAB *(Portunus stanfordi)*
Bright red color, sometimes mottled. Forages at night on volcanic sandy bottoms down to 25 meters. Sometime hides under the cerianthid anemone, *Pachycerianthus fimbriatus*. Subtidal down to 300 meters. Size of carapace five centimeters *(see* photo 241, p.209).
Pacific range: Endemic to the Galápagos.

SALLY LIGHTFOOT CRAB *(Grapsus grapsus)*
Locally known as Zayapa. By waters edge, intertidal zone on rocks and cliffs. Color bright red and turquoise-blue in adults, black in juveniles (for camouflage). Carapace five to 8.7 centimeters. Occurs often in large aggregations, sharing the territory of sea lions and marine iguanas. Feeds on green chlorophyll algae, small fish, animals in putrefaction *(see* photo 242, p.209).
Pacific range: California to Peru, Ecuador, Galápagos. Florida and Caribbean.

HELLER FIDDLER CRAB *(Uca helleri)*
Body color tan to bluish-brown. Pincers of the male are unequal, the large claw is pustulated. Size 3.2 to five centimeters. Sandy mud flats, mangroves, near high tide line. Feeds on algae, bacterias, microcrustaceans. One of the two endemic species of the genus Uca, the other being *Uca galapagensis*, gray to dull with white edges, up to 2.2 centimeters.
Pacific range: Endemic to the Galápagos.

GHOST CRAB *(Ocypode species)*
Currently seen on coral or volcanic sandy beaches, digging holes where it disappears suddenly when startled. Cream color with vertical stick-like eyes. Carapace rectangular, five centimeters wide *(see* photo 243, p.209).
Pacific range: Baja California to Chile, Galápagos.

PANAMIC ARROWHEAD CRAB *(Stenorhynchus debilis)*
Orange to brown, streaked with yellow and black lines in a triangle pattern on back. Distinctive pointed head, like an arrow. Eight long legs, spider like. Forearms of claws long and white spotted. Pincers blue tipped in front of mouth. Carapace one to two centimeters long. On sandy volcanic bottom from 1.5 to 61 meters deep *(see* photo 244, p.210). Forages at night, often seen covered with gray sponges. Lives in symbiosis with the anemone, *Bunodactis mexicana*, taking shelter under its tentacles.
Pacific range: Throughout the Gulf to Chile, Ecuador, Galápagos.

SHAME FACE BOX CRAB *(Calappa convexa)*
Distinctive box shape. Color purple to brown mottled with white. Carapace and claws tuberculate. Size up to ten to 15 centimeters. Capacity to retract claws under the carapace, locked in like a box, and to dig itself quickly into the volcanic sand. Forages at night on sandy bottoms, to depths of 18 to 122 meters *(see* photo 245, p.210).
Pacific range: Throughout the Gulf of California to Ecuador, Galápagos.

YELLOW SNOUT RED SHRIMP *(Rhynchocinetes typus)*
Red, with legs white banded and white spots on rump, white streaks around head. Yellow under the upper mandible of mouth. Subtidal, under rocks. Nocturnal feeder. Found on the west coast of Isabela and around Fernandina in cooler waters. This cleaner shrimp feeds on the parasites of fishes. Length up to five centimeters *(see* photo 246, p.210).
Pacific range: Galápagos to Chile.

BIG EYE SHRIMP *(Metapenaeopsis kishinouyei)*
Translucid body with red streaks longitudinally. Peneid shrimp, with big dark green eyes. Common to Galápagos, subtidal on sandy and gravel bottoms. Length to 6.7 centimeters *(see* photo 247, p.211).
Pacific range: Mexico to Galápagos.

RED-BANDED SHRIMP *(Cinetorhynchus hiatti)*
Conspicuous red and white bands across body. Robust pincers in the first ambulatory legs. Subtidal, under rocks. Nocturnal feeder. Observed in the northern islands, Wolf and Darwin (see photo 249, p.211).
Pacific range: Japan to Loyalty Island, Hawaii, Marquesas, Galápagos.

GIANT KHAKI SHRIMP *(Litopenaeus stylirostris)*
Color greenish to brownish. Top of head is crested like a saw. Long antennae. Globulus, pigmented eyes. On sandy bottoms to 20 meters, down to 90 meters. Nocturnal feeder. Length from 15 to 25 centimeters. (Personal observation during night dive on volcanic sand at Tagus Cove, February 1992 *(see* photo 248, p.211).
Pacific range: Gulf of California to Peru, Galápagos.

GOLD-SPOTTED SHRIMP *(Sicyonia aliaffinis)*
Distinct gold-yellow blotch on the carapace. Dorsally coffee color to green and cream on sides. Diane design with black ring and yellow spot inside. Subtidal on sandy bottoms from four to 240 meters *(see* photo 250, p.212).
Pacific range: Gulf of California to Peru, Galápagos.

SEA STAR SHRIMP *(Periclimenes soror)*
A commensal shrimp associated with the Chocolate chip star, *Nidorellia armata*, and attached to the oral face of the sea star. Bicolored, white on back and orange-red on sides. To depth of 30 meters. Length up to one centimeter *(see* photo 251, p.212).
Pacific range: Gulf of California to Columbia, Galápagos, circumtropical.

DOUBLE PINCERS SHRIMP *(Brachycarpus biunguiculatus)*
This shrimp stands apart with conspicuous, very long pincers. Color translucid to pink with some green streaks. Intertidal between rocks and around caves at depth of three to 15 meters. Observed at Bartolome's Pinnacle on a night dive.
Pacific range: Circumtropical

RED SPINY LOBSTER *(Panulirus penicillatus)*
Red tail and blue markings on spiny head. Distribution throughout the islands. Exploited by commercial fisheries with restrictions at certain times of the year, Jan/Feb. and June/July, to allow reproduction of the species. Hides in cracks and caves during the day. Gregarious species. Likes to live on the edge of reefs exposed to strong waves. Forages at night, in shallow waters two to three meters deep. Feeds on crustaceans and benthic invertebrates, also hermit crabs (Camilo Martinez, CDRS 2000). On rocky substrates, to a depth of nine meters *(see* photo 252, p.212).
Pacific range: Indo-Pacific region, Hawaii, Polynesia, Revillagigedos, Cocos, Clipperton, Galápagos.

TROPICAL ROCK LOBSTER *(Panulirus femoristriga)*
New arrival (Niño, 1998) from the Indo-Pacific. Differs from the red or blue lobsters by the presence of two conspicuous spines on the antennal plate (instead of four in other species) and many white spots on thorax and abdomen. Solitary, nocturnal species. Length up to 35 centimeters.
Pacific range: Indo-Pacific, Japan, Philippines, Taiwan, Micronesia, Galápagos.

BLUE LOBSTER *(Panulirus gracilis)*
Color greenish-blue. Found in shallow waters around two to eight meters (average) to a maximum depth of 30 meters. Hides in caves and among rocks during the day. Forages at night. Usually a solitary species, but sometimes found in 'family nests'. Exploited by commercial fisheries until recent restrictions. Unlike the Red spiny lobster, it does not mind protected bays, and turbid waters. Feeds on crustaceans and benthic invertebrates, also hermit crabs (Camilo Martinez, CDRS 2000). Distribution in Galápagos, mainly on the south and west coast of Isabela (*see* photo 253, p.213).
Pacific range: Mexico to Peru, Galápagos.

SLIPPER LOBSTER *(Scyllarides astori)*
Differs from the two former lobsters in having a smooth carapace with no spines. The head terminates with two flat and rounded lobes extending on both sides of the antennae. Body color, uniformly purple-brown to pink, with small black eyes. Nests in small rounded holes on drop-offs, rock walls. Forages at night to a depth of two to eight meters, maximum 40 meters. Feeds on soft parts of fish, sponges, ascidians and sea urchins (Camilo Martinez, CDRS 2000). Their natural camouflage helps them against the predation of fishermen. Well distributed throughout the Galápagos (*see* photo 254, p.213).
Pacific range: Indo-Pacific, endemic to the islands of the East Pacific.

* On October 1, 2002, a new species of Slipper lobster, *"Parribacus perlatus"* (Holthuis 1967), known from Pascua Island, was identified by Dr.Gary Pore of the Victoria Museum (Melbourne), during a night dive at Wolf Island's anchorage, active at a depth of 6 meters.

Phylum Echinodermata

Class Asteroidea: Sea Stars

ARMORED SAND STAR *(Astropecten armatus)*
Color varies from gray to pink, purple, orange, red or brown. The five arms are fringed with vertical and horizontal rows of spines, movable. On sandy bottoms to a depth of 61 meters. Feed on snails, sand dollars, Purple dwarf olives and also scavenges. Radius up to 15 centimeters (*see* photo 255, p.213).
Pacific range: South California to Ecuador, Galápagos.

SAND STAR *(Luidia foliolata)*
Dark olive. Sandy bottoms. Active at night. Radius eight centimeters *(see* photo 256, p.214).
Pacific range: East Pacific from Alaska to Mexico, Galápagos.

BANDED SAND STAR *(Luidia bellonae)*
Yellowish with brown spots, tiny spines in cluster. Dark spots arranged as bands. Lies buried under the surface. Numerous in western part of the archipelago. Radius ten centimeters.
Pacific range: Gulf of California to Peru, Galápagos.

KEELED SEA STAR (Asteropsis carinifera)
Arms triangular, spines and spores. Thick smooth skin. Wet slimy appearance. Edge of arms with prominent conical spines. Color tan with brick-red pigments on disk and arms. Uncommon, except Rabida. Radius 16 centimeters *(see* photo 262, p.216).
Pacific range: Indo-Pacific, Gulf of California to Panama, Galápagos.

PANAMIC CUSHION STAR *(Pentaceraster cummingi)*
Formerly *Oreaster occidentalis*, also known as Gulf star. Color red, or red mottled with white, orange with dark green. Body wall hard, inflated, with reddish-orange spines. On rocky substrates, reefs, and on sandy coral or volcanic bottoms, where they often gather in colonies (Mosquera) down to 25 meters. Size up to 30 centimeters. The commensal and tiny Sea star shrimp, *Periclimenes soror*, is associated with this species *(see* photo 258, p.214).
Pacific range: Throughout the Gulf to North Peru, Galápagos, Hawaii.

CHOCOLATE CHIP STAR *(Nidorellia armata)*
Color yellow-orange with black spines in a star pattern and all over the body. Pentagonal shape, arms black tipped. Size up to 15 centimeters. On rocky substrates down to 73 meters. Feeds on benthic algae and sedentary invertebrates. Associated with the Sea star shrimp, *Perichimenes soror (see* photo 259, p.215).
Pacific range: Throughout the Gulf to North Peru, Galápagos.

PYRAMID SEA STAR *(Pharia pyramidata)*
Color varies from brownish-yellow with markings to purple. Five tube-like arms, spotted. Size 15 to 20 centimeters. On rocky substrates. Feeds on algae, invertebrates and Pebble coral, *Cycloseris mexicana (see* photo 261, p.215).
Pacific range: Throughout Gulf to North Peru, Galápagos.

BLUE SEA STAR *(Phataria unifascialis)*
Purple-blue bordered with dark bands along length. Stiff, slender body, with long tapering arms. Size ten to 20 centimeters. On rocky substrates, rock walls, down to 139 meters *(see* photo 260, p.215).
Pacific range: Throughout Gulf to North Peru and Galápagos.

TROSCHEL'S SEA STAR *(Evasterias troschelli)*
Reddish-white and mottled, with black spines. Five arms slightly tapering. On rocky substrates down to 70 meters. Radius to 20 centimeters.
Pacific range: Alaska to California, Galápagos.

VARIABLE SEA STAR *(Linckia columbiae)*
Also known as the Pacific comet star. A small sea star with five arms. Central disk is small. Arms with rounded tips. Color goes from red to orange, with pinkish arm tips. Asexual reproduction by splitting into parts. A lone arm is often seen regenerating a new star, comet like. Intertidal among rocks, in caves, under boulders. Subtidal to a depth of 150 meters. Common in the western part of the archipelago. Radius of 3.5 centimeters (*see* photo 257, p.214).
Pacific range: Hawaii, California to Peru, Galápagos.

SMOOTH SEA STAR *(Leiaster veres)*
Large sea star, bright red in color, with long, slender tapering arms. Small central disk. Three dorsal rows and two lateral rows of scales are visible. Habitat varies from rocky areas to sandy or mud bottoms down to depths of 50 meters. Radius up to 20 centimeters. Uncommon in the Islands (*see* photo 263, p.216).
Pacific range: Gulf of California to Panama, Galápagos.

RED SUN STAR *(Heliaster cummingi)*
Central disk large, 32 to 40 rays. Color varies from red to deep blue, black. Rocky shores, mid-littoral in the barnacle zone. Rare after the 1982–83 Niño. Feeds on barnacles and sessile invertebrates. Size nine centimeters.
Pacific range: Endemic to the Galápagos.

24-RAYED SUN STAR *(Heliaster solaris)*
Central disk elevated, 21 to 27 rays. Light gray to greenish-yellow, blotched with gray or black, like bands. Rocky shores. Uncommon before the 1982–83 Niño.
Pacific range: Endemic to the Galápagos.

SUN STAR *(Heliaster multiradiata)*
This starfish looks more like a big, short-spined sea urchin, as it tucks its arms under the body leaving only the appearance of a ball of red-tipped knobs. Size up to 30 centimeters.

BRADLEY SEA STAR *(Mithrodia bradleyi)*
Color pink to pale red. Five tube arms covered with knobs and short, rounded spines of the same color. Rocky substrates, drop offs and wall faces (*see* photo 264, p.216).

GIANT SEA STAR *(Tethyaster species)*
A large, rounded central disk with broad, thick, tapering arms. Crisscrossed red pattern on a whitish background. Arms are red tipped. An unsually huge sea star. On sand and mud from six to 178 meters. Similar to *Tethyaster canaliculatus* found in the Sea of Cortez. Personal observation on a night dive at Punta Vicente Roca. Length up to 50 centimeters (*see* photo 267, p.217).
Pacific range: Central Gulf to Panama, Galápagos.

PRICKLY SEA STAR *(Paulia horrida)*
In the Asterodiscididae family. A little red-orange star with conspicuous spines of different sizes all over the body. Arms are triangular. Found on sand and mud, at depths of 30 meters on average. A similar species is *Amphiaster insignis* found in the Gulf of California. Radius ten to 17 centimeters. Personal observations at Cousin's Rock, Punta Espinosa and Champion (*see* photo 266, p.217).
Pacific range: Central Gulf to Panama, Galápagos.

RATHBUN'S SEA STAR *(Rathbunaster californicus)*
A rather small, red and white star with many delicate arms of various length. Number of arms varies from 12 to 20. Upper body plates with needle-like spines. Diameter up to ten centimeters. Found at depths of 30 meters on coral rubble (Cousin's Rock), on rocks (night dive, Rabida) (*see* photo 265, p.217).
Pacific range: California, Baja California, Galápagos.

Class Ophiuroidea: Brittle Stars

There are 2,000 described species in the world of which 74 species are recorded in Galápagos, 28 species in water less than 20 meters deep. Four species are endemic in Galápagos.

ALEXANDER'S SPINY BRITTLE STAR *(Ophiocma alexandri)*
Slender and flattened long arms, equipped laterally with spines. Arms are banded. Nine to 44 centimeters in diameter. On rocky reefs, under boulders on sand, ledges, down to 70 meters (*see* photo 268, p.218).
Pacific range: Throughout the Gulf to Colombia, Galápagos.

MULTI-COLORED BRITTLE STAR *(Ophioderma variegatum)*
Red and white banded arms. Heart red. Size eight to 18 centimeters. Intertidal zone, under rocks, on rubble and sand, down to 110 meters.
Pacific range: Baja California, throughout Gulf to Panama, Galápagos.

Class Echinoidea: Sea Urchins

PENCIL SEA URCHIN *(Eucidaris thouarsii)*
Ten vertical rows of heavy, stick-like spines, red color to black and gray when encrusted. Diameter of test (skeleton), three to seven centimeters. Spines up to five centimeters. On rocky substrates, holes, crevices, reef depressions to a depth of 150 meters. Encrusting organisms are very present in pencil urchins (*see* photo 269, p.218).
Pacific range: Throughout Gulf to Ecuador, Galápagos.

NEEDLE SEA URCHIN *(Diadema mexicanum)*
A very wide black sea urchin with long, needle-like and venomous spines. Herbivorous species feeding at night. Usually found in the rocky intertidal and submerged zones, also on flat areas of coral rubble where they sometimes gather in large groups. Diameter up to 50 centimeters (*see* photo 270, p.218).
Pacific range: Gulf of California to Colombia, Galápagos.

CROWNED SEA URCHIN *(Centrostephanus coronatus)*
Spines long and black in adult, black and white banded in juveniles. Up to 12 centimeters in size. Carnivorous nocturnal species, unlike most sea urchins which are herbivorous. Spines are slightly poisonous and break easily into one's arm or foot (*see* photo 271, p.219).
Pacific range: Gulf of California, North Peru, Galápagos.

GREEN SEA URCHIN *(Lytechinus semituberculatus)*
Small size, about five centimeters in diameter. Test color is gray-white with short green spines. On rocky substrates, often gregarious (*see* photo 272, p.219).
Pacific range: Columbia to Peru, Galápagos islands.

WHITE SEA URCHIN *(Tripneustes depressus)*
A large, globular urchin. Herbivore, feeds on red filamentous algae, encrusting algae, sponges and other sea urchins. Infra-littoral, over rocky substrates, down to 73 meters. Rather common, depending on the year. Diameter up to 16 centimeters (*see* photo 273, p.219).
Pacific range: California to Ecuador, Galápagos.

FLOWER SEA URCHIN *(Toxopneustes roseus)*
Like a ball of short white spines (up to one centimeter in length) with huge globiferous *pedicellariae* all around it. (*Pedicellariae*: small, pincher-like or vise-like structures on the surface of sea urchins to keep the body surface free of other organisms). General color whitish to pink. On rocks, corals, and sand to a depth of 24 meters. Often seen covered with shell debris, in the northern islands. Highly poisonous. Do not touch. (*see* photo 274, p.220).
Pacific range: Gulf to Ecuador, Galápagos.

GALÁPAGOS SAND DOLLAR *(Encope galapagensis)*
Shape pentagonal, with rounded angles. Color varies, tan, whitish, brown, red-violet or green. Size 7.5 to 20 centimeters. On coral or volcanic sandy bottoms down to 100 meters. Seen on the west side of Isabela (Punta Moreno, Tagus Cove). Also known as Keyhole sand dollar (*see* photo 275, p.220).
Pacific range: Endemic to Galápagos.

HEART URCHIN *(Lovenia cordiformis)*
Also known as Sea porcupine. Heart shaped, 7.5 centimeters long, six centimeters wide. Color white, rose, gray, yellow to purple. Body covered with numerous small and longer spines, brushed aside. Burrows just below the surface of the sand, found to a depth of 140 meters.
Pacific range: South California to Panama, North Peru, Galápagos.

Class Holoturoidea: Sea Cucumbers

Family Holothuridae

Holothuria difficilis	10–12 cms
Holothuria arenicola	10–20 cms
Holothuria impatiens	10–20 cms
Holothuria lubrica	5–15 cms
Holothuria atra	20–30 cms
Holothuria hilla	15–20 cms
Holothuria pandalis	2–10 cms
Holothuria leucospilota	20–40 cms
Holothuria fuscocinerea	20–32 cms
Holothuria imitans	12–20 cms
Holothuria kefersteini	16–20 cms
Holothuria theeli	8–13 cms
Holothuria portovallartensis	8–14 cms
Holothuria maccullochi	18–26 cms

BROWN-SPOTTED SEA CUCUMBER *(Holothuria impatiens)*
Slender body with a bottle shape and a long neck. Knobbly and sandy to the touch. Large tube feet on the underside, in distinctive rows. Length ten to 20 centimeters. Rocky reefs, coral, boulders and on sand to a depth of 46 meters.
Pacific range: Throughout Gulf to Ecuador, Galápagos.

SULFUR SEA CUCUMBER *(Holothuria lubrica)*
Color dull to gray, brown or black. Soft body skin, with 20 large tentacles around mouth. Small *papillae* (pimple-like projections) on the body surface. Large sulfur-colored tube feet on the underside. Size five to 15 centimeters. In rocks and crevices down to 55 meters. Feeds day and night in areas of current.
Pacific range: Gulf to Ecuador, Galápagos.

SEA CUCUMBER, PEPINO *(Stichopus fuscus)*
Large with thicks flanks, underside flat. Smooth skin covered on top and sides with numerous warts (in juveniles), which tend to develop as soft spines in adults. The mouth is directed downwards, the species grazes on rocks and reefs. Rocky reefs, boulders, occasionally on sand, down to 61 meters (*see* photo 276, p.220).
Pacific range: Throughout Gulf to Ecuador, Galápagos.

GIANT SEA CUCUMBER *(Stichopus horrens)*
Color green to orange, brown, mottled. Long, soft, conspicuous spines. Active at night, when the big ones may be seen standing erect on their backsides, apparently feeding on plankton, with their head and soft spines bent towards the current. Length to 25 centimeters. (*see* photos 277, 278, p.221).

WARTY SEA CUCUMBER *(Holothuria fuscocinerea)*
A very distinctive species that cannot be mistaken for any other in Galápagos. Large, slender, cylindrical body covered by warts pierced on the top. Ventral surface is flat and pale. Color cream to light coffee. Found in rocky areas where it remains exposed day and night. Habitat intertidal, where it feeds on sandy and coral rubble bottoms. Often seen in association with *Holothuria kefersteini*. Length up to 30 centimeters (*see* photo 279, p.221).
Pacific range: Hawaii, south of Mexico, Galápagos.

CAMOUFLAGED SEA CUCUMBER *(Holothuria kefersteini)*
A long sea cucumber with rough skin covered with soft spikes. Color black to reddish in some individuals. Juveniles are black, covered with tubercles. Exposed day and night, but always coated in sand or rubble as a perfect disguise, mimetic of the bottom. Habitat intertidal and subtidal on sandy coral bottoms. Length up to 20 centimeters (*see* photo 280, p.222).
Pacific range: Mozambique to Hawaii, Clipperton, Cocos, Galápagos.

DIVING SITES

RECOMMENDATIONS BEFORE DIVING

Although diving in the Galápagos started about 30 years ago, dive tourism is relatively new to the islands. The first land-based dive center was established in Puerto Ayora (Santa Cruz Island) in 1992 and the sport has become increasingly popular. There are now three main dive centers in Puerto Ayora and a number of smaller operations have also started up, albeit perhaps less professional. A recommended Santa Cruz dive center is, "Scuba Iguana" (Mathias Espinosa) at the former Hotel Galápagos, Puerto Ayora, Santa Cruz Island, tel./fax: (593) (5) 526 497 or 526 330; email: info@scubaiguana.com; www.scubaiguana.com. The price (as of early 2006) was US$115 for two boat dives including lunch, dive equipment, guide, boat trip, shower and towel.

Three dive centers operate from Puerto Baquerizo Moreno, on San Cristobal Islands:

"Chalo Tours" (established 1997), email: chalotours@hotmail.com.
"Wreck Bay Dive Center" (established 2004), email: insofacto@hotmail.com.
"Galakiwi" (established December 2004), email: galakiwi@yahoo.com.

PADI OWSI instructor, Pierre Constant will open his "Scubadragon Dive Center" on Puerto Villamil (Isabela Island) in early 2007, if all goes according to plan! For information, fax: (331) 4621 7736; email calaolife@yahoo.com or check the websites www.calaolife.com and www.scubadragongalapagos.com.

The decompression chamber, at the 'Centro Medico Protesub' in Puerto Ayora is open from 9:30am-12:30pm and 3:30pm-5:30pm, tel: (05) 2526 911 or mobile: (09) 855 911. Created in 2001 by Henry Schaeffer (dec.), it is now owned by Mexican Maurico Moreno's company SSR International. The doctor-in-charge of the hyperbaric chamber is Dr. Gabriel Idrogo, tel: (099) 283 990 (24 hours) or (05) 2526 101 (home). For diving emergencies, call Dr. Lopez (24 hours) at (099) 283 995.

WATER TEMPERATURE
Galápagos is usually considered to be a region of cold waters, despite its equatorial position. The existence of three main water currents explains this phenomenon; two cold currents (coming from the west and the southeast) and one warm flow (coming from the northeast, Panama). The water temperature is, of course, influenced by the seasons. Sea surface temperatures may range from 17°C to 27°C depending on whether it is the cold season (May to December) or the warm season (December to May). In the Galápagos, temperatures

tend to be warmer in the northern islands, cooler in the central and southern islands and frankly, cold on the west of Isabela Island (down to 13°C to 15°C degrees).

During Niño years, however, sea surface temperatures will range evenly all over the islands from 25°C to 30°C whatever the season. Whatever time of the year, it is necessary to wear a wet suit (5mm to 7mm thick) when diving. For more details on seasons and temperatures, refer to Chapter 2, Part One.

WATER CLARITY

All waters are usually clear during the cold season, although the ocean surface can be agitated in August and September. The warm season can bring rather murky waters depending on the site.

CURRENTS

These can be strong, up to three to seven knots, and treacherous in the Galápagos region. Compass navigation underwater is necessary. Divers should always check the direction of the current before commencing a dive; drift diving is compulsory in this case and for security reasons, a safety sausage is a 'must' at all times. Unfortunately, divers have been lost and never found again.

DANGERS

Galápagos is certainly not a place for novice divers. Therefore, advanced certification is recommended. Divers should not take risks exploring submarine caves as these can actually be very long and tricky tunnels created by wave action. 'Remolinos' (also known as eddies or whirlpools) are related to down current effects and should not be taken lightly, especially at the end of a dive! If caught in one, do not try to fight it. Get out of it at once by swimming sideways, across it and away from the rocks. Its intensity—the sucking effect—will decrease as you swim towards the blue. 'Remolinos' are associated with converging currents around a rocky point, or along a rock wall, etc. (e.g. Gordon Rocks, Darwin, Wolf Islands).

Sharks are neither dangerous nor aggressive unless they are provoked. However, an attitude of respect is necessary; maintain distance and have a proper refuge or hiding place close by, in case it is needed. (Also refer to p.163)

Fortunately, the one poisonous sea snake in the Galápagos waters, Pelamis platurus (Hydrophiidae family), is rarely seen. It is a pelagic migratory sea snake, mostly seen during warm Niño years. About 50 centimeters in length, its dorsal and upper sides are black and ventrally it is bright yellow. The venom is stronger than that of a cobra. It should not be approached.

The long needle-like spines of the black sea urchin are slightly poisonous, and will break easily in your arm or leg. The pain and numbness may continue for two to three days. 'Flower sea urchins' should not be touched as they are highly poisonous and can inflict a painful sting (refer to p. 241).

LIST OF DIVING SITES

Classification: Snorkelling   < 3 meters   [SN]
                  Skin diving   < 10 meters   [SK]
                  Scuba diving > 10 meters   [DIV]

	SN	SK	DIV
CENTRAL ISLANDS			
Around Santa Cruz			
El Bajo (Academy Bay)			*
El Barranco (Academy Bay)			*
Gordon Rocks			*
Guy Fawkes (west)			*
Island Coamaño (Academy Bay)	*		*
Mosquera Island (west beach and east)	*	*	*
Punta Carrion (north)			*
Punta Estrada (Academy Bay)	*	*	*
Sin Nombre (west)			*
Southern Channel (Itabaca)	*	*	
South Plaza (lagoon and cliffside)	*	*	*
Tortuga Negra (north)			*
Venecia (west)			*
North Seymour (south coast) (northeast point)	*	*	
Daphne Mayor			*
Daphne Minor			*
Santa Fé (northeast lagoon)	*	*	*
Northeast Bay (lagoon and rocks)	*	*	*
Around Santiago			
Bainbridge Rocks			*
Bartolomé Island (beach, Pinnacle Rock)	*	*	*
Beagle Rocks (islets)	*	*	*
Bucaneer's Cove (around north point)	*	*	*
Cousin's Rock			*
East Bartolomé Island			*
James Bay (Puerto Egas and grottos)	*	*	*
Piedra blanca (north of Buccaneer's Cove, west coast)			*
Rabida Island (beach and west cove) (north point)	*	*	*
Roca Don Ferdi (east)			*

	SN	SK	DIV
Sombrero Chino (lagoon)	*		
Sullivan Bay	*		
Pinzon			
Islote Onan			*
EAST			
Around San Cristobal			
Cerro de las Tijeretas (cove, Puerto Baquerizo)	*	*	*
Five Fingers rock (west)			*
Isla Lobos (north west)			*
Kicker's Rock (Stephens Bay)			*
Punta Pitt (east)			*
Roca Ballena (south)			*
Roca Este (east)			*
Roca Pitt (east)			*
NORTH			
Genovesa			
Darwin Bay (beach side)		*	
Darwin Bay (western reef)	*	*	*
Entrance reef (Darwin Bay)			*
Prince Philip's Steps			*
Marchena Island			
Punta Espejo			*
Punta Montalvo (north)			*
Punta Mejia (northwest)			*
Darwin Island			
Eastern tip and rock arch			*
La Botella (west cove)			*
Fondeadero (north east)			*
Wolf Island			
East cliff and corals			*
El Derrumbe (middle east)			*
El Pinaculo (northeast)			*
La Banana (north)			*
Islote La Ventana (southwest)			*
Pinta			
Cape Ibbetson (southeast)			*
Rocas Nerus (north)			*

	SN	SK	DIV
WEST			
Around Isabela			
Cape Marshall (northeast)			*
Crossman Islands			*
Cuatro Hermanos (Crossman Islands)			*
Elizabeth Bay			*
El Triangulo (south Tortuga Island)			*
Islote Cowley (east)			*
Las Marielas (Elizabeth Bay)			*
La Viuda (south Villamil)			*
Punta Albermarle			*
Punta Moreno			*
Punta Moreno (west)			*
Punta Vicente Roca		*	*
Roca Blanca (Cartago Bay)			*
Roca Redonda			*
Roca Union (south)			*
Tagus Cove			*
Tortuga Island (south of Puerto Villamil)	*		*
WEST			
Fernandina			
Punta Espinosa	*		*
Cape Douglas			*
Cape Douglas (northwest)			*
Cape Hammond (southwest)			*
SOUTH			
Around Floreana			
Caldwell Island			*
Champion Island	*	*	*
Devil's Crown (Onslow)	*	*	*
Enderby Island			*
Frank's Finger Rock (west)			*
Gardner Island			*
Punta Cormorant (Olivine beach and rocks)		*	*
Roca Orca (southeast)			*
Around Española			
Gardner Bay (rocks)		*	*
Gardner Island			*
Punta Suarez	*	*	
Xarifa Island	*		*

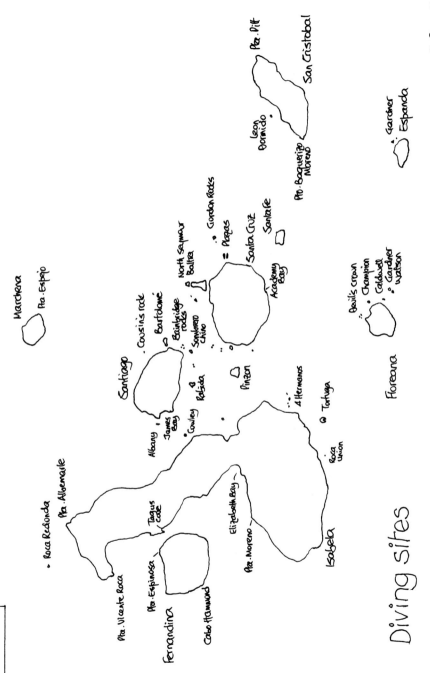

Diving sites

© Piroco 2002

Darwin

Wolf

Pinta

Marchena
Pta. Espejo

Roca Redonda
Pta. Albemarle

Pta. Vicente Roca

Fernandina
Pta. Espinosa

Cabo Hammond

Tagus Cove

Elizabeth Bay

Pta. Moreno

Isabela

Roca Redonda

Santiago
Cousins rock
Bartolome
Bainbridge rocks
Sombrero Chino
Rabida
Cowley
Albany
James Bay

Pinzon

4 Hermanos
Tortuga

Roca Union

North Seymour
Baltra
Gordon Rocks
Plazas
Santa Cruz
Santa Fe
Academy Bay

Leon Dormido
Pto. Baquerizo Moreno

Pta. Pitt
San Cristobal

Devil's crown
Champion
Caldwell
Gardner
Watson

Floreana

Gardner
Espanola

	SN	SK	DIV
OTHERS			
Guy Fawkes Island			*
Hancock Bank			*
McGovern Bank			*
Punta Bowditch (Conway Bay, Santa Cruz Island)	*	*	

MAPS OF DIVING SITES

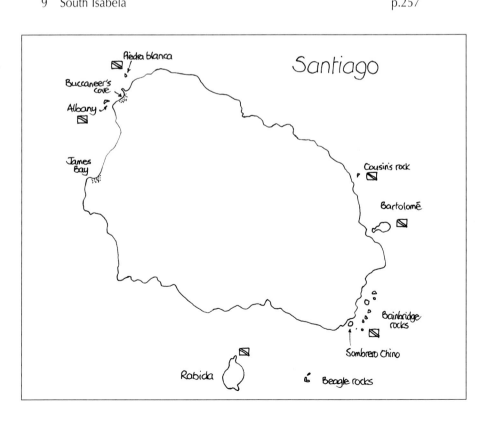

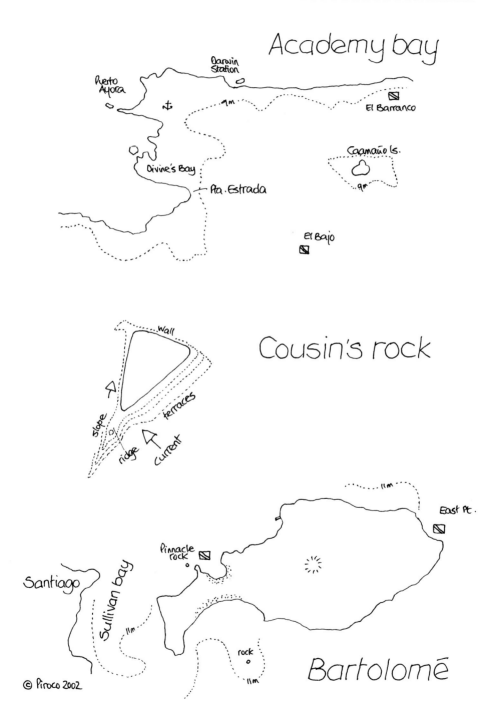

Academy bay

Darwin Station

Puerto Ayora

9m

El Barranco

Caamaño Is.

Divine's Bay

Pta. Estrada

9m

El Bajo

Cousin's rock

Wall

slope

ridge

terraces

current

11m

East Pt.

Pinnacle rock

Santiago

Sullivan bay

11m

rock

11m

Bartolomé

© Piroco 2002

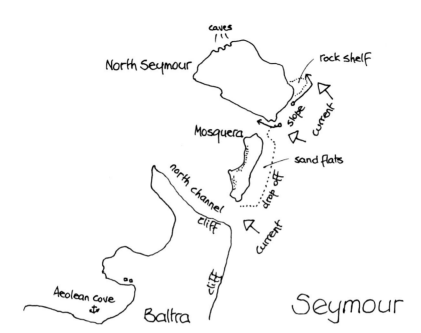

caves

North Seymour

rock shelf

slope

current

Mosquera

sand flats

north channel

drop off

cliff

current

cliff

Aeolean cove

Baltra

Seymour

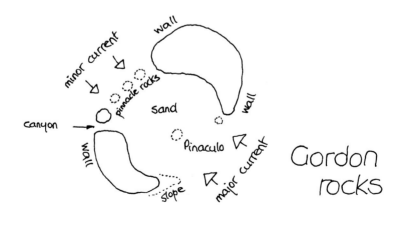

wall

minor current

pinnacle rocks

sand

wall

canyon

wall

Pinaculo

major current

slope

Gordon
rocks

© Piroco 2002

San Cristobal

Caleta Tortuga

Punta Pitt

Islote Pitt

Leon Dormido

Stephens Bay

Isla Lobos

Pto. Baquerizo Moreno

Bahia Rosa Blanca

Roca Este

Roca Ballena

Española

Pta. Suarez

Gardner
Osborn
Xarifa

Pta. Cevallos

Corona del diablo

Enderby
Champion

Floreana

Black Beach

Caldwell

Gardner

Watson

© Piroco 2002

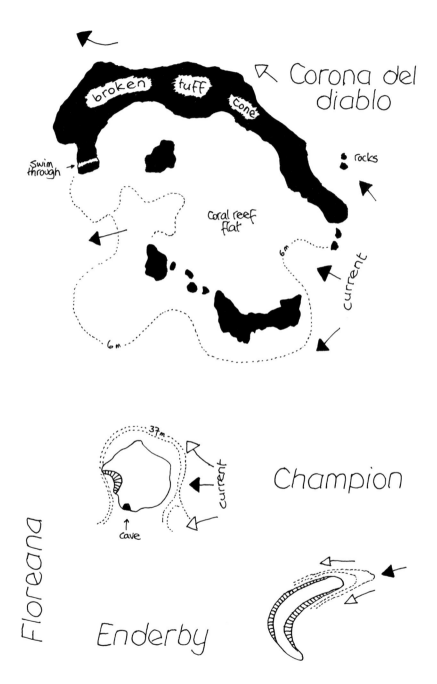

broken   tuff   cone

Corona del diablo

rocks

swim
through

Coral reef
flat

6 m

6 m

current

37 m

current

Champion

Floreana

cave

Enderby

© Piroco 2002

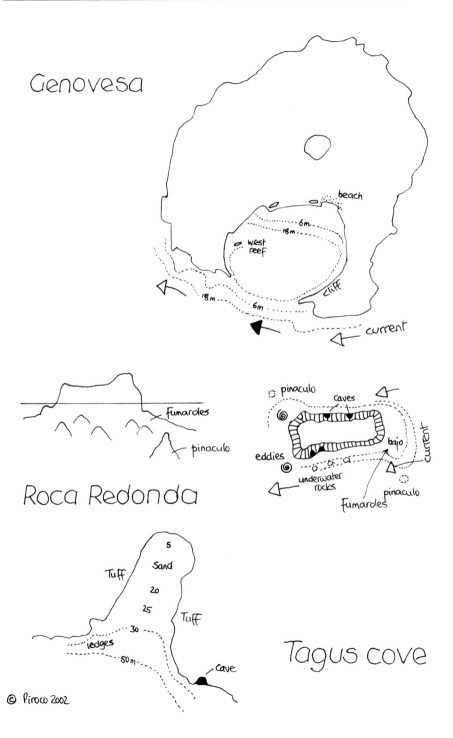

Genovesa

beach
6m.
18m
west reef
cliff
18m
6m
current

Roca Redonda

Fumaroles
pinaculo

pinaculo
caves
eddies
underwater rocks
Fumaroles
pinaculo
bajo
current

Tagus cove

Tuff
Sand
5
20
25
30
Tuff
ledges
50m
cave

© Piroco 2002

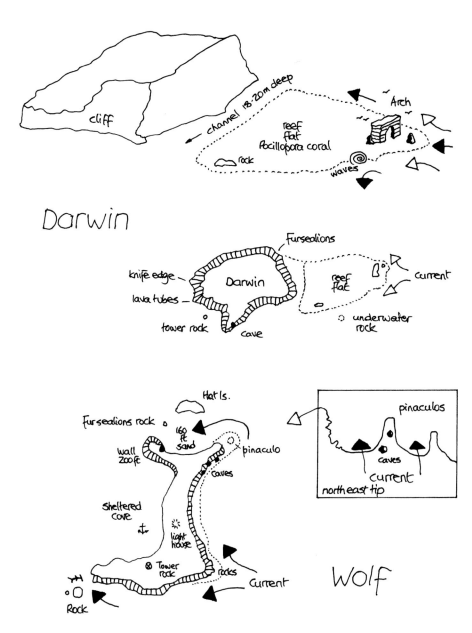

Darwin

Wolf

© Piraco 2002

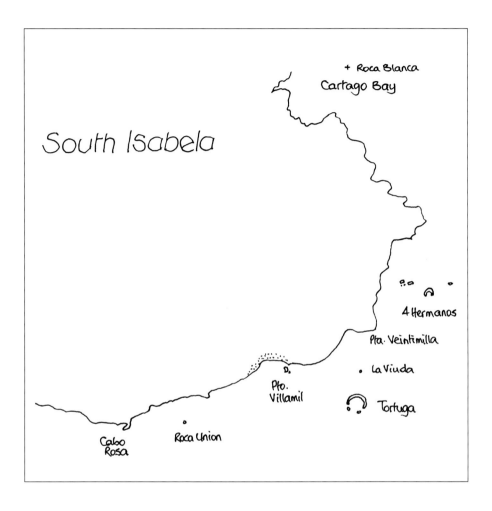

South Isabela

+ Roca Blanca
Cartago Bay

4 Hermanos

Pta. Veintimilla

La Viuda

Pto.
Villamil

Tortuga

Cabo
Rosa

Roca Union

THE GALÁPAGOS MARINE RESERVE

* MASTER PLAN * OBJECTIVES * HUMAN USE * ADMINISTRATION * ZONING * NORMS * MANAGEMENT PROGRAMS

THE 1998 MASTER PLAN

The first mention of a marine reserve of two miles around the Galápagos Islands dates back to 1974. In the following two years, Gerry Wellington, an American scientist and Peace Corps volunteer, studied the potential of a marine reserve between cold and warm waters. Twenty years of conflicts were to follow a first attempt at management.

In 1986, the Reserve of Marine Resources of Galápagos (RRMG), with a 15-mile extension, was created and involved seven entities, the so-called "7-headed monster" (Pippa Heylings, personal communication), composed of the Department of Energy, the Department of Foreign Relations, the National Counsel, the National Institute of Fisheries (INP), the Department of Industries, the Fisheries Department and the SPNG (Servicio Parque Nacional Galápagos).

Consequently, the first Master Plan was approved in 1992, but revisions were soon necessary. These led to a document, released in 1994, that compiled all agreements signed by the various sectors involved.

> 0–2 miles would be the artisanal fishing zone
> 2–5 miles would be the shark fishing and semi-industrial fishing zone
> 5–15 miles the industrial fishing zone

In 1996, many changes to the administrative structure of Ecuador influenced the management of the Marine Reserve. In October 1996, the new Ministerio del medio Ambiente (MMA) was created, the Department of the Environment, as executive authority for the environmental politics of Ecuador. The INEFAN or Instituto Nacional Ecuatoriano Forestal y Areas Naturales, formerly part of the MAG (Ministerio de Agricultura y Ganaderia) was integrated into the MMA and assigned the administration of protected areas of the state. In November of the same year, INEFAN took control of the RRMG and declared it a Biological Reserve, the administration of which would be the responsibility of the Galápagos National Park (formerly SPNG, renamed PNG in 1995).

This unilateral declaration was therefore killing the interests of other sectors previously involved. This meant a new restrictive use of the RRMG, where fishing was still allowed, but not to the satisfaction of these other parties. Abuses were soon being made as a show of discontentment by the fishermen. UNESCO then threatened to declare the

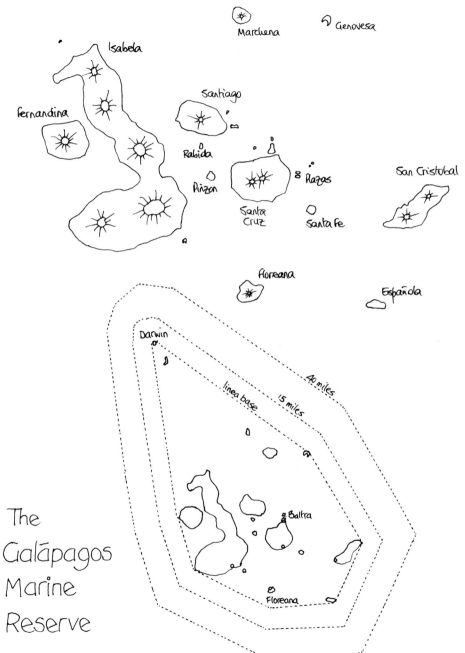

Pinta

Marchena

Genovesa

Isabela

Santiago

Fernandina

Rabida

Pinzon

Plazas

San Cristobal

Santa
Cruz

Santa Fe

Floreana

Española

Darwin

40 miles

linea base

15 miles

The
Galápagos
Marine
Reserve

Baltra

Floreana

© Pierre Constant 2002

Galápagos a World Heritage Site in danger of destruction. This was bad news for the Ecuadorian government, who had to act accordingly and quickly, before international funds were cut off.

In April 1997, the interim president Fabian Alarcon released Decreto #245 which launched the Autoridad de Manejo de la RRMG, a management authority presided over by the MMA, the sub-secretary of fisheries resources and DIGMER, the Direccion General de la Marina Mercante. An Interinstitutional Commission of Control and Vigilance (CICV), mentioned in the original 1992 Master Plan, was also formed. In May 1997, the leaders of the Cooperativas de Pesca Artesanal de Galápagos (Cooperative Fisheries) signed a document in front of the National Congress, which recognized the role of the PNG in the control and vigilance within the Galápagos Marine Reserve, but requesting that the control and exploitation of marine resources also involved the INP (National Institute of Fisheries), the Charles Darwin Research Station (CDRS) and PNG. The necessary revision of use of the RMG initiated a process of local participation to resolve the problems and conflicts among users, with the objective of a drawing up new Master Plan.

In June 1997, the Department of Environment instructed the Director of the Galápagos National Park to coordinate this process. A seminar was organized between June 5–7, which led to the formation of a so-called Grupo Nucleo (cell group), composed of the Tourism sector (Galápagos Chamber of Tourism and Asociacion de Guias), the Artisanal Fishing sector represented by the Cooperativas de Pesca of Santa Cruz and Cristobal (and Isabela in 1998), CDRS and PNG (el Jefe de la Unidad de Recursos Marinos in 1998), DIGMER, represented by the Port Captain of Santa Cruz and the subdirection of fisheries in the Galápagos.

The Grupo Nucleo worked for 15 months, with facilitators Felipe Cruz, Pippa Heylings and Rodrigo Jacome, and held a total of 74 meetings and three seminars. Finally, from an historical context of antagonism and incompatibilities regarding the use of the Marine Reserve, the situation concerning the management radically changed to consensus and collaboration. The formulation of the "Special Law for the Conservation and the Special Use of the Galápagos Province" directed by the Ministerio del Medio Ambiente, was approved in March 1998. The new Marine Reserve was created as a new category of protected area within the National Heritage of Pro tected Areas. Originally 15 miles, the Galápagos Marine Reserve was extended to 40 miles, excluding industrial fishing within the reserve zone.

THE CDF STRATEGIC PLAN 2006–2016

In the face of rapid change in the Galápagos and new and emerging challenges to the conservation of this World Heritage Site, in 2006 the Charles Darwin Foundation (CDF) launched a new ten-year Strategic Plan. It outlines the major hurdles that must be overcome if the Galápagos, a global icon of conservation and evolutionary history, is to be conserved for the world.

OBJECTIVES

The main objective of the 1998 Master Plan for the Galápagos Marine Reserve is as follows:

"To protect and conserve the marine coastal ecosystems of the archipelago and its biological diversity for the benefit of humanity, the local population, science and education."

SPECIFIC OBJECTIVES:
- Protect and conserve marine and coastal ecosystems to maintain evolutionary ecological process in the long run.
- Complement the protection of land biota by marine and coastal biota of the Galápagos ecosystems.
- Protect endemic marine and coastal species.
- Insure conservation and protection, also recuperation of populations of species of fisheries resources, which have great importance for commercial fishing.
- Facilitate the fact that Galápagos fishermen maintain and improve their socio-economic base, making sure of the realization of fishing activities compatible with biodiversity.
- Conserve marine coastal ecosystems as an economic base for tourism activities, with control of the environmental impact.
- Provide and promote scientific activities to increase knowledge of marine biodiversity, sites and species exploited and monitor the ecological impacts caused by human activities.
- Install a system of adaptive and participative management of the Galápagos Marine Reserve, which can use data collected, with the object of modifying the management according to updated information as well as to socio-economic and environmental considerations.
- Create and strengthen structures and financing through the Galápagos National Park for the function of the Junta de Manejo Participativo of the Galápagos Marine Reserve.
- Insure protection and conservation of the scenic values of the marine and coastal systems of the Galápagos.
- Establish basic scientific and technical requirements which insure environmental protection and conservation of the natural resources of the RMG and its sustainable development.

LAW

"Special Law for the Conservation and sustainable development of the Galápagos province."
(Law #67, Registro Oficial #278, 18 March 1998)

- Maintain the ecological systems and the biodiversity of the Galápagos province, especially native and endemic, and allow the evolutionary process under a minimal human interference, taking into consideration the genetic isolation between islands, and between the islands and the continent.
- Sustainable development and control of the capacity (to sustain pressure) of the ecosystems of the Galápagos province.
- Favoured participation of the local community in the development activities and in the economic benefits, within the structure of special models of production, education, formation and work.
- To reduce the risks of introduction of diseases, pests, species of plants and animals exotic to the Galápagos province.
- The quality of life of the residents of the Galápagos province must correspond to the exceptional characteristics of a World Heritage Site.
- To recognize the existing interactions between the inhabited zones and the marine and terrestrial protected areas, and therefore the need of an integrated management.
- A principle of care in the execution of works and activities which may cause damage to the environment or to the islands ecosystems.

HUMAN USE

Human use in the Galápagos Marine Reserve occurs in four main areas; artisanal fishing, marine tourism, scientific research and the navigation and maneuvers of the Ecuadorian Navy.

ARTISANAL FISHING

It all started with the hunting of whales and fur sea lions at the beginning of the 19th century. After the islands became colonized by Ecuador in 1832, fishing became a daily affair for the *colonos*, the pioneers. Industrial fishing has continued since the 1940s, not only by Ecuadorian boats, but also by international fleets from the United States, Panama, Costa Rica and Japan, which were primarily interested in tuna. Although these boats were a source of communication and business for the early settlers, most operations were clandestine and furtive. In the 1950s, Ecuador officially claimed a 200-mile exclusive zone as territorial waters to protect its rights against foreign abuses. Purse seine and long line fishing boats arrived in the 1970s. In 1985, Ecuador initiated a program which authorized Japanese and Taiwanese long liners to operate in national waters under the

Ecuadorian flag. But this program was terminated in 1996. When the American Navy base was established in Baltra (around 1940), it boosted the economy for the fishermen of Santa Cruz and San Cristobal, because they provided fresh fish for the US military. Towards the end of the 1940s, the Sociedad Pesquera de Galápagos (known as La Predial) started operations in San Cristobal, and *Rose Marie* the first Ecuadorian tuna boat took loads of fish to the nearby continent. Due to bad management, this company collapsed in 1955. Some American industrial fishing boats, *Lucy* and *Jane* began working in the Galápagos at the beginning of the 1960s and brought prosperity to the island. A new fleet of twenty 30-foot boats operating from San Cristobal in 1970 to 1972, increased the profits. Four large boats from Panama, *Beatriz, Codiakk, Chicuzen Maru* and *Patao*, came to the islands to buy fishing products.

Fishing operations diminished in the 1980s due to the sudden boom of tourism, which diverted some of the fishermen from their usual line of business. Around the mid-1980s, lobster fishing techniques included the technology of diving with compressed air. Fishermen soon became organized into Cooperativas, catching fresh fish for local consumption, lobsters for exportation and 'seco salado' or salted dry fish for the continent. Favorite species were *lisa* and *bacalao*.

In the last 20 years, new fisheries opened: pepinos or sea cucumbers, tuna in pelagic waters and shark fins (illegally). The number of boats and fishermen increased tremendously between 1997 and 2000, from 270 to 341 boats and from 457 to 682 registered fishermen, between the three islands of Santa Cruz, San Cristobal and Isabela. (after Informe 1999–2000, Fundacion Natura, Quito).

MARINE TOURISM
Marine tourism started in 1969, with cruises around the islands and occasional snorkeling. Scuba diving gradually became more popular during the 1980s. Commercial and recreational tourism soon led to different options to discover the Galápagos Islands.
- 'Tour Navegable' is the classical cruise around the islands, to both the National Park and the Marine Reserve, where passengers sleep on the boat.
- 'Tour Diario' is a day trip, where the visitors do not sleep on board, but return to a port.
- 'Tour de Bahia y Buceo', also a day trip, where visitors can dive as well, then return to port.
- Other activities related to marine tourism involve: sea kayaking, surfing and sailing. The proposed activity of 'sport fishing' was banned in 2005.

SCIENCE
Following Charles Darwin's visit in 1835, a number of scientific expeditions out of Europe or the United States came to the Galápagos: Hopkins Stanford Galápagos Expeditions 1898–99; William Beebe 1924; Allan Hancock Pacific Expeditions 1932–38. Then the Charles Darwin Research Station (CDRS) became active in 1964 and was followed by the

establishment of the Galápagos National Park (SPNG) in 1972. Gerard Wellington came between 1973 and 1975 to help CDRS and SPNG with the evaluation of the marine environment.

In the 1980s, research was mainly done by the Instituto Nacional de Pesca (INP) and the CDRS. Cooperative work was also done by the Instituto Oceanographico de la Armada (INOCAR) and CDRS.

Since the 2000s, the marine laboratory "Biomar" of the Charles Darwin Research Station, has been actively taking responsibility for all research programs. In December 2003, the 'Area de Investigacion y Conservacion Marina' of the Darwin Foundation together with the Galápagos National Park, published a 140-page document on 'El Turismo en la Reserva Marina de Galápagos', under the direction of the Department Head, Eva Danulat. During July–August 2005, Mathias Espinosa and Jaime Navas worked as consultants for the Galápagos National Park, on the elaboration of new Rules and Regulations for diving in the Galápagos Marine Reserve. However, nothing came out of it and a year later, nothing has been implemented.

ECUADORIAN NAVY AND AIRFORCE

The *Armada del Ecuador* has been present in the islands since the 1920s. The Galápagos archipelago was later declared *Segunda Zona Naval* on the 14th of February 1958. Port captains are now found on the five inhabited islands of Santa Cruz, San Cristobal, Seymour, Isabela and Floreana.

The Instituto Oceanografico de la Armada (INOCAR) has helped the navigation in the islands with the installation of buoys and lighthouses, also by providing actualized marine charts for the use of fishing and tourist boats, as well as for the merchant marine. The 2nd Naval Zone conducts operations known as Search and Rescue (SAR) complying therefore with its function of rescue, coordination center of the insular region and saving lives of people lost at sea. Other operations involve aeromaritime explorations such as reconnaissance, vigilance, patrol, search (Rebusca), identification and pursuit. Through the various Capitanias de Puerto (Port Captains), the Direction of the Merchant Marine (DIGMER) ensures the rules and regulations are applied to guarantee navigation in its respective areas.

Civic actions of a medical nature are also provided by the Ecuadorian navy to take care of the well being of the population in isolated locations.

The Ecuadorian navy regularly conducts operations such as rescue, logistics and help to the community, instruction, antideliquency and control of illicit activities. The Galápagos Marine Reserve is an area of 133,000 square kilometers within the 40-mile exclusion zone. The Ecuadorian navy is the only legal authority able to arrest and capture illegal boats. The Galápagos National Park has no jurisdiction in the matter. A naturalist guide has no right to come aboard a suspicious boat, unless given permission by the captain or skipper. By law, a cargo boat has to navigate 60 miles off the Galápagos archipelago.

A radar base with a 96-mile radius is located in the Bolivar Channel (west Isabela).

Other bases are scheduled for Punta Albemarle (north Isabela), Puerto Villamil (south Isabela) and Progreso (San Cristobal) within the next four years, and should have been operational by 2005. The headquarters and main communication center is now based in Puerto Ayora (Santa Cruz) where the information is collected.

Illicit activities include illegal fishing, drug trafficking between boats, as well as smuggling people using so-called *coyoteros*, the boats involved in the illegal transport of people towards the United States. The most famous stowaway was the former Peruvian minister Montesinos in 2000, who arrived one night in Puerto Villamil on a private yacht asking for a room. Fishing aboard a tourist boat is now prohibited in the visitors' sites in between the islands.

A new officer in charge of Control and Vigilance is now posted at the Galápagos National Park office in Puerto Ayora. For any reports of illegal boats or suspicious activities contact: Ramiro Morejon, Control y Vigilancia (PNG), mobile: (09) 219950.

The Ecuadorian navy has recently created a Comando de Operaciones Insular, based on San Cristobal. It has a Corvette, an helicopter and a Beechcraft airplane to carry out detection and maritime exploration. The SPNG boat *Tiburon Martillo* will take care of the Control and Vigilance of Darwin Island in the far north of the archipelago. It was sponsored by the company Galamazonas (*Aggressor* fleet) and Jean Michel Cousteau.

The Ecuadorian airforce is based on San Cristobal, Isabela and Baltra. It takes care of the control and operations of the respective airports.

Definitions
(SAR): to provide personnel and assistance to people and properties in danger.
(RCC): Rescue Coordination Center: to carry on functions of SAR within the different regions.
(EAM) (ES): Aeromaritime and superficial explorations are control and vigilance by air or by sea, to detect with anticipation or in an opportunistic manner, the presence of units involved in illicit activities.
(Rebusca): Vigilance by air or sea to bring into evidence a contact within a definite area, with previous information or suspicion of being, which actual position or intent is unknown.
(Seguimiento): Operation with the aim of permanent control over one or many contacts. The efficiency of the monitoring is measured by the capacity of the means used, to obtain and report the information.

ADMINISTRATION AND MANAGEMENT

AIM (AUTORIDAD INTERINSTITUCIONAL DE MANEJO)
The highest authority in charge of the RMG (ie. politics and jurisdiction at government level) is the Autoridad Interinstitucional de Manejo (AIM). It is the executive body that approves or negates the Master Plan, makes sure that it is applied and distributes the

resources assigned to the Galápagos Marine Reserve. It also approves the calendar of fisheries, volumes, dimensions, species and fishing techniques allowed in the islands. And finally, it allows participative studies and scientific investigations with the purpose of improving the politics of conservation and development of marine fisheries.

The AIM is composed of seven members:

* The Department of Environment
* The Department of National Defense
* The Department of International Trade, Industries and Fisheries
* The Department of Tourism
* The Galápagos Chamber of Tourism
* The Conservation, Science and Education Sector of the Galápagos province
* The Artisanal fishing sector of the Galápagos province

The Director of PNG acts as technical secretary of the AIM, having the responsibility of administration and managment of the RMG. It also coordinates actions with the Ecuadorian Navy for control and patrol; with the Subsecretary of Fishing Resources for the correct exploitation of marine resources; with the INP/INOCAR for programs of research and monitoring.

JUNTA DE MANEJO PARTICIPATIVO (JMP)

The JMP is the instance of participation of the users of the RMG which, in cooperation with the Direction of PNG has the power to put into effect the participation and responsability of the users in the management of the area. Decisions are followed in this manner: the JMP analyzes and decides the viability of the proposal; the PNG or the AIM approves or negates.

The JMP is composed of four members:

* delegate of the Artisanal Fishing sector
* delegate of the Galápagos Chamber of Tourism
* delegate of CDRS
* delegate of PNG

Among the general attributes of the Junta de Manejo Participativo (Junta of Participative Managment), these are some significant issues:

• to analyze and propose modifications to the Master Plan
• to analyze and propose revision of the Zonification of the RMG
• to insure the realization of studies related to the environmental impact, within the RMG
• to coordinate the participation of the users
• to promote development of the educational and scientific use of the Marine Reserve
• to analyze and propose new activities
• elaboration and proposal to reforms of the laws

(cf. *Organigram of Functions of the Galápagos Marine Reserve*)

Zoning

As a means of managment, zonification helps to protect different areas of the Galápagos Marine Reserve. This has the effect to normalize and regulate human activities, including the use of resources, as well as to conserve and protect the biodiversity. Eventually, to sustain the economic benefits of the RMG.

Zonification is in no way a rigid concept, for both the JMP and the Director of PNG will make changes that will be approved by the AIM, ideally and logically for a better managment of the RMG. Four zones are considered: tourism, fishing, science and education. A general distinction is made between multiple use zones and limited use zones. The first category concerns deep open waters, inside or outside the Linea base (first imaginery perimeter around the islands). The limited use zones are better defined into three sections:

Zona de Exclusion (five percent)
Also known as Subzone of Comparison and Protection, this zone serves as test or control area, to study ecology and biodiversity in the absence of human impact. Only science and education will be allowed here.

Zona de Uso no Extractivo (18 percent)
Also known as Subzone of Conservation and non-extractive use, it relates to aquatic tourism, but also science, conservation and education. In this zone snorkeling, diving, *panga* rides and whale watching from boats are permitted.

Zona de Extraccion (77 percent)
Known as Subzone of Conservation and Extractive use, it involves artisanal fishing, education, science, tourism, patrol, SAR and military manoeuvres.

Finally, on the top of these zones, some areas could be temporarily managed with the purpose of experiments or recuperation (regeneration). For example, if an area has suffered damage from over-exploitation or contamination, then it may be protected for some time. This case has occurred for the fishing of *pepinos* and lobsters.

However, Camillo Martinez, an Ecuadorian scientist from the CDRS thinks that 25 percent of the zonification should be kept for scientific investigation and other purposes. The 1998 Master Plan stipulates that after the first two years, in 2001, the JMP will present a report to the AIM, on the initial effects of the zonification, bearing recommendations for the next two years. Once the zonification is definitive, monitoring will go on to evaluate and revise the zonification if necesary, as part of the objective of the Master Plan.

NORMS

Fishing techniques forbidden in the RMG
- with explosives
- with chemicals (natural or synthetic)
- oceanic and drifting nets
- *Trasmallo* or passive nets
- submarine pistols, harpoons, with compressed air

Requirements to be a fisherman and to practice artisanal fishing in the RMG
- to be a permanent resident
- to be affiliated to a cooperative legally bound to the Special Law of Galápagos
- to have the license of DIGMER
- to have the license of PARMA (Pescador Artisanal de la Reserva Marina de Galápagos)

Tourist activities forbidden in the RMG
- water skiing
- jet ski or motorized skiing
- other motorized artefacts that may cause environmental impact
- subaquatic fishing or fishing from tourist boats

Requirements to offer scuba diving
- a guide licensed by PNG, with international Divemaster certification for every eight divers
- license of DIGMER
- personnel trained in the use and maintenance of compressors and first aid
- dive tourists should present minimum level of diving with international certification Open Water Diver
- minimum equipment of first aid and communication
- oxygen on board
- in case of big boats, a *panga* is needed for each dive guide
- international dive flag should be present on dive sites

Scientific activities forbidden or subject to specific rules
- bioprospection studies will be permitted only if impact on the ecosystem is minimum
- mining or search for minerals for commercial exploitation
- handling without ethics or abuses of organisms
- transplant or change of species between islands
- realization of studies which imply ecological impact, non-justifiable in its scientific or practical value

Requirements for scientific activities
- institutions or individuals must have prior authorization from PNG, based on technical and scientific criteria defined by PNG/CDRS
- all visiting scientists must provide two copies of their project to PNG. Two copies of their publication will be given to CDRS library
- a proper authorization from PNG will be needed for any collection of specimen from the Marine Reserve. The approval should be granted for taxonomic identification

MANAGEMENT PROGRAMS

* Administration and Direction
* Research and Monitoring
* Control and Vigilance
* Environmental education and Communication

In the sub-program of administration and managment which insures proper financing of the RMG, as well as the necesary infrastructure and equipment, the consequent activities include:
- insure that the percentage of the entrance fee to the Galápagos National Park assigned to the RMG, actually reverts to the managment of the latter
- guarantee funds for the conservation and development of the Galápagos
- maintain actualized marine charts
- issue licenses for naturalist dive guides
- issue licenses for the artisanal fishermen of Galápagos
- provide fishing permits for boats
- provide permits for boats which offer scuba diving
- issue authorizations for commercial, educative or scientific filming, in accordance to regulations
- realization of private external audits
- judge and sanction infractions perpetuated in the RMG

RULES AND REGULATIONS FOR DIVING IN THE GALÁPAGOS MARINE RESERVE

Following the first Naturalist Dive Guide's course for the Galápagos Marine Reserve held in Puerto Ayora, Santa Cruz, by the Galápagos National Park, from July 9 to 27, 2001, a set of proposed rules and regulations has been drawn up by the 20 guides present. The author attended the course, sharing his views, as did quite a few 'old timers'.

- The dive guide has to be a recognized Dive Master with a minimum of 100 dives and an adequate experience of diving in the Galápagos.

- The dive guide has to know the dive sites before taking tourists to dive. He has to be trained by experienced dive guides, who have experience of difficult and potentially dangerous dive sites in the Galápagos. A dive guide with clients cannot dive a site he does not know.
- The dive guide must master the English language and must be able to give a proper dive briefing in English prior to the dive.
- The dive guide must have a good physical and psychological condition, as well as good air consumption.
- The dive guide must show example and enforce the rules of not touching and not feeding fish and marine life. He shall also follow the rules himself. No collection of shells, corals or marine life is allowed. Scientists may be an exception to this rule, but only with prior approval and with a permit from the Galápagos National Park and not during a tourist dive cruise. They will have to comply with the requirements of their scientific occupation and whereabouts.
- In order to avoid erosion or destruction of the marine environment the diver will be required to master and practice neutral buoyancy, so as not to kick the bottom, corals or gorgonians.
- The dive guide has to have a good knowledge of the marine fauna and flora as an underwater naturalist. Likewise, he shall know about cleaning stations, marine life interactions, symbiotic relationships etc.
- The dive guide must have a basic knowledge of underwater photography and video, in order to provide suggestions during briefings. However, the guide should keep in mind and be aware that his personal use of photography or video, although not expressly forbidden, may jeopardize the care and safety of the dive tourists.
- The dive guide should evaluate individually the level of all divers before the dive, keep an eye on problematic divers, take care of weak or poorly experienced divers underwater.
- Because diving in the Galápagos is hazardous due to currents and other potential risks factors, a minimum level of Advanced Open Water Diver (or equivalent) is required from dive tourists on a diving cruise.
- The dive guide will strive to return to the surface with the group, but he has no obligation to do so if circumstances or emergency situations require otherwise. However, the guide will make sure that all divers are back on the boat, safe and sound, before sailing off.
- Divers should wear a proper wetsuit (5 to 7mm), have a regulator with octopus, carry a safety sausage and a whistle on all dives, or alternatively a dive flag or dive alert, in the unfortunate event of getting lost.

DIVE BRIEFINGS

- Mention emergency equipment and their location on board: DANO2 oxygen tank, first aid kit etc.
- Mention the hyperbaric chamber in Puerto Ayora.
- Have all divers sign the liability release and show proof of dive insurance.
- Encourage the practise of buddy teams.
- Mention that a dive briefing will be given at every dive site.
- Be clear on the maximum depth of the dive: PADI < 40 meters, *Agressor* fleet: 110ft, Galápagos average: 30 meters. Anything deeper is out of the guide's responsibility.
- Nobody should return to the surface with less than 500 PSI or 40 bars.
- Maximum time of one hour per dive.
- Compulsory safety stop of three minutes at five meters, with visual contact with the rocks, cliff or *bajo*.
- No decompression diving in the Galápagos recommended.
- If lost in the blue, divers should be back to the surface in three minutes, except for Darwin Arch where one should exit straight away before being carried away by strong currents.
- If current is too strong, cancel the dive.
- Review of international signals, signals between diver and *pangero*.
- Each diver should check his own air at all times during the dive.
- Regulator and console should be kept close to the body.
- Roll over from the *panga* in a synchronized manner.
- Immerse with your buddy straight away.
- At the end of a dive, inflate BCD at the surface.
- Teach the *pangero* to retrieve camera from diver at the end of the dive, and how to pull tanks properly out of the water without grabbing the first stage or the hoses.

APPENDIX

LIST OF GALÁPAGOS FISHES, WHALES, DOLPHINS AND MARINE INVERTEBRATES

Reference to color photographs	Photo:	Yes	No	Page
Cornetfishes, Trumpetfishes, Pipefishes				
Reef cornetfish	*Fistularia commersonii*	x		49
Trumpetfish	*Aulostomus chinensis*	x		49
Fantail pipefish	*Doryrhampus melanopleura*		x	
Pacific seahorse	*Hippocampus ingens*	x		50
Needlefishes, Halfbeaks, Flyingfishes				
Pike needlefish	*Strongylura exilis*	x		50
Halfbeak	*Hyporhampus unifasciatus*	x		51
Ribbon halfbeak	*Euleptorhamphus longirostris*		x	
Longfin halfbeak	*Hemirhampus saltator*		x	
Sharpchin flyingfish	*Fodiator acutus*		x	
Flyingfish	*Cheilopogon dorsomaculata*		x	
Flyingfish	*Exocoetus monocirrhus*	x		51
Flyingfish	*Prognichthys seali*		x	
Parrotfishes, Wrasses				
Blue chin parrotfish	*Scarus ghobban*	x		51–2
Bumphead parrotfish	*Scarus perrico*	x		52
Bicolor parrotfish	*Scarus rubroviolaceus*	x		52–3
Azure parrotfish	*Scarus compressus*	x		53
Mexican hogfish	*Bodianus diplotaenia*	x		53–4
Harlequin wrasse	*Bodianus eclancheri*	x		55
Cortez rainbow wrasse	*Thalassoma grammaticum*	x		56
Green wrasse	*Thalassoma lutescens*	x		56
Chameleon wrasse	*Halichoeres dispilus*	x		57
Spinster wrasse	*Halichoeres nicholsi*	x		57
Dragon wrasse	*Novaculichthys taeniourus*	x		58
Banded wrasse	*Liopropoma fasciatum*	x		58
Galápagos sheephead	*Semicossyphus darwinii*	x		58–9
Pacific beakfish, Tigris	*Oplegnathus insigne*	x		59

	Photo:	Yes	No	Page
Surgeonfishes, Angelfishes, Damselfishes, Butterflyfishes				
Yellow tail surgeonfish	*Prionurus laticlavius*	x		59
White tail surgeonfish	*Acanthurus glaucopareius*	x		60
Yellow fin surgeonfish	*Acanthurus xanthopterus*	x		60
Convict tang	*Acanthurus triostegus*	x		60
Moorish idol	*Zanclus canescens*	x		61
King angelfish	*Holocanthus passer*	x		61
Barberfish	*Heniochus nigrirostris*	x		61–2
Scythe butterflyfish	*Chaetodon falcifer*	x		62
Three-band butterflyfish	*Chaetodon humeralis*	x		62
Meyer's butterflyfish	*Chaetodon meyeri*	x		63
Racoon butterflyfish	*Chaetodon lunula*		x	
Threadfin butterflyfish	*Chaetodon auriga*		x	
Panama sergeant major	*Abudefduf troschelli*	x		63
Dusky sergeant	*Abudefduf concolor*	x		63
Rusty dameselfish	*Nexilosus latifrons*		x	
Yellow tail damselfish	*Eupomacentrus arcifrons*	x		64
Acapulco damselfish	*Eupomacentrus acapulcoensis*	x		64
Galápagos whitetail damsel	*Stegastes leucorus beebei*	x		64
Giant damselfish	*Microspathodon dorsalis*	x		81
Bumphead damselfish	*Microspathodon bairdii*	x		81
White spot chromis	*Chromis atrilobata*	x		82
White-striped chromis	*Chromis alta*	x		82
Black spot chromis	*Azurina eupalama*		x	
Puffers, Porcupinefishes, Boxfishes				
Galápagos pufferfish	*Spheroïdes angusticeps*	x		84
Concentric pufferfish	*Spheroïdes annulatus*	x		82
Guineafowl puffer	*Arothron meleagris*	x		83
White-spotted puffer	*Arothron hispidus*	x		83
Spotted sharp-nosed puffer	*Canthigaster punctatissima*	x		84
Balloonfish	*Diodon holocanthus*	x		84
Porcupinefish	*Diodon hystrix*		x	
Galápagos blue porcupinefish	*Chilomycterus affinis galapagoensis*	x		85
Pacific boxfish	*Ostracion meleagris*	x		85–6
Triggerfishes, Filefishes				
Yellow-bellied triggerfish	*Sufflamen verres*	x		86
Black triggerfish	*Melichthys niger*	x		86
Pink tail triggerfish	*Melichthys vidua*		x	

		Photo:	*Yes*	*No*	*Page*
Blunthead triggerfish	*Pseudobalistes naufragium*		x		87
Finescale triggerfish	*Balistes polyepsis*		x		87
Red tail triggerfish	*Xanthichthys mento*		x		87
Blue-striped triggerfish	*Xanthichthys caeruleolineatus*		x		88
Scrawled filefish	*Aluterus scriptus*		x		88

Blennies, Tube blennies, Labrisomid blennies, Gobies

		Yes	*No*	*Page*
Large banded blenny	*Ophioblennius steindachneri*	x		88
Sabretooth blenny	*Plagiotremus azaleus*	x		89
Barnacle blenny	*Acanthemblemaria castroii* (E)	x		89
Galápagos four-eyed blenny	*Dialommus fuscus* (E)		x	
Cheekspot labrisomid	*Labrisomus dentriticus* (E)	x		89–90
Large mouth blenny	*Labrisomus xanti*		x	
Jenkins clinid	*Labrisomus jenkinsi* (E)		x	
Porehead blenny	*Labrisomus multiporosus*		x	
Galápagos triplefin blenny	*Lepidonectes corallicola* (E)	x		90
Spotblenny goby	*Malacoctenus zonogaster* (E)		x	
Afuera goby	*Malacocotenus afuerae*		x	
Throatspotted blenny	*Malacoctenus tetranemus* (E)		x	
Galápagos blenny	*Starksia galapagensis* (E)		x	
Orange brotula	*Ogibia deroyi* (E)		x	
Pink brotula	*Ogilbia galapagoensis* (E)		x	
Tagus goby, mystery goby	*Chriolepis tagus* (E)		x	
Blackeye goby	*Coryphopterus urospilus*		x	
Galápagos sleeper	*Eleotrica cableae* (E)		x	
Galápagos blue-banded goby	*Lythrypnus gilberti* (E)	x		90
Goby species	*Lythryphus rizophora*		x	
Tailspot brotula	*Calamopteryx jeb*		x	

Groupers, Seabasses, Grunts, Mojarras, Snappers, Seachubs

		Yes	*No*	*Page*
Flag cabrilla	*Epinephelus labriformis*	x		91
Spotted cabrilla grouper	*Epinephelus analogus*		x	
Panama graysby	*Epinephelus panamensis*	x		91
Mutton hamlet	*Epinephelus afer*	x		91
Leather bass	*Epinephelus dermatolepis*	x		92
Misty grouper, mero	*Epinephelus mystacinus* (E)		x	
Bacalao, yellow grouper	*Mycteroperca olfax*	x		93
Bacalao, yellow grouper	*Mycteroperca olfax* (yellow phase)	x		93
Gray threadfin seabass, plumero	*Cratinus agassizi*	x		93
Camotillo, white-spotted seabass	*Paralabrax albomaculatus*	x		94
Barred serrano	*Serranus fasciatus*	x		94

	Photo:	Yes	No	Page
Creolefish	*Paranthias colonus*	x		94–5
Cortez soapfish	*Rypticus bicolor*	x		95
Gray grunt	*Haemulon scudderi*	x		95
Forbes grunt	*Orthopristis forbesi*	x		96
Yellowtail grunt	*Anisotremus interruptus*	x		96
Graybar grunt	*Haemulon sexfasciatum*	x		96, 113
Brassy grunt	*Orthopristis chalceus*	x		113
Peruvian grunt	*Anisotremus scapularis*	x		113
Black-striped salema	*Xenocys jessiae*	x		114
White salema	*Xenichthys agassizi*	x		114
Pacific flagfin mojarra	*Eucinostomus californiensis*		x	
Spotfin mojarra	*Eucinostomus argenteus*		x	
Yellowfin mojarra	*Gerres cinereus*		x	
Blue and gold snapper	*Lutjanus viridis*	x		114
Yellowtail snapper	*Lutjanus argentiventris*	x		115
Mullet snapper	*Lutjanus aratus*	x		115
Pacific dog snapper	*Lutjanus novemfasciatus*		x	
Jordan snapper	*Lutjanus jordani*		x	
Spindle snapper	*Lutjanus inermis*	x		115
Dusky chub	*Girella fremenvillei*	x		116
Cortez chub	*Kyphosus elegans*	x		116
Blue bronze chub	*Kyphosus analogus*		x	
Rainbow chub	*Sector ocyurus*	x		116
Shiner perch	*Cymatogaster aggregata*		x	

Squirrelfishes, Bigeyes, Cardinalfishes

		Yes	No	Page
Crimson soldierfish	*Myripristis leiognathos*	x		117
Big scale soldierfish	*Myripristis berndti*		x	
Sun squirrelfish	*Sargocentron suborbitalis*		x	
Tinsel squirrelfish	*Adyorix suborbitalis*	x		117
Glasseye	*Priacanthus cruentatus*	x		117
Popeye catalufa	*Pseudopriacanthus serrula*	x		118
Pink cardinalfish	*Apogon pacificus*	x		118
Blacktip cardinalfish	*Apogon atradorsatus*	x		118–9
Tail spot cardinalfish	*Apogon dovii*	x		119

Scorpionfishes, Hawkfishes

		Yes	No	Page
Stone scorpionfish	*Scorpaena plumieri mystes*		x	120
Rainbow scorpionfish	*Scorpaenodes xyris*	x		120
Bandfin scorpionfish	*Scorpaena histrio*		x	

		Photo:	Yes	No	Page
Red scorpionfish	*Pontinus furcirhinus*			x	
Stalkeye scorpionfish	*Pontinus strigatus*		x		121
Hieroglyphic hawkfish	*Cirrhitus rivulatus*		x		121
Coral hawkfish	*Cirrhitichthys oxycephalus*		x		122
Longnose hawkfish	*Oxycirrhites typus*		x		122

Goatfishes, Searobins, Lizardfishes

Galápagos searobin	*Prionotus miles* (E)		x		119
Mexican goatfish	*Mulloïdichthys dentatus*		x		123
Sauro lizardfish	*Synodus lacertinus*		x		123
Spotted lizardfish	*Synodus scituliceps*			x	
Lizardfish	*Synodus jenkinsii*			x	
Marchena lizardfish	*Synodus marchenae* (E)			x	

Anchovies, Herrings, Remoras, Silversides

Anchovy	*Anchoa naso*			x	
Galápagos thread herring	*Opisthonema berlangai* (E)		x		124
Peruvian Pacific sardine	*Sardinops sagax sagax*			x	
Remora, sharksucker	*Remora remora*		x		124
Silverside	*Eurystole eriarcha*			x	
Silverside	*Nectarges nesiotes* (E)			x	

Porgies, Bonefishes, Tilefishes, Dolphins

Pacific porgy	*Calamus brachysomus*			x	
Galápagos porgy	*Calamus taurinus*		x		147
Galápagos seabrim	*Archosargus pourtalesi*		x		147
Bonefish	*Albula vulpes*			x	
Tarpon	*Elops affinis*		x		148
Ocean whitefish	*Caulolatilus princeps*		x		145
Dolphinfish	*Coryphaena hippurus*		x		145

Jacks, Pompanos

Gafftopsail pompano	*Trachinotus rhodopus*			x	
Paloma pompano	*Trachinotus paitensis*			x	
Steel pompano	*Trachinotus stilbe*		x		125
African pompano	*Alectis ciliaris*		x		125
Green jack	*Caranx caballus*		x		126
Pacific crevalle jack	*Caranx caninus*			x	
Black jack	*Caranx lugubris*		x		126
Gold-spotted jack	*Carangoïdes orthogrammus*			x	

	Photo:	Yes	No	Page
Big eye jack	Caranx sexfasciatus	x		126
Horse eye jack	Caranx latus		x	
Bluefin jack	Caranx melampygus	x		127
Tille jack	Caranx tille	x		127
Rainbow runner	Elagatis bipinnulatus	x		127
Almaco amberjack	Seriola rivoliana	x		128
Yellow tail amberjack	Seriola lalandei	x		128
Big eye scad	Selar crumenophthalmus		x	
Yellowtail scad	Decapterus santae helenae	x		128
Mexican scad	Decapterus muroadsi		x	

Barracudas, Mackerels, Tunas, Swordfishes, Marlins, Sunfishes

	Photo:	Yes	No	Page
Pelican barracuda	Sphyraena idiastes	x		124
Wahoo	Acanthocybium solanderi	x		145
Sierra mackerel	Scomberomorus sierra	x		146
Pacific bonito	Sarda chilensis		x	
Oriental bonito	Sarda orientalis	x		146
Skipjack tuna	Euthynnus pelamis	x		146
Black skipjack	Euthynnus lineatus		x	
Yellowfin tuna	Thunnus albacares	x		147
Albacora	Thunnus alalunga		x	
Bigeye tuna	Thunnus obesus		x	
Chub mackerel	Scomber japonicus		x	
Ocean sunfish	Mola mola	x		148
School of Tarpon	Elops affinis	x		148
Swordfish	Xiphias gladius		x	
Pacific sailfish	Istiophorus platypterus		x	
Black marlin	Makaira indica		x	
Striped marlin	Makaira mazara		x	

Croakers, Drums, Mullets, Snooks

	Photo:	Yes	No	Page
Galápagos rock croaker	Pareques perissa		x	
Wide eye croaker	Odontoscion eurymesops		x	
Galápagos croaker	Umbrina galapagorum		x	
Striped mullet, blacktail mullet	Mugil cephalus	x		149
Orange-eyed mullet	Xenomugil thoburni		x	
Galápagos mullet, lisa	Mugil galapagensis	x		149
Snook	Centropomus nigrescens		x	

	Photo:	Yes	No	Page
Batfishes, Frogfishes				
Red-lipped batfish	Ogcocephalus darwinii	x		149–50
Sanguine frogfish	Antennarius sanguineus	x		150
Bandtail frogfish	Antennarius strigatus		x	
Galápagos batfish	Dibranchus species		x	
Flounder, Soles, Tonguefishes				
Bigmouth sanddab	Citharichthys gilberti		x	
Speckled sanddab	Citharichthys stigmaeus		x	
Blue-eyed flounder	Bothus mancus	x		150
Leopard flounder	Bothus leopardinus	x		151
Striped sole	Achirus fonsecensis		x	
Reticulated sole	Aseraggodes herrei	x		151
Rainbow tonguefish	Symphurus atramentatus	x		151
Morays, Snake eels, Conger eels, Freshwater eels				
Hardtail moray	Anarchias galapagensis		x	
Blackspot moray, hourglass moray	Muraena clepsydra	x		152
Panamic green moray	Muraena castaneus	x		152
Jewel moray, lentil moray	Muraena lentiginosa	x		153
Fine-spotted moray	Gymnothorax dovii	x		153
Unidentified moray		x		153
Magnificent moray, white-spotted	Muraena argus	x		154
Zebra moray	Gymnomuraena zebra	x		154
Night moray, freckled moray	Echidna nocturna		x	
Snowflake moray	Echidna nebulosa		x	
Yellowmargin moray	Gymnothorax flavimarginatus		x	
Black moray	Gymnothorax buroensis		x	
Masked moray	Gymnothorax panamensis		x	
Olive moray	Gymnothorax funebris		x	
White mouth moray	Gymnothorax meleagris	x		154
Paint-spotted moray	Siderea picta		x	
Slenderjaw moray	Enchelycore octaviana	x		155
Mosaic moray	Enchelycore lichenosa		x	
Peppered moray	Uropterygius polysticus		x	
Rusty moray	Uropterygius necturus		x	
Longhead moray	Uropterygius macrocephalus		x	
Galápagos snake eel	Callechelys galapagensis (E)		x	
Pouch snake eel	Paraletharchus opercularis (E)		x	
White snake eel	Apterichtus equatorialis (E)		x	
Tiger snake eel	Myrichthys tigrinus (M. maculosus)	x		155

	Photo:	Yes	No	Page
Pacific snake eel	*Ophichthus triserialis*	x		156
Galápagos garden eel	*Heteroconger klausewitzi*	x		155
Blackfin conger	*Paraconger californiensis*	x		156
Galápagos brotula	*Ophidion species*	x		156
Freshwater eel	*Anguilla marmorata*	x		157

Stingrays, Golden rays, Eagle rays, Mantas

Whiptail stingray	*Dasyatis brevis*	x		157
Black-blotched stingray	*Taeniura meyeri*	x		157
Longtail stingray	*Dasyatis longus*		x	
Golden cownose ray	*Rhinoptera steindachneri*	x		158
Spotted eagle ray	*Aetobatus narinari*	x		158–9
Giant manta	*Manta birostris*	x		159–60

Sharks

Galápagos shark	*Carcharhinus galapagensis*	x		177
Blacktip shark	*Carcharhinus limbatus*		x	
Silvertip shark	*Carcharhinus albimarginatus*	x		177
Gray reef shark	*Carcharhinus amblyrhynchos*		x	
Silky shark	*Carcharhinus falciformis*		x	
Bignose shark	*Carcharhinus altimus*		x	
Sandbar shark	*Carcharhinus plumbeus*		x	
Oceanic whitetip	*Carcharhinus longimanus*		x	
Bull shark	*Carcharhinus leucas*		x	
Whitetip reef shark	*Triaenodon obesus*	x		160, 177
Blue shark	*Prionace glauca*		x	
Whitenose shark	*Nasolamia velox*		x	
Tiger shark	*Galeocerdo cuvieri*		x	
Smooth hammerhead	*Sphyrna zygaena*		x	
Scalloped hammerhead	*Sphyma lewini*	x		178
Great hammerhead	*Sphyrna mokarran*		x	
Galápagos hornshark	*Heterodontus quoyi*	x		178–9
Mexican hornshark	*Heterodontus mexicanus*		x	
Speckled smoothhound	*Mustelus mento*		x	
Broadnose smoothhound	*Mustelus species*		x	
Spotted houndshark	*Triakis maculata*		x	
Longnose catshark	*Apristurus kampae*		x	
Panama ghost catshark	*Apristurus stensensi*		x	
Combtooth dogfish	*Centroscyllium nigrum*		x	
Cookie cutter shark	*Isistius brasiliensis*		x	
Bigeye thresher	*Alopias superciliosus*		x	

		Photo:	Yes	No	Page
Thresher shark	Alopias vulpinus			x	
Pelagic thresher	Alopias pelagicus			x	
Whale shark	Rhiniodon typus		x		179
Shortfin mako	Isurus oxyrinchus			x	
Longfin mako	Isurus paucus			x	
Great white shark	Carcharodon carcharias			x	

Baleen whales: Rorquals

Blue whale	Balaenoptera musculus			x	
Fin whale	Balaenoptera physalus			x	
Sei whale	Balaenoptera borealis			x	
Bryde's whale	Balaenoptera edeni			x	
Minke whale	Balaenoptera acutorostrata			x	
Humpback whale	Megaptera novaeangliae			x	

Toothed whales, Ocean dolphins

Sperm whale, cachalot	Physeter macrocephalus			x	
Pygmy sperm whale	Kogia breviceps			x	
Dwarf sperm whale	Kogia simus			x	
Cuvier's beaked whale	Ziphius cavirostris			x	
Blainville's beaked whale	Mesoplodon densirostris			x	
Lesser beaked whale	Mesoplodon peruvianus			x	
Gingko-toothed whale	Mesoplodon gingkodens			x	
Southern bottlenosed whale	Hyperoodon planifrons			x	
Killer whale, orca	Orcinus orca		x		222–3
Pygmy orca	Feresa attenuata			x	
Melon headed whale	Peponocephala electra			x	
False killer whale	Pseudorca crassidens			x	
Short finned pilot whale	Globicephala macrorhynchus			x	
Long finned pilot whale	Globicephala melas			x	
Risso's dolphin, gray grampus	Grampus griseus			x	
Common dolphin	Delphinus delphis			x	
Bottle-nosed dolphin	Tursiops truncatus			x	
Spotted dolphin	Stenella attenuata			x	
Spinner dolphin	Stenella longirostris			x	
Striped dolphin	Stenella coeruleoalba			x	
Rough-toothed dolphin	Steno bredanensis			x	
Fraser's dolphin	Lagenodelphis hosei			x	

	Photo:	Yes	No	Page

MISCELLANEOUS

		Yes	No	Page
Black turtle	*Chelonia agassizi*	x		222
Sea lion		x		223
Galápagos penguin	*Apheniscus mendiculus*	x		224

MARINE INVERTEBRATES

PHYLUM CNIDARIA
Class Anthozoa: Anemones, Corals, Gorgonians

		Yes	No	Page
Pacific tube anemone	*Pachycerianthus fimbriatus*	x		181
Mexican anemone	*Bunodactis mexicana*	x		179–80
Anemone	*Bunodosoma species*		x	
Leopard-spotted anemone	*Antiparactis species*	x		180
Anemone	*Anthopleura species*		x	
Zoanthid	*Palythoa species*		x	
Zoanthid	*Zoanthus species*		x	
Golden sea fan	*Muricea species*		x	
Orange cup coral	*Tubastrea coccinea*	x		182
Tagus cup coral	*Tubastrea tagusensis*		x	
Yellow polyp black coral	*Antipathes galapagensis*	x		183
Pink cup coral	*Tubastrea species*		x	
Black coral	*Antipathes panamensis*	x		223
Pebble coral	*Cycloseris elegans*		x	
	Cycloseris mexicana		x	
Reef building corals	*Gardineroseris planulata*		x	
	Psammocora stellata		x	
	Psammocora brighami		x	
	Pocillopora damicornis		x	
	Pocillopora elegans		x	
	Pocillopora capitata		x	
	Agaricella species		x	
	Porites lobata		x	
	Pavona clavus		x	
	Pavona gigantea		x	
	Pavona varians		x	

PHYLUM ANNELIDA
Class Polychaeta: Segmented worms

		Yes	No	Page
Common fireworm	*Eurythoe complanata*	x		185
Ornate fireworm	*Chloeia viridis*	x		185

		Photo: Yes	No	Page

PHYLUM MOLLUSCA

Class Polyplacophora: Chitons

		Yes	No	Page
Rippled chiton	Chiton sulcatus		x	
Chiton	Chiton goodallii		x	

Class Cephalopoda: Cephalopods

		Yes	No	Page
Galápagos twin-spot octopus	Octopus oculifer	x		191
Enope squid	Abraliopsis affinis		x	
Enope squid	Pterygioteuthis giardi		x	
Purpleback flying squid	Sthenoteuthis oualaniensis		x	
Glass squid	Liocranchia reinhardti		x	
Pacific argonaut	Argonauta pacificus		x	

Class Bivalves

		Yes	No	Page
Magnificent scallop	Nodipecten magnificus		x	

Class Gastropoda: Snails, Sea slugs, Sea hares, Nudibranchs, Flatworms

		Yes	No	Page
Panamic horse conch	Pleuroploca princeps	x		185
Chief rock snail	Hexaplex princeps	x		186
Grinning tun	Malea ringens	x		186
Little deer cowrie	Cyprae cervinetta		x	
Thin-shelled helmet	Cypreacassis tenuis		x	
Galápagos abalone	Haliotis dalli		x	
Galápagos black sea slug	Onchidella steindachneri (E)		x	
Starry flatworm	Pseudobiceros species 6 (E)	x		186
Orange spotted nudibranch		x		187
Panama aglaja	Navanax aenigmaticus	x		187
Carolyn doris	Platydoris carolinae (E)	x		187
Warty sea slug	Pleurobranchus areolatus	x		188
Apricot slug	Berthellina engeli	x		188
Warty seacat, sea hare	Dolabrifera dolabrifera		x	
Blue-striped sea slug	Tambja mullineri (E)	x		188–9
Starry night nudibranch	Hypselodoris lapizlazuli (E)	x		189
Carnivorous nudibranch	Roboastra species	x		
Galápagos discodoris	Discodoris species (E)	x		189
Roboastra nudibranch		x		189
Walking seahare	Aplysia cedrosensis	x		190
Spanish shawl	Flabellina species	x		190

PHYLUM ARTHROPODA

Class Crustacea: Crabs, Shrimps, Lobsters

		Photo: Yes	No	Page
Galápagos pebblestone crab	*Mithrax species*		x	
Giant hermit crab	*Petrochirus californiensis*	x		192
Hairy hermit crab	*Aniculus elegans*	x		192
Bar-eyed hermit crab	*Dardanus fucosus*	x		192
Swimming crab	*Cronius ruber*		x	
Stanford swimmer crab	*Portunus stanfordi*	x		209
Sally lightfoot crab	*Grapsus grapsus*	x		209
Ghost crab	*Ocypode species*	x		209
Heller fiddler crab	*Uca helleri*		x	
Panamic arrowhead crab	*Stenorhynchus debilis*	x		210
Shamed face box crab	*Calappa convexa*	x		210
Yellow snout red shrimp	*Rhynchocinetes typus*	x		210
Giant khaki shrimp	*Litopenaeus stylirostrsis*	x		211
Banded coral shrimp	*Stenopus hispidus*		x	
Red-banded shrimp	*Cinetorhynchus hiatti*	x		211
Big eye shrimp	*Metapenaeopsis kishinouyei*	x		211
Sea star shrimp	*Periclimenes soror*	x		212
Gold-spotted shrimp	*Sicyonia aliaffinis*	x		212
Double pincers shrimp	*Brachycarpus biunguiculatus*		x	
Red spiny lobster	*Panulirus penicillatus*	x		212
Blue lobster	*Panulirus gracilis*	x		213
Slipper lobster	*Scyllarides astori*	x		213
Tropical rock lobster	*Panulirus femoristriga*		x	

PHYLUM ECHINODERMATA

Class Asteroidea: Sea stars

		Yes	No	Page
Armored sand star	*Astropecten armatus*	x		213
Sand star	*Luidia foliolata*	x		214
Banded sand star	*Luidia bellonae*		x	
Panamic cushion star	*Pentaceraster cummingi*	x		214
Variable sea star, pacific comet star	*Linckia columbiae*	x		214
Chocolate chip star	*Nidorellia armata*	x		215
Blunt-rayed seastar	*Asterina species*		x	
Pyramid sea star	*Pharia pyramidata*	x		215
Blue sea star	*Phataria unifascialis*	x		215
Troschel's sea star	*Evasterias troschelli*	x		
Keeled sea star	*Asteropsis carinifera*	x		216
Smooth sea star	*Leiaster veres*	x		216
Bradley sea star	*Mithrodia bradleyi*	x		216

	Photo:	Yes	No	Page
Giant seastar	Tethyaster species	x		217
Prickly seastar	Paulia horrida	x		217
Rathbun's seastar	Rathbunaster californicus	x		217
Sun star	Heliaster multiradiata		x	
Red sun star	Heliaster cumingi (E)		x	
24-rayed sun star	Heliaster solaris		x	
Crown of thorns	Acanthaster planci		x	

Class Ophiuroidea: Brittle star

Simple brittle star	Ophiactis simplex		x	
Savigny brittle star	Ophiactis savigny		x	
Alexander's spiny brittle star	Ophiocoma alexandri	x		218
Black spiny brittle star	Ophiocoma aethiops		x	
Schmitt's brittle star	Ophiocomella schmitti		x	
Smooth brittle star	Ophioderma teres		x	
Multi-colored brittle star	Ophioderma variegatum		x	
White-banded brittle star	Ophionereis albomaculata		x	
Three-spined brittle star	Ophionereis perplexa		x	
	Ophiophragmus species		x	
Hancock's brittle star	Ophioplocus hancocki		x	
Glass-spined brittle star	Ophiothrix spiculata		x	
Epizoic brittle star	Ophiothela mirabilis		x	

Class Echinoidea: Sea urchins

Pencil sea urchin	Eucidaris thouarsii	x		218
Needle sea urchin	Diadema mexicanum	x		218
Crowned sea urchin	Centrostephanus coronatus	x		219
Green sea urchin	Lytechinus semituberculatus	x		219
White sea urchin	Tripneustes depressus	x		219
Flower sea urchin	Toxopneustes roseus	x		220
Galápagos sand dollar	Encope galapagensis	x		220
Heart urchin, sea porcupine	Lovenia cordiformis		x	
Grooved heart urchin	Agassizia scobiculata		x	
Keeled heart sea urchin	Brissus obesus		x	
Cushion sea urchin	Astropygia pulvinata		x	
Coffee sea urchin	Caenocentrotus gibbosus		x	
Pacific sea urchin	Cassidulus pacifica		x	
Purple sea urchin	Echinometra vanbrunti		x	
Oblong pencil sea urchin	Echinometra oblonga		x	
Rounded sea biscuit	Clypeaster rotondus		x	
Ocre sea biscuit	Clypeaster ochrus		x	

	Photo:	Yes	No	Page
Class Holothuroidea: Sea cucumbers				
Brown-spotted sea cucumber	*Holothuria impatiens*		x	
Sulfur sea cucumber	*Holothuria lubrica*		x	
Sea cucumber, pepino	*Stichopus fuscus*	x		220
Warty sea cucumber	*Holothuria fuscocinerea*	x		221
Giant sea cucumber	*Stichopus horrens*	x		221
Camouflaged sea cucumber	*Holothuria kefersteini*	x		222

(E) Endemic

GLOSSARY

Acute	Sharp, pointed.
Adipose fin	Behind the dorsal fin, a fleshy fin without supporting rays.
Baleen	Fibrous plates in parallel rows. Upper jaw of some whales.
Band	Oblique or diagonal line, pigmented.
Bar	Vertical line, short, broad, pigmented.
Barbel	A fleshy tentacle like projection on the head, usually around the mouth, often threadlike.
Benthic	Living on the ocean bottom.
Breach	To leap above the water surface.
Caudal	Belonging to the tail.
Compressed	Flattened from side to side, so that the fish is higher than it is wide.
Ctenoid scale	A scale with spine(s) along the rear margin or exposed surface.
Cycloid scale	Smooth scale without spine.
Demersal	Organisms living near the ocean bottom.
Depressed	Flattened from top to bottom. Fish is wider than it is high.
Dimorphism	Two distinct forms of the same species.
Falcate	Strongly curved or lunate.
Fathom	A measure of water depth, one fathom = 1.8 meters.
Filament	Long thread-like structure.
Finlet	Isolated fin-rays behind dorsal or anal fins.
Flukes	Horizontal tail fin in cetaceans.
Fusiform	Spindle-shaped, tapering at each end.
Keel	Sharp ridge located on the back, belly or caudal peduncle.
Krill	Shrimp-like crustaceans eaten in huge numbers by baleen whales.
Lateral line	Series of tubes or pored scales associated with the sensory system; from opercule to base of caudal fin.
Lunate	Moon-shaped or crescent-shaped.

Melon	Bulging forehead in toothed whales; often contains oil.
Nape	Area on the back extending from head to dorsal fin.
Opercle	Flat bone covering most of the gill chamber.
Oviparous	In reproduction: laying eggs, not giving birth to live young.
Ovoviviparous	In reproduction: giving birth to live young hatching from eggs, held inside the body without receiving nutrients from the mother.
Peduncle	The trunk-like part of the body to which the tail is attached.
Pelagic	Organisms living in open waters, rather than close to the shore.
Plankton	Microscopic plants and animals drifting near the surface of open waters.
Protractile	Mouth capable of forward extension.
Reticulate	Marked with a network of lines, often chain-like.
Rostrum	Forward projection of the snout in fish; beak-like in whales.
Serrated	Saw-toothed or jagged.
Spiracle	Respiratory opening located on the back part of head, above and behind the eyes (sharks, rays and related fish); blowhole in whales.
Striated	Marked with narrow, parallel grooves or lines.
Stripe	Thin horizontal line or area of pigment.
Swim bladder	Air-filled sac located under the backbone in fish. Used in buoyancy regulation.
Truncate	Having a blunt end.
Vermiculate	With fine, wavy lines; worm-like.
Viviparous	In reproduction: bearing live young that have received nutrients from the mother.

USEFUL WEBSITES

Calao Life	www.calaolife.com
Chamber of Tourism	www.galapagoschamberoftourism.org
Charles Darwin Foundation (Galápagos Conservancy, USA)	www.galapagos.org; www.darwinfoundation.org
Freunde der Galápagos Insein (Switzerland)	www.galapagos-ch.org
Fundacion Wild Aid	www.wildaid.org
Galápagos Conservation Trust (UK)	www.gct.org
Nordic friends of Galápagos (Finland)	www.galapagopsnordic.org
Moonrise Travel (Pto.Ayora, Galápagos)	www.galapagosmoonrise.com
Scubadragon Dive Centre	www.scubadragongalapagos.com

RECOMMENDED READING

Abbott, Donald P. *Factors influencing the zoogeographic affinities of Galápagos inshore marine fauna.* in: The Galápagos, Ed. R.I. Bowman Proc. Symp. GISP, 1966. p.108–122.

Allen, G.R. and Robertson D. Ross. *Fishes of the Tropical Eastern Pacific.* University of Hawaii Press, 1994/Crawford House Press, Bathurst NSW 2795, Australia 1994.

Armas, Jenny. *The Galápagos rays.* in: La Garua, July 1984 n°2. Club de Guias de Galápagos, Santa Cruz, Galápagos.

Audubon Society. *Field guide to the North American fishes, whales and dolphins.* A. Knopf, New York, 1983.

Baldridge, H. David. *Shark attack: a program of data reduction and analysis.* Contrib. Mote Mar. Lab, 1974.

Beebe, William. *Rays, mantas and chimaeras.* Eastern Pacific expedition, New York Zoological Society, 1941.

Broadus, J.I. Pires and A.Gaines. *Coastal and marine resources management for the Galápagos Islands.* Woods Hole Oceanographic Institution, 1984.

Burkov, V.A. *Symposium on equatorial circulation in the Pacific.* Abstract of symposium papers. Tenth Pac. Sci. Congr., Honolulu, Hawaii, 1961.

Cañon, Jose. *Oceanogrphy of the eastern equatorial Pacific.* Manus., CDRS, 1977.

Carwardine, Mark. *Whales, dolphins and porpoises.* Dorling Kindersley, London, 1995/ed. espanola, Ed. Omega SA, Barcelona, 1995.

Christensen, Niels Jr. *Observations of the Cromwell Current near the Galápagos Islands.* Deep sea research vol.18, 1974, pp.27–33.

Compton, Gail. *Manta rays and stingrays.* Oceans, Jan. 1977.

Constant, Pierre. *The Galápagos Islands: A Natural History Guide.* 7th edition, Airphoto International, Hong Kong, 2006.

Corliss, John B. *The thermal springs of the Galápagos rift: implications for biology and the chemistry of sea water.* Pacific division 1983, pp.25–31.

Danulat, Eva, M. Brandt, P. Zarate, M. Montesinos & S.Banks. *El Turismo en la Reserva Marina de Galápagos* (2003), Parque Nacional Galápagos + Fundacion

Darwin, Charles. *Puerto Ayora, Santa Cruz, Galápagos*

Dempster, Robert P. and Earl S. Herald. *Notes on the hornshark; Heterodontus francisi.* occ. Pap. Calif. Acad. Sci. n°33, 1961.

Ebeling, Alfred W. *Mugil galapagensis, a new mullet from the Galápagos islands, with notes on a related species* Copeia n°3, 1961, p.295–305.
Elliott, Melinda and Tom Keating. *Galápagos marine research.* Manus., CDRS, 1979.

Fitter, Julian + Daniel & David Hoskins. *Wildlife of the Galápagos.* Collins Safari guide (2000)
Finet, Yves and Hickmann, Cleveland Jr. *A field guide to the marine mollusks of the Galápagos.* Sugar Spring Press, Lexington, Virginia, 1999.
Fowler, Henry. *The fishes. Galápagos Islands.* in: The results of the fifth George Vanderbilt expedition (1941), Acad. Nat. Sci. Phil. Monogr. N°6, 1944.

Galápagos Islands Explorer (Visitor's Map of the Galápagos Islands, Ecuador), Created and published by Ocean Explorer Maps, 2005, www.oceanexplorer.net
Galápagos National Park. *Naturalist guide's course notes.* Pierre R. Constant, 1980, 1982, 1986.
Garrick, JAF and Leonard P. Schultz. *A guide to the kinds of potentially dangerous sharks.* in: Sharks and survival. Gilbert, Perry W., 1975.
Gilbert, Charles H. *A supplementary list of fishes collected at the Galápagos islands and Panama.* Scientific results of explorations by US fish commission steamer *Albatross.* n°XIX Proc. Nat. Mus. 13. n°840, pp.449–455, 1891.
Gilbert, Perry W. *The shark: Barbarian and benefactor.* Bioscience, 18, 946–950, 1968.
The visual apparatus of sharks. in: Sharks and survival, 283–326, 1975.
Advice to those who frequent or find themselves in shark infested waters. in: Sharks and survival, 1975.
Glynn, Peter W. *Coral reef community.* undated article, CDRS, post-1975.
Glynn, Peter and Gerard Wellington. *Coral and coral reefs in the Galápagos Islands.* Univ. California Press, Berkeley, 1983.
Grove, Jack. *Peces de las islas Galápagos Instituto National de Pesca.* Bolt. Cient. Tecn. vol.VII, n°2, Guayaquil, 1984.
Influence of the 1982–83 El Niño event upon the ichthyfauna of the Galápagos archipielago. in: El Niño in the Galápagos Islands, the 82–83 event. Gary Robinson, Quito, 1985.
Grove, Jack and Lavenberg, R.J. *Fishes of the Galápagos Islands.* Stanford University Press, California, 1997.
Gudger, E.W. *Natural history of the whale shark: Rhincodon typus.* Zoologica, 1(19) 349–389, 1915.
A second whale shark at the Galápagos islands. Nature, 132, p.569, 1933.
Gotshall, Daniel W. *Marine animals of Baja California: a guide to the common fishes and invertebrates.* Sea challengers and Western marine entrerpr. Ventura, Calif, 1982.

Halstead, Bruce Walter. *Venomous stingrays*. in: Poisonous and venomous animals of the world. vol.3. Lib. of Congress, Washington, 1970.

Hedgpeth, Joel. *The oceanographic setting of the Galápagos Research proposal*. Manus. Galáp. Internat. Sci project, 1964.

Hickman Jr., Cleveland. *Guia de campo sobre Estrellas de Mar y otros equidermos de Galápagos* (1998) Sugar Spring Press, Lexington, Virginia, USA

Hickman Jr., Todd Zimmerman *Crustaceos de Galápagos* (2000), Sugar Spring Press, Lexington, Virginia, USA

Houvenagel, Guy T. *Oceanographic conditions in the Galápagos and their relationships with life on the islands*. from: Upwelling ecosystems. Ed. R. Boje and M. Tomczak, Springer, Berlin, 1978.

Hubbs, Carl L. *Ogcocephalus darwinii: a new batfish endemic at the Galápagos islands*. Copeia, n°3, 1958.

Jimenez, Roberto. *Mise en évidence de l'upwelling équatorial à l'Est des Galápagos*. ORSTOM, ser. oceanogr. 16, n°2, 1978.

Jimenez-Prado P. & Bearez, Ph. Marine Fishes of continental Ecuador, Simbioe/Nazca/IFEA, Tome 1 (130 pages), Tome 2 (401 pages), Quito, 2004

Johnson, R.H. *Requins de Polynésie*. Ed. du Pacifique, Tahiti, 1978, 1983.

Jordan, D.S. and Charles H. Bollman. *Description of new species of fishes collected at the Galápagos islands* (Cruise of the steamer *Albatross*, from Norfolk to San Francisco). Indiana Univ., 1887–88.

Karl, D.M. *Deep sea primary production at the Galápagos hydrothermal vents*. Science, vol.207, 1980.

Kerstich, Alex. *Sea of Cortez Marine Invertebrates*. Sea Challengers, Monterey, Calif., 1989.

Leatherwood, Steve and W.E. Ewans. *Whales, dolphins and porpoises of the eastern north Pacific*. Naval Undersea Center, San Diego, Calif., 1972.

Levéque, Raymond. *Notes sur quatre cétacés de l'océan pacifique*. Mammalia, 27 n°4, 1963.

Marine environment and protection in: Key Environments: Galápagos, Ed. by Roger Perry, Pergamon Press, Oxford, 1983.

Maxell, Clifford Dwayne. *Marine productivity of the Galápagos archipelago*. Thesis, Ohio State Univ., 1974.

McCosker, John E. *The moray eels of the Galápagos islands*. Proc. Calif. Acad. Sci. 4th series, n°13, 1975.

McCosker, John E. *Galápagos underwater*. Pacific discovery, 31 (2), 1978.

McCosker and Rosenblatt. *Galápagos shorefishes* in: Key environments: Galápagos. Ed. by Roger Perry, Pergamon Press, Oxford, 1984.

Merlen, Godfrey. *A field guide to the marine mammals of the Galápagos (Cetacea and Pinnipeds)*. Fundacion Charles Darwin, 1998.

Merlen, Godfrey. *Cetaceans in Galápagos waters*. Handout from Naturalist Guide's course, CDRS, Galápagos, 1985.

Minasian, Stanley M., Kenneth Balcomb III and Larry Foster. *The world's whales complete illustrated guide*. Smithsonian books, Washington D.C., 1984.

Mitchell, E.D. *The status of the world's whales*. Nature Canada, vol 2, Ottawa, 1973.

Peterson, R.L. *Recent mammal records from the Galápagos Islands*. Mammalia, 30. N°3, 441–445, 1966.

Pike, Gordon. *Whale identification. Guide to the whales, porpoises and dolphins of the North-East Pacific and Arctic waters of Canada and Alaska*. Fisheries Research Board of Canada, Biological Station, Nanaïmo B.C., 1956.

Poll, M. and N. Leleup. *Un poisson aveugle nouveau de la famille des Brotulidae provenant des iles Galápagos*. Bull. Classe. Sci. Acad. Royale Belgique, 51, 5th series, 464–474, 1965.

Robinson, Gary and Eugenia M. del Pino. *El Niño in the Galápagos Islands, The 1982–1983 event*. Charles Darwin Foundation for the Galápagos, Quito, 1985.

Rodriguez, José. *El fenomeno de El Niño y sus efectos en el littoral insular de Galápagos*. CEDIG. N°4 pp.65–83, CDRS library, 1983.

Roy, Tui. *Discovering a new species: Caecogilbia deroyi*. Pacific Discovery, 27, N°3, 12–14, 1974.

Sarbone, Rosenberg, Steve & Ellen. *The Diving Guide: Galápagos Islands* (2004), Cruising guide Publications, Dunedin, Florida, USA

Schroeder, Robert E. *Philippine Shore Fishes of the western Sulu Sea*. Bureau of fisheries and aquatic resources. Nat. Media Prod. Center, Manila, 1980.

Scott, Peter. *Some Galápagos fishes—drawings and notes*. Manus., 6pp, CDRS Library, 1976.

Sibert, John. *Some oceanographic observations in the Galápagos islands*. American Zoologist, 11 pp.405–408, 1971.

Snodgrass, Robert Ewans and Edmund Heller. *Shore fishes of the Revillagigedos, Clipperton, Cocos and Galápagos islands*. (Papers from the Hopkins-Standford Galápagos expedition 1898–1899.) Proc. Wash. Acad. Sci. vol. 6, 1905.

Springer, Stewart. *Anti-shark measures* in: Sharks and Survival, by Ch. Gilbert, 1975.

Standford oceanographic expedition. *Eastern tropical Pacific, equatorial current system and Galápagos archipelago*. vols.17, 19, 20, CDRS library, 1968.

Stevens, John. *A fish with double vision: Dialommus fuscus*. Natural History, 89, N°1, 62–67, 1980.

Thomas, D.A., L.T. Finley, A. Kerstich. *Reef fishes of the sea of Cortez*. Univ. Arizona Press, Tucson, Ariz., 1987.

Tricas, Timothy and McCosker. *Predatory behavior of the white shark: Carcharodon carcharias, with notes on its biology*. Proceed Calif. Acad. Sci. vol. 43. N°14, 221–238, 1984.

Undersea wonders of Galápagos. National Geographic, 154 (3), 1978.

Walker, Boyd W. *Origin and affinities of the Galápagos shore fishes*. Galápagos Islands symposium, 8 pp., 1964. Symposium of Bowman, p.172–174, 1966.

Wellington, Gerard. *The Galápagos coastal marine environment*. Resource report to Dept. Nat. Park and Wildlife 1–341, Quito, 1975.

Williams, David L. *The Galápagos spreading center lithospheric cooling and hydrothermal circulation*. Geophys. J.R. astr. Soc. 38, pp.627–634, 1974.

Wyrtki, Klaus. *Oceanography of the eastern tropical Pacific Ocean*. Oceanogr. Mar. Biol. Ann. Rev, 4, 1966.

Note: The main source of information, documents and books is the Charles Darwin Research Station (CDRS) Library, Puerto Ayora, Santa Cruz, Galápagos Islands.

INDEX OF COMMON NAMES
ENGLISH–FRENCH–SPANISH

English	French	Spanish	Page
Lobsters	Langoustes	Langosta	234
– Blue	– bleue	Langosta azul	237
– Red	– rouge	Langosta roja	236
– Slipper	Cigale de mer	Langostino	237
Mackerels	Maquereaux	Macarela	108
– Sierra	Maquereau sierra	Sierra	108
Mantas	Raies mantas	Manta raya	144
Marine iguana	Iguane marin		–
Marlin	Marlin	Pez espada	129
– Black	– noir	Picudo	129
– Striped	– raye		129
Mexican goatfish	Surmullet mexicain	Salmonete barbon	100
Mexican hogfish	Vieille mexicaine	Vieja de piedra	45
Milkfish		Lisa diabla	–
Mojarras	Mojarras		79
– Pacific flagfin	Mojarra du pacifique	Chaparra	79
Molas	Poisson lune	Pez luna	112
Moorish Idol	Idole maure	Idolo moro	65
Moray	Murene	Morena	136
– Black	– noire	– negra	136
– Fine-spotted	– mouchetee		137
– Hardtail	– a queue dure		136
– Hourglass (Blackspot)	– a pois noir		137
– Lentil (Jewel)	– lentigineuse		137
– Magnificent	– magnifique		136
– Masked	– masquee		138
– Night	– nocturne	– nocturna	138
– Paint-spotted	– blanche		137
– Panamic green	– verte de Panama	– verde	136
– Peppered	– poivree		139
– Rusty	– rouille		138
– Slenderjaw	– a dents longues		138
– White mouth	– a pois blanc		137
– Yellowmargin	– a frange jaune		137
– Zebra	– zebree	– zebra	137
Mullet	Mullet	Lisa	130
– Galápagos	– des Galápagos	Lisa	132
– Orange-eyed	– a oeil orange		132
– Striped	– raye		130
Mutton hamlet	Loche hamlet	Cherna, guaseta del Pacifico	76

English	French	Spanish	Page
Sand dollar	dollar des sables		241
Sardine			
– Peruvian Pacific	Sardine du Pacifique	Sardina	103
Scorpionfishes	Poisson scorpion	Pez escorpion	99
– Rainbow	Scorpion arc en ciel		99
– Red	scorpion rouge	Brujo	99
– Stone	scorpion		99
Seahorse	Hippocampe	Caballito de mar	43
Scrawled filefish	Robe de cuir		71
Seabass	Merou, loche	Mero	75
– Gray threadfin	Merou a filament	Plumero	77
– White-spotted rock	Loche mouchetee	Camotillo	76
Seabream			
– Galápagos	Porgy a raies bleues	Camiseta, sargo camiseta	111
Sea chub	saupe	Chopa	
– Blue bronze	– de bronze		97
– Cortez	– de Cortez		80
– Dusky chub	Saupe serieuse		80
– Rainbow	saupe arc en ciel		97
Sea cucumber	Concombre de mer	Pepino de mar	243
Sea lion	Otarie	Lobo de mar	–
– Fur	Otraie a fourrure	Lobo de dos pelos	–
Searobin	Grondin		100
– Galápagos	Grondin des Galápagos	Gallineta, gallina	100
– Orange throat	Grondin a gorge orange		–
Sea snake	serpent de mer	Culebra de mar	–
Sea star	Etoile de mer	Estrella de mar	237
Sea turtle	Tortue de mer	Tortuga	–
Sea urchin	Oursin de mer	Erizo de mar	240
– Crowned	oursin diademe		241
– Flower	oursin fleur		241
Shark	Requin	Tiburon	166
– Blacktip	– a pointes noires	– punta negra	166
– Bull	– taureau		168
– Galápagos	– des Galápagos	– de Galápagos	166
– Great white	– blanc	– blanco	173
– Gray reef	– gris	– gris	166
– Horn	– a cornes	– gato, dormilon de Galápagos	170
– Silvertip	– aileron blanc		166
– Tiger	– tigre	– tigre	169

INDEX OF SCIENTIFIC NAMES

Where two or more entries are listed, the main entry is marked in **bold**.

APGB/23/02